"A SHOCKING, FORCEFULLY WRITTEN ACCOUNT of a young woman's journey to the edge of dying and back again . . . Her anger comes through loud and clear, and she makes many thought-provoking comments."
*Chicago Tribune*

"EXHILARATING AND HOPEFUL . . . A BRAVE AND HONEST BOOK."
*Glamour*

"A HORROR STORY, GRUESOME AND FRIGHTENING. AND TRUE . . . BRILLIANTLY WRITTEN . . . Cook is honest: having lived through death, she wants life at face value. This is a disturbing, beautiful, and profoundly insightful book. What it says about illness and death is not nice; what it says about life is real: we can, if we want to, save our own lives."
*Philadelphia Enquirer*

"LEAVES YOU REELING AND DEVASTATED . . . SEARING . . . UNFORGETTABLE." *After Dark Magazine*

"THIS IS A TRUE STORY, FRIGHTENING ENOUGH TO MAKE ONE'S OWN PERSONAL NIGHTMARES PALE . . . A detailed confession, shocking in its absolute, unsparing candor . . . *Second Life* will move readers deeply."
*People*

# SECOND LIFE

## STEPHANI COOK

———◆———

BALLANTINE BOOKS • NEW YORK

Library of Congress Catalog Card Number: 81-8919

ISBN 0-345-30675-9

This edition published by arrangement with Simon & Schuster, Inc.

Printed in Canada

First Ballantine Books Edition: October 1982

*The author is grateful for the permission of the following publishers to quote copyrighted material from the following works:*

"Santa Claus is Coming to Town," by Haven Gillespie and J. Fred Coots, copyright 1934, renewed 1962, Leo Feist, Inc. Used by permission, all rights reserved.

Excerpt from Mary Gordon's "The Parable of the Cave or: In Praise of Watercolors" in *The Writer on Her Work*. Janet Sternburg, ed., W. W. Norton, 1980. Used by permission.

FOR JIM
AND
FOR TONY

. . . Why was I so susceptible to the bad advice of men? . . . [Perhaps because] I learned the pleasures of being a good girl.

And I earned, as a good girl, no mean rewards. . . . Bestowing pleasure upon a loved father is much easier than discovering the joys of solitary achievements. It was easy for me to please my father; and this ease bred in me a desire to please men—a desire for the rewards of a good girl. They are by no means inconsiderable: safety and approval, the warm, incomparable atmosphere created when one pleases a man who has vowed, in his turn, to keep the wolf from the door.

But who is the wolf? . . .

Mary Gordon: "The Parable of the Cave or: In Praise of Watercolors"

# AUTHOR'S NOTE

THIS STORY WAS HARD TO TELL, BUT I HAVE TOLD IT just as I remember it, as carefully and fairly as I could. I have changed names and identifying details where it seemed necessary.

It is a true story, and one that is particular to its time and place: advances in medical technology and research have rendered obsolete many of the procedures, treatments, and, I hope—in all fairness to the profession—attitudes.

There are many people to thank for their help to me. Some appear in the book—Barbara and Anya among them—and some of them do not: Geoffrey and Alice and my sister Madelon. These people helped me pull through my ordeal as surely as did any doctor or drug. "Michael" *was* wonderful to me during that period, and I don't know how we would ever have managed without his parents' unflagging support and generosity.

There are also people who were instrumental in getting me to write this book against massive conscious and unconscious resistance. Julie Houston and Carol Eisen Rinzler made me think about it first and encouraged me to think of myself as a writer; my editor Nan A. Talese was nurturant, perspicacious and endlessly patient; Dennis Krieger did a thorough friendly reading, as did Barbara Gorin; and Jim Carse helped me to think through most of the underlying philosophical issues. But I would never have gotten started—I would never have kept going—without Frank Snepp, who convinced me that this story could and should be told, and that I should tell it. All of it.

# PROLOGUE

# SEPTEMBER 1974

———◆———

NO APOLOGIES. NO EXPLANATIONS. IT WAS EASIER AND not quite a lie to let everyone think it was a kind of accident, that it was the fever and I had been made delirious, and that that was why my darkest impulses had boiled to the surface on that unseasonably warm Indian summer afternoon. It was certainly more impulse than gesture because I didn't plan it. On the other hand it was clear to me that I knew what I meant to do.

Still if I hadn't been sick, if I hadn't had to go ahead with Alexandra's sixth birthday party, if I hadn't been overtired and desperate, I probably wouldn't have cracked . . . and once cracked, wouldn't have broken.

It was one of my brittle periods.

I leaned against a wall—grateful for one less direction to fall down in—and sweated out of all proportion to the heat of the day: there were too many kids, there was too much noise, and I couldn't see straight. I had made it through the wild greetings at the door; I had made it through the evisceration of the presents and the strewing of their colorful entrails; I had made it through Pin-the-Smile-on-the-Face. But now as I watched the little girls, flushed with their own excitement, wheeling in splendid, vivid confusion around the hub of my beautiful daughter—my moon-child, silver-smooth child; now as I watched her little brother Zachary—sunny and irrepressible, squealing with laughter and festooned with ribbons—my head felt like one of the huge pink helium-filled balloons that moved with the children, riding the fractured air, and I could tell I was not going to make it through the cake—a large sheet of glutinous yellow sponge curtained with icing, on which I had carefully laid out a miniature farm complete with duck pond, barn, animals, and farmer, the grass green sugar crystal, the fences licorice. The road was paved with jelly beans.

I caught Michael's eye and he ambled over, a man rarely given to change of pace. He would have to manage the cake with its saccharine landscape. He would have to manage the rest of the games. He would have to manage all these little girls in their party dresses and he would have to manage the matching of child to parent when the party was over. But he was good at that.

"I don't feel well," I said. "I have to go to bed." Michael's expression of annoyance—disconcertingly like his ordinary expression—faded into disapproval. "I'm sorry," I offered, "but I can't help it. I've got to get out of here." I ducked his glare. Don't look at me that way, I thought. Don't look at me.

Maybe chaos is catching.


"Look at yourself," I hissed to the white face in the bathroom mirror—the white face floating above the white body, the white body in the white nightgown, the white tile glittering like blind eyes behind me. I could barely hear the children now; their shouts of laughter were like the far-off chirping of insects on a summer night. "Just *look* at yourself."

There in the mirror, floating on its surface like a dead body—decomposed by myopia—was the image of a woman, almost thirty—thin, pale, with close-cropped hair (kept that way, since the illness, both in penance and defiance). I hardly recognized myself. From two and a half feet, I could have been anybody or nobody.

That wasn't always true: I used to be *somebody*, a familiar array of all the appropriate American-girl dreams and hopes and traits, my life a wealth of adolescent fantasy: a Seven Sisters education; a glamorous life of modeling, travel, and money; an appropriate marriage to an intelligent, handsome husband with a promising future; a comfortable life in New York City. I had been what every girl wanted to be. Or thought she wanted to be. I had had what everyone wanted to have.

Until I got sick. Until my body came apart and then like a bad joke, so did my head. Or maybe it was my head and *then* my body . . . not that it mattered in the end.

Until I got well.

To be cured is not to be healed.

I leaned forward on the old-fashioned, broad-edged sink. The heat drained through my hands where they had laid themselves on the cold porcelain; it drained through my feet in their cotton socks where I stood on the white tile. I blinked to clear my vision, making my eyes sting. What I saw in the mirror repelled me: a woman, emptied of resources; a victim, deprived of any-one else to blame; a collection of omissions in search of a committee. These things don't happen by accident.

When I opened the door of the medicine chest my reflection slid off the edge, vacuumed into the white.

Because I only wanted to cut my wrist and not my fingers, I had to wad tissues over the top of the razor blade to protect them. I had an intense memory of sneaking a look at the cunning box that held my moth-er's shaving paraphernalia when I was about Alexan-dra's age. I had been warned against opening that box, and even more expressly warned against touching its contents. I had of course examined it at the first oppor-tunity, running my fingers over one of the neat blades set on edge to determine for myself—the beginnings of a largely unproductive empiricism—their actual danger quotient and then felt only a sweet ache as I was cut to the bone. I had since then had a healthy respect for (1) other people's opinions and (2) the deceptive nature of appearances.

The tight sleeve of the nightgown, pushed above the elbow, functioned as a kind of tourniquet: I was careful, wanting a slow, languorous bloodletting rather than some obscene exsanguination. Choosing a tender stretch of forearm—halfway between wrist and elbow—I made six precise inch-long cuts, lined up like birthday candles, in a delta of blue-green veins. As a giddy afterthought I added one—to grow on—and watched, fascinated, as all seven lit with streaks of red that flamed into fat beads and melted into the white bowl of the sink.

This is what I found out: cutting into oneself with even a new, sharp razor blade is not quite the dramatically simple deed it is made out to be. It hurt rather more—and bled rather less—than I had hoped. After I stopped the bleeding with a compress, I cleaned myself up, bandaged myself up, and got into bed like a good girl, feigning coma for the rest of the afternoon.

It was some hours before Michael came into the bedroom. The party was long over. "Feel better?" he asked, and continued into the bathroom. I held my breath. Then, "What have you done?" he yelled. "What is this?" I knew he was looking at the spattered sink, mullioned with dried blood. He stormed back into the bedroom. "What have you done?"

Quite obviously, not much. There I was in bed with the pillow over my head.

They fluttered around me like bats: Michael, my internist Dr. G., my closest friends. Mostly I looked out the window, into the soft, black night.

"For shame," they squeaked, not understanding, "to tempt death—even to entertain the idea—after what you've been through."

# PART ONE

———◆———

*The doctor—a philosopher manqué—said: "There are two things we want to know. First, what are the factors intrinsic to the pathogen which potentiate its capacity to invade; and second—conversely—what are the factors in the host which allow for invasion, contribute to the pathology of infection, and then ultimately lead to resistance?"*

# JUNE 1970

DR. B. HAD PROMISED THAT I WOULDN'T HAVE THE baby for two weeks yet, so it was ridiculous to worry about the fact that he was going away for the weekend.

"You women—you're all the same!" he said. (He wasn't being unkind.) "You get so excited. I told you I'd be here for this baby, and I will. Trust me."

Trust me. Why do so many men say trust me? You can alter those words with cadence, inflection, expression, and they all say the same thing to me: give over. Give in. Give up. But if you can't trust your doctor, who, as they say, *can* you trust? Still, I had this rumble of prescience—like thunder barely heard—and said again: "All I know, Len, is that if you're not here, I'll go into labor. I don't know how I know, but I know."

"Look." He leaned over his desk paternally and put down his pen. For some reason I couldn't look away from his hands; one was caught by the other, as if he were preventing its escape. "Even if by some chance you were to go into labor, you know Dr. S. is around. That's what a group practice is for: we cover for each other. He's okay—you've met him, haven't you? There's nothing to worry about. He's very capable." The trapped hand had worked itself free and was picking at the calendar book that lay in front of him on the green blotter. He creased the corner of a page, then smoothed it. It was a gesture of dismissal.

I liked Len, but I didn't like Dr. S. He had a whiny voice and fingers like stalks of white asparagus. And I was used to Len. I had already established the necessary intimacy with him, and, as I suppose is true with most young expectant mothers, I was a little bit in love, although it was less with him than with his power—his knowledge of the secret, the forbidden—his magical assumptive capacity to heal the primal female wound, a wound not of loss but of brokenness. Dr. S. was not a healer, he was just a doctor.

I shifted in my chair to show Dr. B. that his infinitesimal gesture of dismissal had not been missed: signaling one's willingness to go is a classic technique for eking out a few more moments of attention from a doctor. My folded hands rested on the enormous pregnancy, heavy in my lap, that pressed up under my ribs so I couldn't breathe. I comforted the fetus with a proprietary pat.

"Okay, Len. Terrific. But you'll see." I tried to sound both ominous, so he'd see I was serious, and facetious, so he wouldn't take it that way.

"Women's intuition?" He laughed softly as he swung around to get up from behind his desk. "You'll probably deliver just to teach me a lesson."

I made a face and launched myself out of his red leather armchair. He was already next to me, facing me, standing perhaps a little closer than necessary. We blinked at each other for a moment from behind our respective corrective lenses as if we were looking through those magnifying peepholes that let you check possible intruders, and then he pushed me gently ahead of him to the door, opening it.

"Don't worry. Trust me." He smiled in a fatherly sort of way, nodding, then looked past me and gestured with a jerk of his head to one of the women arranged like expensive plates against the grass-cloth walls of his waiting room.

I was right, of course; I tend to be right about all the wrong things. And I was right on schedule. My schedule.

Maybe it was anxiety that brought my labor on. Maybe it was the fabled last-minute rush to get things done: I spent that afternoon on my hands and knees painting the floor of the room into which Alexandra would be moved, ceding the nursery to the new baby. It was also not inconceivable that it was pure orneriness, that I did want to teach Len a lesson, did want to demonstrate that I could be right, even though I was only the patient.

I had the first contraction as I completed the last square, wiped my hands with a turpentine-soaked rag, and straightened to stretch, pulling myself up by a door handle. ("Guess what?" I announced, feeling the weight of my ambivalence, when Michael got home from work.) I carefully had very little to eat that night, called Dr. S. to alert him, and went to bed. The contractions had gone from fifteen minutes apart to eight minutes apart and they were fairly steady. Michael and I lay next to each other, holding hands, remembering out loud Alexandra's birth twenty months before—an event that seemed to have had even more impact on him than me, exciting in him a rare and vivid enthusiasm.

Lying there together with the sheets thrown off in the summer heat, we faded into drowsy enchantment, watching the contractions—which could be seen as well as felt—as they gathered like waves and then broke on the beach-head of one or the other hipbone. There was something infinitely reassuring about the simplicity and regularity—the predictability—of nature, and something amazing in the seismic surges of movement the small being nestled inside of me was capable of even in that tight space. The taut skin of my belly shivered and thumped, reminding me of a child giggling under a blanket. Our mood was light, and the rich jasmine-like smell that somehow finds its way out of New York City parks in the early summer—overwhelming even bus exhaust and the fetid smell of decay—was a soporific.

I was able to sleep only a couple of hours before the contractions awakened me. I couldn't get comfortable and finally gave up trying about 3:00 A.M., moving into the living room where I spent the next few hours alternately reading and pacing. The contractions refused to speed up but just as obstinately refused to go away. The night felt very long, so when the new sun finally turned the looming glass-and-steel sentinels on the Palisades across the Hudson into pillars of fire, I was relieved and exhausted. As soon as the hour was decent, I checked in with Dr. S. We went through what was to become a familiar litany: no, the contractions had not speeded up—still eight minutes apart—but they did seem stronger; no, there was no "show" (the bloody plug of mucus that stoppers the womb and is forced out during labor); no, the water hadn't broken. I felt a distinct failure under his questioning: there were no dramatic physical corroborates of what I was afraid he thought a suspicious and typical story.

I was particularly uneasy about exposing my own anxieties—and my need for reassurance—to Dr. S. I didn't mind too much if Len thought I was a bit dizzy; at least he never brought it up to me, never shamed me with it. Len's easy capacity to understand and forgive his female patients the apparent weaknesses of the all-too-weak flesh was one of the singular qualities—not encountered in my parade from unsatisfactory gynecologist to unsatisfactory gynecologist—that made me want him around. If he was a little reserved toward the concerns of his patients, he also treated them without disdain, taking time with them, encouraging them to ask questions, and providing sound, untechnical information. He knew the value of some good old reassurance and avoided smug lectures.

But you could never tell what doctors thought privately—even if they treated you well—so there was probably a little colored flag affixed to the outside of my medical file signaling high neuroticism, the tendency to overreact, hypochondria. The good Dr. S. instructed me not to worry. I should call "when something happens."

Nothing had happened by the time I called him back that afternoon, and I did so sheepishly, apologetically. I knew I was tired, and probably imagining things, but the contractions felt stronger and stronger. No, they hadn't speeded up. No, nothing else had happened. However, I was coming up to the neighborhood of the hospital to take Alexandra to see *her* doctor: in that absolutely predictable way of small children in which the simplest endeavors become complicated, she had awakened that morning with a temperature of 104 degrees. Didn't he want to see me? Just to check me out? But he was busy; unless this was some kind of a crisis it simply wasn't possible. I could always go to the Emergency Room, of course, and get checked. But call when something happened.

Alexandra's pediatrician wasn't so sanguine. She kept glancing at me nervously while she patted and prodded Alexandra's tender little body, turning her on her back and over again like a pancake on a griddle. "What's the matter with you? Are you in labor? How far apart are the contractions? Have you called your doctor?" Because she was echoing some of my building concern I felt defensive: "He thinks it's false labor. Nothing to worry about. I've checked with him every few hours." My own unsureness made my voice tremble. She pursed her lips and her faint mustache quivered slightly. Her German accent thickened. "I think you should be checked."

Home again, I put Alexandra to bed and flopped onto the sofa. I'd been in this slow but definite labor for almost twenty-four hours. Dr. S. may think it false labor, or hysteria, but it felt real enough to me and I worked at convincing myself that the labor *felt* so intense because I was overtired, and my fatigue was magnifying my discomfort. I checked with Dr. S. once more. He sounded exasperated. "Do you want us to induce you?" (He made it sound so medieval. I thought of forceps, of lowered Apgar scores, of the risk of messing with Mother Nature.) "You're probably not ready yet because you're not due yet. Do you want to take that chance? Why don't you wait till Len gets back?

This 'labor' will unquestionably slow if you stay off your feet."

I probably should have been angry with him and at his tone. Instead I was angry with myself for not being properly reassured, for letting my body get the better of me this way, as it had with the violent morning sickness which had attended both pregnancies. I felt mortified and neurotic. The doctor had *said* I wasn't in real labor—only in a holding pattern—so I must distract myself and act normal, not feel the pain, refuse the temptations of hysteria. I promised myself not to call the doctor again until something had definitely *happened*.

Dinner out and maybe even a movie seemed normal and therefore a good idea, so when Michael trailed in after his long subway ride up from Wall Street, I was dressed and determinedly cheerful. I waddled behind him up to Broadway, to our favorite restaurant, where I gorged myself on Indonesian food, thinking it might bring on the labor in earnest.

It didn't intensify labor, but it did make me feel funny, so we abandoned the movie idea and headed home. I climbed into bed with a book, dreading another long night.

At nine thirty, Michael came in and sat on the edge of the bed. "How's it going?"

The stopwatch with which I was timing the contractions was lying next to me. I covered it with my hand and could feel the ticking like a tiny pulse. Suddenly I was so disheartened, felt so bullied and out of control; I was ashamed I wasn't stronger, wasn't the woman I wanted to be. I swallowed to get control of myself, but the tears pushed through and I began to bawl. The words all ran together in a slick of misery: "I'm so tired, and this baby is never going to come, and I'm sick of talking to that damn doctor, he makes me feel like a fool, and I've changed my mind, I want to be induced, because if this is the first stage of labor, I can't go through the whole damn thing from here, it hurts too much, I'm too worn out, and maybe I can't even go

through with the natural childbirth, maybe they'll have
to put me to sleep."

I paused, gulping for air. Michael looked worried,
knowing how much, all along, I had wanted *not* to be
anesthetized.

"I think," he said carefully, getting up from the bed
so that I weltered like an overloaded ship at anchor as
the mattress straightened out, "I think we should call
Dr. S. and tell him we're coming in to the hospital.
You've had enough of this."

"It's only that the contractions feel so strong, and I
guess I'm finally afraid," I sniffed, as a new wave of
crying threatened to make me unintelligible. "I don't
think I can take the pain if this is only the beginning. I
simply got myself too tired out." I should have gone in
earlier, and what they thought of me be damned. Alexandra was induced after the first twelve hours of labor,
and Len had broken the amniotic sac with a wicked-
looking knitting-needle thing. And *still* that had taken
five more hours. As Michael stood next to the bed, I
swung around, putting my arms around his knees and
my head on his thigh. He smoothed my hair. "Let's just
go to the hospital," he said very softly.

As if God had heard, the next contraction came on.
It was five minutes since the previous one. "That does
it," said Michael. "I'm calling the doctor and we're
going."

I lumbered into the kitchen, needing to write out the
schedule on which Alexandra was to get her medicine
for Mina, my adopted grandmother and our temporary
housekeeper: sweet Mina, who had come from Ger-
many between the wars, when my mother was seven, to
raise two generations of our family; devoted Mina, who
loved us all more than we deserved. As I wrote, Michael called Dr. S.'s answering service to say we were
on our way to the hospital and would meet him there.
The answering service said Dr. S. was not on call, but
that Dr. K., the third member of the group practice,
would call back in a couple of minutes. "You'd better
change your clothes," I said over my shoulder to

Michael, oblivious to the necessity of changing mine: I was still wearing a robe with nothing underneath but my huge belly. In spite of the June heat, the tile floor of the kitchen was cold, and I shifted from one foot to the other as I wrote "8 AM one teaspoonful . . ."

Another contraction came on. I glanced at my wristwatch and saw that again five minutes had elapsed. Now I was satisfied, vindicated, and felt elated even as it peaked a little early. But my elation evaporated as the peak lasted, and I began to gasp, holding onto the edge of the kitchen counter with both hands, feeling like laundry on a line in a gale of pain, anchored only by the two points of connection. Then with a great rush and splash, my water broke. It streamed down the inside of my thighs and drizzled over my insteps onto the white floor. I couldn't move as it puddled around my feet. I put my head down into my arms on the top of the dishwasher and the uncompleted instructions for Alexandra's aspirin, penicillin, and phenobarbital, so I would not pass out. I was still gasping when Michael came in.

"Oh, my *God*. Is that the water? Did the water break?"

"Now it's all right to go," I whispered. "Now something's happened."

He glanced at the trickles of fluid spiraling around my ankles, at the pink-streaked mess on the floor. "Do you think we ought to wait for the doctor to call?" But he wasn't looking for an answer—he'd already decided—and picking up the phone, called the answering service again, saying we would meet Dr. K. at the hospital, that the water had broken. He spoke sharply to me. "Get dressed now. I think we ought to go."

"Let me just finish these instructions. Mina won't know when Alexandra is supposed to have her medicine if I don't write it down." Looking impatient, Michael said, "I'm going to put on my shoes, and then I'll get the car. I want you to be ready."

I tucked my old ragged terry-cloth robe up between my legs to dry them off and stepped onto a pile of paper towels I had yanked off the roll and dropped at my feet. I called to Mina, already in bed in the little room off the kitchen. Wrapping and rewrapping her robe around her, she joined me at the dishwasher, looking dubiously at the wet floor while I went over the schedule. The lenses of her thick glasses that corrected for cataracts had a way of making her eyes look huge and loose in her face, and as she nodded her head the brilliant opaque reflections caught there flipped up and down, obscuring her eyes and then as suddenly revealing them, making me feel dizzy.

Another contraction began to build. I checked my watch: only three minutes had passed since the last one. "Three minutes," I hollered to Michael. "We're in business."

Michael walked into the kitchen a moment later. "What are you *doing*? Why aren't you getting dressed? Let's *go!*"

For that moment—once again paralyzed, pilloried by another contraction—I could do nothing but look at him helplessly, terrified, and when I opened my mouth to say something, to answer him, a voice that wasn't mine came out, a kind of cow sound, a mooing, an urgent bellow that rose to something just short of a scream. I couldn't ever remember hurting so much. He pried my fingers from the counter edge and turned me to him, but I couldn't straighten up—much less walk—and hung from his shoulders like a small monkey on its mother. I wanted to apologize for making such an ungodly sound (what *must* the neighbors think?), but I couldn't talk through the blaze of pain, could only make monstrous animal moans. Panting, I dropped my head on his chest until the contraction began to ease off. "We're in trouble," I said between set teeth. "I'm having the baby."

"I *know* you're having the baby." Michael sounded a little panicky himself. "That's why I want you to hurry up! C'mon! Should I bring your clothes?" He peeled my arms from around his neck. "I'll get your clothes, and then I'll run down and get the car."

"Don't get the car," I said dully. "There's no time."

"A taxi! You want a taxi? I'll get a taxi. That'll be faster." I had a sense of distance, of disassociation; I felt very busy . . . somewhere . . . else. Michael was talking to himself, making little reflexive motions toward the bedroom. His eyes glittered. He was halfway out the door.

"Wait. Don't go. Don't get a taxi."

"All right, you don't want a taxi. You're right. I'll get the car. It'll just take a second. Can you make it downstairs by yourself? No, come with me. Don't change your clothes. It doesn't matter." He pulled me a little toward the door but I resisted, grabbing at the dishwasher and hanging on as if to let go would be to venture into deep water when I couldn't swim.

"No."

"No? *NO?* . . . What do you *mean* no? Don't be silly. Let's not waste any more time." He was panting like me.

"I'm having the baby right now. Right here." I didn't want him to misunderstand. "Right. Now."

He stopped dead still and drew back. "You're kidding." I could see he couldn't decide whether to believe me or to believe his own good, well-ordered sense that suggested that reasonable people plan things better.

"I'm not kidding. I can feel the head." Little spurts of fluid splashed onto the floor in emphasis, while Michael stared at me as if he expected the head to show itself somehow, perhaps popping out of my shoulder or falling out of my mouth.

"Oh my Lord. Oh my Lord." He made two quick trips the length of the kitchen, the only pacing he was going to get in. "What'll we do? Can you get back to the bedroom?"

I wasn't going anywhere; even letting myself down onto the floor seemed to be more than ought to be required of me at such a moment. The thing was to have this baby however it had to be had; beyond the fact—the immediacy—of this birth, my coping mechanisms stalled. "I think I'd better stay here," I said with the exaggerated dignity of someone who is declining an invitation for which she had no adequate excuse. "We'll just have to handle it ourselves." (*Handle* it? What was I *talking* about?) I was very frightened, but I wanted to seem calm.

Another contraction began to gather with the massive roll of a mountainous storm cloud; I knew it was a birth contraction. It might have been a bowling ball that was pushing against the top of my thighs and I squeezed them together as I had when I was little and couldn't get to the bathroom fast enough. The baby was going to drop out on its head in front of the dishwasher, into the soggy piles of paper towels. "It's coming. It's coming," I wailed.

Propping me back against the kitchen counter, Michael spun around and grabbed the kitchen phone, dialing the number of the doctor's answering service. He shouted into the mouth piece, holding the receiver away from his head as if he were broadcasting. "You-tell-that-doctor-to-get-over-here-right-away-we're-having-the-baby." He slammed the phone down, and in spite of being so distraught, I began to laugh.

"Michael! You didn't say who we were, or where we were, or anything!" He laughed too, breaking the tension, looking sheepish. It was okay, we would be okay. We would manage by ourselves. "It's coming now," I said again, more calmly. It was almost a whisper.

"Lie down," Michael commanded. And to Mina, whom we'd forgotten and who was standing motionless, astonished, he said, in very measured tones, "Go downstairs. Tell the doorman to call one of the doctors in the building. Tell the doorman we are having the baby and we need help." Mina ran out the front door without a word. Michael helped me to the floor; I certainly would have remained standing, bewildered, if he hadn't given me a little push. So much for Pearl Buck and her women of the fields. Here I had an opportunity to try a better way of giving birth, a more natural way, a way I would never have been indulged in in the hospital, and recent conditioning took over. Michael had said Lie down! and obediently I slid onto the floor. My long terry robe seemed to be everywhere—I felt wrapped in it, trapped in it—but while Michael washed his hands and watched me nervously, I managed finally to get clear of the fabric and part the robe beneath the still tightly tied sash under my breast. I bent my knees, pulled them up. It was good enough: with my legs opened toward Michael, he could see the head crowning—a convex disc of rosy purple, bulging like an eye. I was no longer thinking, just feeling the tremendous pressure, as if a cantaloupe were trying to be born. I would burst, a bomb of flesh; my viscera would push through and plop out, I would lose control in all the bearing down and make a shameful stinking mess on my nice white floor. I strained and puffed, trying to do the Lamaze breathing that was supposed to slow the progress of birth, trying to keep the pile driver of the baby's head from splitting me up the middle like a pea pod, convinced that if I could just give us a little time to think, everything would be all right. I put my hands between my legs to feel the head, to determine what was happening, perhaps to ease, somehow, the baby's passage, but Michael pushed them away gently. "I'll do it."

I remembered the movies of births I'd seen in my Lamaze class, the ones from the Continent, in which no episiotomy (the surgical slitting of the perineum—the thin skin just behind the vaginal opening) was performed. The doctors there prevented tearing of the delicate membranes by controlling the speed of the birth and allowing the perineum to accommodate the baby's head, as if easing it through a sweater with a tight neck. "Try to stretch the perineum so I don't get ripped up," I managed to say, but I might as well have suggested to a sky diver with a failed chute that he bend his knees for the landing: birth at this stage has the insistence and uncontrollable urgency of vomiting. I could feel myself tearing backward and forward, but it no longer hurt. I was as separate from the pain—though not from the sensation—as if it were my robe tearing, rather than me.

My body gave one more tremendous heave which I experienced but had no control over, and with a wrenching, sucking noise, the baby's head fell out of the vagina and lolled against my buttocks. It felt awful, terrifying, and painless.

"That's the head, isn't it?" I felt disoriented, as if I were rolling downhill and couldn't stop. I was a macabre, garish, surrealistic painting—like those I had seen by the Mexican artist, Frida Kahlo-Rivera—lying there on the chaste white tile, my ugly mustard-colored robe in wings under me, my thighs smeared with blood, and a glistening bulb of baby-head, the eyes swollen and the face blue, hanging out of my body.

I knew the baby ought to be turned, the shoulder ought to be helped out because it was a bulky part, but everything seemed in such slow motion, and from such a great distance, that I didn't realize how fast first one shoulder and then the other squeezed out after the head. With the shoulders freed, the rest of the baby's body followed easily, flopping out wetly onto Michael's hands.

"A boy," Michael said, sounding satisfied. Then his voice picked up a tone of elation. "It's a boy." He held him up, as if he were displaying a luxury item aimed at the upper-income consumer. Sure enough. It was a baby, it was a boy. There was a tiny penis. And he seemed to have all the right parts in their prescribed number. (I was counting fast.) Looking at him, all I could think of were those round rubber babies that were called Dydee dolls in the forties; I had had one I loved unashamedly into my teens.

He was perfect. And while his face had been discolored at the moment of birth, a healthy pink had come up quickly. Probably because of his fast trip, he was very beautiful, perfectly proportioned without the misshapen head that is usual after birth. He had a wisp of a smile on his face, still coated with the waxy white vernix. And he was sound asleep. Or unconscious.

Or dead.

My heart almost stopped. All the fear flooded back.

"Is he breathing?" I was almost shouting, half sitting up, the blood and water and mucus tipping forward out of me and flooding toward Michael where he knelt between my legs, wetting his new chinos at each knee. "For God's sake turn him over. Turn him upside down." It was all I could think of. Isn't that what they did to clear the air passages? Trying to stay calm I pushed my fingers into the baby's mouth to make sure there were no obstructions, waking him up. He hollered in protest. "It's good that he cries," I said no less than three times, reassuring myself and Michael, who seemed to need no reassurance.

Michael put the baby into my arms, and I jiggled the tiny boy gently to keep him crying until I could be sure that he was not in a coma, that he was not going to die, that he was breathing easily and nothing was wrong. He waved his small wet fists at the cold noisy world that had intruded into his blissful prenatal slumber. I pushed myself up slightly, so that I could lean my back against the wall and cradle the baby more expeditiously, putting him to my breast, now wanting him to stop crying, to be comforted. I also hoped that if he nursed, my uterus would contract again and push out the placenta, which energetic and then halfhearted bearing down hadn't dislodged: it should have been expelled right after the baby, and it was damned uncomfortable. I was impressed with nature's cleverness—the cord was exactly long enough for me to hold the baby while we were, in a sense, still one person—but I didn't like sitting in that clammy, gelatinous puddle with the rubbery, tumescent cord that coiled from my body nasty and slithery under me.

The baby was still crying when Mina rushed back through the front door, her robe untied, her round dumpling body bobbling under her pink nylon nightgown. How hard it must have been for her—in her sixties and always modest and deferential, especially toward men—to have to confront Albert, our eighty-year-old doorman, with whom she maintained a polite flirtation, in her nightie.

"Look what we did, Mina!" I must have looked and sounded like a demented child presenting a mud pie or some other equally unappetizing mess for a parent's approval. "Michael and I did it ourselves. It's a boy, Mina."

She reached out to the wall for support; I was afraid she might faint. Michael moved quickly to her side and put one arm around her, steadying her. She leaned into him ever so slightly, and, looking dazed, reported that she and Albert were unable to find any medical help. Two of the four doctors in the building were out for the evening (it was a Friday night), one was retired and felt he couldn't get involved, and the final one said that obstetrics was not his specialty, that he had no instruments, and that we would do better to call an ambulance . . . which Albert had done. Michael walked Mina into the darkened living room and left her there to collect herself.

Now there was a banging at the kitchen door; Michael opened it for the superintendent, who looked out of breath and worried. I was conscious of the immodest position in which I faced the door—my knees were still bent and spread, though I had pulled the sodden robe up between my legs. The super decently looked away and suggested to Michael that he get a sheet to cover me. Ramirez confirmed what Mina had said about the doctors, shaking his head as if he had a hard time understanding how people who lived in such relative comfort could care so little for their neighbors. One had the sense that any of the people *he* knew—the ones who sat around on stoops and yelled at each other's kids and lived in real neighborhoods—would have found ways to be much more helpful. He told Michael that the police had been called, and an ambulance, and that he would try personally to talk to the two doctors in the building.

"Tell them," said Michael, "that we've already *done* everything. The baby's born already. We just want to make sure that everyone's all right. Get them just to come and check Stephani and check the baby and see that he is breathing properly. They don't need instruments. We just want a little reassurance. Any doctor knows more than we know."

I nodded in agreement. "We don't need anything, really. I just want to make sure that everything's all right." My voice shook, either with the cold of the floor, or fright. "It may be too late, if something's wrong, by the time the police and the ambulance get here. Just ask them to come and *look* at us. Surely one of them could do that?"

Mr. Ramirez dashed down the service stairs on his errand of mercy. Alone again, Michael and I looked at each other. What now? The baby had stopped crying, and though I was urging him to suckle, he wanted to sleep. I held his still-wet body next to my own, wrapping the upper part of my robe around both of us. It was delightful, holding my naked newborn that way; I regretted not having been able to share such a moment with my daughter. He was exquisite. He looked pleased with himself. I relaxed as Michael crouched next to me, looking at the baby. We began to giggle, and then to laugh, singing "We did it, we did it" to each other. We felt wonderfully satisfied and wonderfully close.

"If this weren't so terrifying, it would be very funny," I said. "And how much nicer, all around—if you planned it, of course," I added hastily—"to have the baby at home. We should have had Alexandra this way. And you did such a good job." Michael beamed.

We kissed each other. Michael touched the cheek of the sleeping baby.

"Oh, Lord! Alexandra!" In the excitement we had completely forgotten her. Was she awake? Frightened by the noise? Michael ran to check her. I was feeling more and more accomplished. Having a baby wasn't so hard. I made another feeble attempt to expel the afterbirth, even though the cord was still slightly rigid. I had read somewhere that until the cord detumesces completely, it should not be cut: vital nutrients would still be flowing through it. I also was more and more aware of my discomfort: the placenta seemed to be stuck partway through the cervix (at least that's what it felt like) and I was beginning to cramp severely—undoubtedly the attempt of the uterus to be done with its job of giving birth. It was also apparent that in spite of the lack of sensation in the vagina during the birth itself, the baby had done considerable damage with his passage. When Michael came back—Alexandra hadn't even awakened —I asked him to check me. With the continuing trickle of fluid and the caked blood, however, he couldn't tell where I was torn.

"You'd better call the doctor back, in case he's coming here."

"That goddamn doctor," Michael said as he reached for the phone, which was on the wall above my head. "He hasn't even called *back* yet."

He had a brief conversation with the answering service, and when he hung up, he shook his head.

"You're not going to believe this," he said, "but they still haven't been able to get the guy who's on call. He's at a *party* in New Jersey, and someone has had the phone tied up. They're sending the police to the house to get him." His face was shadowed, and he looked angry. "It's a goddamn good thing that nothing went wrong, but you can bet that Dr. B. is going to hear about this. This is totally unacceptable. One or both of you could have *died*. You should have been in the hospital much earlier." Sometimes Michael gets a look on his face that makes him look as if he's bitten into an apple that turned out to be wormy.

"It's okay, though, Pea," I said, using my pet name for him. "We're both all right. Nothing did happen. Everything's *perfect*. We did it all by ourselves! Alexandra's even still asleep."

He turned away and stood for a moment, his hands in his pockets, the wet stains on the knees of his pants creeping around now and almost meeting at the back crease. "I'd better check on Mina." Who, it turned out, was standing where he had left her, looking out a window at the city's night lights.

"She was probably in shock," he said later.

\* \* \*

We managed to shock Michael's parents as well, but shocking them provided us with more consistent amusement than shocking anyone else: their life had always been so well-planned and sensible that getting them riled with the unexpected was a diverting sport for both Michael and me. It was late—10:45—and ordinarily they retired early, but they wouldn't have forgiven us for not letting them know about the arrival of their new grandson. I felt a kind of demonic glee (we had outdone ourselves this time in being chaotic and unpredictable) as I urged Michael to call them, intruding once more on the orderliness and comprehensibility of their comfortable lives in the near suburb in which they had raised their two boys. Michael's conversation with his mother was a masterpiece of ellipsis, a monologue over what he reported to be her stunned silence.

"Hi! . . . Did I wake you? We thought you'd want to know we had a baby! It's a boy!" (Pause.) "Oh, he's fine. She's fine too. They're *both* fine." (Pause.) "Oh yes, the delivery went very smoothly, just great!" (Pause.) "Well of *course* I could tell. I was *there*, wasn't I? I . . . uh . . . I even helped deliver him. . . . Actually, I guess it would be more accurate to say that I delivered him myself," Michael said with great dignity (Pause.) "He didn't have anything to say about it; he wasn't there." (Pause.) "Well . . . probably because we're still at home. . . ." Michael held the receiver away from his ear and rolled his eyes. Gingerly resettling it, he continued: "It just happened too fast. We never made it to the hospital." (Pause.) "No, really, they're both fine, there's nothing to worry about." (Pause.) "No, you don't have to do that, it's not necessary. Everything's under control. . . ."

And then Michael was holding the receiver away from his ear again, looking at it as if he expected to see tiny tendrils of smoke puffing out of the circle of little holes.

"She hung up on me. She said they'd be right in."

"They don't have to come."

"I know, but she's already hung up."

"What did she say?"

"Nothing, except that they'd be in right away. She didn't say anything else."

(Later my mother-in-law said that she and my father-in-law had been asleep when Michael called, and that she was groggy. After she had hung up she went back to sit on her bed and collect her thoughts. After a few moments of silent reflection, she said, "Did I just answer that phone?" "Yes," my father-in-law sleepily replied. "Who was it at this hour?" "Oh God," she said. "Get dressed. I was praying I'd dreamed it." It is the only time she has ever left her house with the beds unmade.)

Now there was further commotion outside the back door: the police had arrived. We could hear the sirens and see the red flashes from the squad car bouncing around the quiet dark walls of the hallway. Two officers marched authoritatively through the door, looking around in police-like fashion for perpetrators. Ramirez, the super, hung behind them.

The first one came up and stood over me. I felt another stab of self-consciousness, lying there like that, although now I had a sheet draped over me in which my knees made a little tent.

"Are you okay? Pain? Bleeding?" He had red hair and freckles. "Should we take you to the hospital in the squad car, or can you wait for an ambulance?"

"I'll wait," I said in a tiny voice, feeling as if I had somehow affronted them by no longer needing them. The second patrolman stood on my other side.

"It's a good thing you already had it," he said, as much to his partner as to me. "I never delivered a baby before."

"Don't they train you to do that?" I was trying to seem interested and hospitable. Maybe I should offer them tea or cookies.

"Oh, yeah," he answered. "I just never *did* it." There was an awkward pause during which we looked at each other and then, variously, at the ceiling, the floor, and some empty middle distance.

"How did this happen?" asked the redhead, picking up the conversational ball. Michael grimaced and I was too tired to go into it.

"It just did."

"Didn't you have any warning?" They were persistent. They must have been expected to write a report about my extravagant behavior, offering some seemly reason for it.

"We just guessed wrong," I said dismissively, busying myself with the baby so that I wouldn't have to talk to them anymore, but would not seem unsociable either. The afterbirth was still caught somewhere inside; I was hurting and edgy. I was also aware of how ridiculous and disheveled I must look, and how the cord, now completely flaccid, snaked up from under my robe, over the sash, and back in again where it was still attached to the baby I held in my arms next to my body. To make matters worse, I was beginning to worry that if the afterbirth weren't expelled soon—and the cord properly cut—it might mean that something had indeed gone wrong.

"Maybe we should try to cut the cord," I said to Michael. "Do you think we should?"

"Naw," said the cop, whose responsibility I apparently now was. "The ambulance will be here in a few minutes. They'll do it. There'll be a doctor on the ambulance. You'd better wait for them." He leaned over me and peered at the baby. "Cute baby. Usually they don't look too good right after they're born. Mind if I smoke?"

I pointed to the end of the kitchen. "Over there, please." His heavy boots made a scratching, clacking sound against the ceramic tile. He stepped absentmindedly over the evaporating pool of amniotic fluid. "I dunno," he said, as he sauntered toward the back door, "*my* wife wouldn't have been able to do that. Jesus. On the kitchen floor."

"Your wife may not have had any more choice than I did," I said, but only Michael heard me.

The policemen talked and looked around for nonexistent ashtrays, eventually dropping their ashes into their cupped hands. Their presence was reassuring while we waited for the ambulance that finally arrived with much screeching of tires and the siren going full blast. By now I was sure that most of the inhabitants of Eighty-first Street were leaning out their windows, looking for the cause of all the excitement, as New Yorkers tend to do.

The ambulance attendants first tried to get a stretcher up the back elevator, and then a stretcher up the front elevator, and in the end settled on a wheelchair—the only conveyance that would fit in either one of them. The medic ran in, sweating heavily and looking like an older version of the teenagers I see in the park with radios grafted to the sides of their heads.

"Well, you *took* long enough," Michael chided them. "Do you realize we called almost forty-five minutes ago?"

"We couldn't get here any sooner," replied the medic in a surly tone. "Friday's a real busy night," added the driver, who ran in too, jostling the policemen. There were now seven people and one baby in a space about three by ten.

"Do you think I *like* this job, buddy?" asked the medic. "I mean, like, I was supposed to be off *duty* at eleven, and now *this*." He looked tragically at his watch. "Other people got plans too, you know. It's Friday night. You oughta be glad we came. We coulda called in off duty." He rolled his eyes and shook his head, quite clearly washing his hands of us. "The people in this city!" he muttered.

"Are you a doctor?" Michael asked with a trace of sarcastic self-righteousness. "Where's the doctor? They said they were sending a *doctor*." The medic gave him a withering look.

"Hey. Buddy. Ya think they can spare doctors to run around in ambulances and do stuff like this? I'm *trained*.

You got nothing to worry about. Like I said, you oughta be glad you got *us*." He turned to me. "You cut the cord yet?"

"A doctor!" said Michael, his voice rising. "They promised a *doctor*." The medic ignored him, moving toward me and flipping open the top of my robe to get a better look at the baby. "He seems okay. He breathe right away?" He was fumbling in his case for something.

"Do you know how to cut a cord?" Michael's voice had an almost imperceptible tinge of hysteria.

"I know what I'm doing," the medic snarled. "Why I've cut probably about *twelve* cords. So I know how to cut a cord. Just stand back, buddy, and don't worry. We'll take care of everything."

"The placenta is still in there," I offered meekly. "It doesn't seem to want to come out. Do you think maybe you could pull it out?"

The medic tugged experimentally at the cord. The red-haired policeman dropped a long ash from the end of his cigarette, and the superintendent turned away, clearing his throat. It didn't budge. I was afraid that something would tear—or worse yet, that the cord might somehow snap and leave the placenta inside me, where my imagination already had it festering; then they'd have to go fishing for it in the hospital. I must have looked scared, because the medic stopped pulling the cord and sort of handed the slack up to me. I didn't know what to do with it either.

"Naw, we'd better leave it. They'll fix it in the hospital." He set to work clipping and cutting the cord. The other attendant pulled a sterile paper sheet from its plastic bag and instructed me to lay the baby on it. I didn't want to surrender his soft little body to the dry, crinkly paper.

"Your husband can carry him," the medic volunteered.

They wrapped the baby boy up as if he were a package, tying string around him to keep the sheet in place. I was lifted off the floor, the cord dragging obscenely behind me like a lifeless tail, and helped to lower myself gingerly into the wheelchair. Everything was cold and wet and sticky and crusty. It felt as though I were sitting on a recent road kill.

In the meantime, Mina had ventured out of the living room, blinking and pale. She still hadn't said a word. I patted the hand she was resting on the arm of the wheelchair as if she were a child who didn't want to see her mommy go.

"I'm fine," I said, "and Michael's parents will be here soon. Why don't you clean up that mess in front of the dishwasher? You know how his mother is." My attempt at levity—a reference to my mother-in-law's well-known fastidiousness—didn't take. Mina nodded slowly, as if she were dreaming. "Take good care of Alexandra. I'll be home in a couple of days." I leaned closer to her as the ambulance attendant looked at his watch. "You did good, Mina. Thanks.

In a moment we were out the front door of the apartment and into the elevator. I tried to arrange the bloody part of the robe so that it couldn't be seen, knowing that by now the lobby would be lined with co-tenants: New York City is the home of the spectator sport of disaster watching. The attendant snatched the wheelchair out of the elevator and then ran, pulling it backwards over the Persian carpets. I felt doubly undignified, being raced blindly through the lobby like a huge, terry-cloth covered garbage bag on a hand dolly. "Slow down," I hollered as I waved to my neighbors and tried to look jaunty. Michael tripped through the lobby after us, carrying his large white parcel—in which no baby was apparent—trying to keep up.

Because I was able only to look behind me, I didn't see my in-laws until I passed them. (They had made a speechless trip in from the suburbs in record time.) The picture they made, looking uncharacteristically disheveled themselves, their heads swiveling to catch the whole parade, their mouths open, was unexpectedly comic.

"Hold it!" I shouted to the attendant, who was hell-bent on getting me out the door and was moving faster than ever. "Those are my *relatives*! I want to *talk* to them!" But the attendant, belatedly whipped into a frenzy of urgency, must have thought that at last I had cracked under the strain, shouting and gesticulating behind him, and continued out the door. "Don't worry," I yelled through cupped hands at my in-laws, who stood side by side, transfixed.

Michael dashed past them, giving a weak little smile, afraid of being left behind. He proffered the crackly white bundle briefly, then realizing that no baby was visible and his bestowal looked like a rolled shroud, he drew it back.

"Don't worry, there's nothing the matter with the baby. I'll call you from the hospital," was all he managed to get out as he fled out the door after me. The onlookers in the lobby rubbed their hands and nodded to each other in satisfaction at the little drama.

The attendants chucked me and my wheelchair into the back of the ambulance together; outside it looked like a converted panel truck, inside, like a two-person submarine.

Michael was handed onto a small seat which was bolted to the portholed steel divider that sealed us off from the men in front. We took off up Riverside Drive after a brief tussle about whether I would be taken to the city hospital that had dispatched the ambulance, or to the private hospital where my third-string doctor—I hoped—awaited me. It appeared that I was somehow now the property of the city hospital, and it took no little convincing to get them to take us where we wanted to go.

As if the baby weren't now an hour and fifteen minutes old, and as if everything that we had to worry about medically hadn't been seen to, it was suddenly an emergency call and we raced uptown, sirens wailing and rubber burning. I had to brace both feet against the

divider and hang onto the door handle with one hand
while steadying a wheel of the chair with the other to
avoid being tossed around like the clapper of a bell.
Michael was no help: he was having trouble staying on
his own little seat, trying to keep the baby from being
flung across the back of the ambulance as we alternated
between startling accelerations and momentum-defying
stops, holding the bundle well out in front of him so
that his arms would absorb the jolts of the potholes. He
looked as if he were trying to keep an incompetently
packaged tiered cake level. When we paused for an instant for a turn, Michael tried banging on the divider
and shouting that there was no need to hurry now, that
the rough ride was even worse back where we were. But
the driver, triply insulted, steadfastly refused to acknowledge us and dipped and swerved over the New
York City streets all the way to the hospital.

On our arrival, the baby was taken from Michael,
with reassurances that he was all right and promises
that he would be returned to me for the 6:00 A.M. feeding in the morning. I wanted very much to establish a
good nursing routine as soon as possible and didn't rel-
ish being thwarted—as I had been with Alexandra—by
hospital schedules, which are inflexibly alien to babies' schedules. A couple of months before, I had come
here to speak with the head nursing administrator in the
vain hope that I might convince her of my ability to
care for my newborn infant a forbidden twenty-four
hours a day (which I would have to do when I got
home anyway), but in spite of my pleas and protestations of competence, I was rebuffed. The administrator—who looked as though she chewed nails and spit
rust—informed me huffily that modified rooming-in
(for the eight daylight hours) was for the *mother's* benefit, so she could get her rest. I argued, cajoled, promised
to be good, and threatened, but no dice: the hospital
knew best what was right for "its" babies and "its"
mothers. I could of course always get myself another

hospital. (In retaliation I intended to be released as soon as possible, denying them a couple extra days of their exorbitant prices.)

Dr. K. arrived soon after we did, rescued from his pool party in New Jersey. From his attitude, I couldn't tell whether he was chagrined about what had happened, or simply out of sorts because his evening had been interrupted. He installed me in an operating room and tackled the messy job of cleaning me up. Now that the excitement was over, I could feel the tears—five of them, by my count, and all forward, with two into the clitoris. They reopened as he pulled the cord that still hung out of me—limp and iridescent, moon-gray—and finally dislodged the reluctant placenta which slurped out with a voluptuous wet pop that sounded ridiculously sexual. It was cursorily examined by Dr. K., and discarded—having presumably been adjudged to be perfectly normal in spite of its tenacity.

Compromised by fatigue and aftershock, I was trembling so badly I had to be strapped down. Then, as Dr. K. pierced me again and again with the knifelike little needles used for suturing, I relinquished any show of bravery I had managed to maintain up until now and squealed like a pig being slaughtered. He was hurting me. He was hurting me a lot, and I no longer cared what he or anybody else thought.

Michael heard me screaming from the hall outside the operating room where he stood waiting for me, and tried to get in, insisting on his right to be with me and lend whatever support he could, but Dr. K., a man I had never met, was having none of it and barred him, making me feel even more punished than I already did and throwing Michael at last into the rage that had been brewing for hours. By the time the suturing was finished, I was thoroughly worn out. So was Michael, who looked worse after having had to stand outside the operating room listening to me howl than he had after the many exhausting hours of labor we had gone through together with Alexandra. He tenderly kissed me good night and I fluttered my fingers at him as I was wheeled off to a room in the silent night-dimmed hospital.

At seven the next morning I awoke with a start. I could hear the babies out on the floor, but nobody had brought me mine. I desperately wanted to see my little boy and reassure myself once more that he was none the worse for our experience of the night before. I also wanted to nurse him. Now.

I rang the nurse. Why hadn't my baby been brought out with the others for the 6:00 A.M. feeding? She had been instructed, she said, not to wake me because I hadn't been admitted until midnight. "I'm awake now, as you can see," I politely submitted, "and I would like to have my baby as soon as it is convenient." She promised that he would be brought shortly. Then she disappeared.

At eight I corralled another nurse. I must understand, she said brusquely, that with all the other babies out on the floor the nurses were terribly busy and could not be expected just to drop everything simply because there was something I wanted. I would have to wait.

"I can't imagine," I tossed at her retreating back, "that two minutes cannot be found to bring me my baby." A baby was not what could be termed an unreasonable request. "I can go get him on my own," I said. "He's *hungry*. It's not fair to make him wait!" But I was talking to myself.

By eight forty-five I was fuming. Clearly nothing was going to be done unless I made some sort of scene, which I was entirely willing to do on behalf of my defenseless infant. So I stalked out to the nurse's station— an uncomfortable endeavor: a spread-eagled shuffle would have come more naturally but it lacked what I thought was the necessary forthrightness—to demand my rights and my baby's rights. The nurse at the desk was evasive, referring me to the woman in charge, who, after more evasiveness, admitted that I was not to have the baby at all. Because he had been born outside the hospital he was in quarantine and could not be removed.

I was free to go in and see him, and to nurse him
on a chair in the isolation nursery, but he could not
be brought "onto the floor" to be with me in my
room—even for that dinky "modified rooming-in."
(The precise term she used in reference to my poor innocent little fellow was "contaminated.") She pointed
to a small, pale-blue glass enclosure at the end of the
hall. (*Contaminated?*)

I tried to reason with the nurse—a wildly optimistic
gesture. Did it make sense that my son was any different from the other babies because he had been born at
home? They didn't disinfect the *women* who came in
here, who handled their babies all day, and then returned
them to the common nursery at night—to say nothing
of the fathers and grannies and cousins and other visitors who also handled, breathed on, and generally compromised the babies' "sterility." The nurse was not to
be swayed: the baby could not be removed from the
isolation nursery until we were both discharged from
the hospital.

I stomped off to the end of the hall to nurse my
baby. Holding him, feeling his small body against me
while he rooted blindly, blissfully, at my breast, I began
to feel the considerable anger I had suppressed or deflected the last two days surfacing like oil from a
wreck: all that anxiety, resentment, and guilt; all the
disgust at myself for not having had the sense and
confidence to believe in my own body, of perhaps having very nearly caused my baby's death because *I* didn't
want to be thought neurotic. I had been required, too
often, to abdicate my conviction that I knew what was
best for myself and my baby. I felt more and more de-
personalized, judged, and railroaded. *I* had been pregnant, *I* had given birth, and ever since I had been
packed into this hospital I had had no control over
what was done with me and my baby, and no voice in
the decision making that would determine how he spent
the important first few days of his life. How *dare* they?
How could *I*?

I settled my tiny boy into his plastic bin and gently

tucked the receiving blanket around him. He sucked his own lips for a moment and then was mercifully asleep. I knew what I woud do. It was simple. I walked back to the nurse's station.

"I'm leaving," I said calmly to the woman at the desk. "If it's such a big problem to have my baby with me, I'm going home. I *had* him without anybody's help, and I can manage the rest of it without any help. So you'd better do whatever needs to be done to release us. Just wrap him up in something while I get dressed," I finished very matter-of-factly, ignoring the horrified expression on her face, "and I will take him as he is. Thank you very much." I turned to leave, feeling as if I'd just ordered a take-out dinner.

The nurse grabbed my forearm through her little window. "Ah . . . just wait a second," she said. "There must be some way to work this out. . . ."

"Do I get my baby?" I interrupted.

"You know we can't do that, it's against the rules. . . ."

"You work it out then," I said, "because I'm going home."

"You can't do that, you can't do that," she said, her arm still extending through the window to where her hand was attached to me. "Now don't get excited." She looked around quickly, as if she might need some help controlling me, perhaps for a couple of able-bodied men to throw me to the floor and restrain me until I regained my senses. (Crazy patient here, declaring her independence from the hospital's policy and arbitrary benevolence.) She pressed a buzzer and two more nurses hurried down the hall toward us: reinforcements!

"I'm not excited," I said, "but I *am* going home."

"You *can't* leave," she insisted. "Nobody's released you. And you certainly can't take the baby. It's against regulations."

"Oh, but I *can* leave. And I intend to leave. And you're going to have a hard time preventing me from taking the baby with me. And now you *will* excuse me,"

I said, a mocking tone slipping into my voice, "I have to call my husband."

I wheeled around as purposefully as I could, considering the fact that when I walked it felt as if I'd sat in a rosebush and had caught the thorny part of it between my legs. Back in my room, I telephoned Michael to tell him please to come and retrieve us.

As so often seems to happen, irate protest was more effective than a reasonable plea. It turned out that I didn't have to leave—although by now I sincerely wanted to. It turned out that there were . . . avenues . . . to be pursued in just such "extraordinary" cases, and that arrangements could and would be made for the twenty-four-hour-a-day rooming-in that was permitted in such cases . . . the same twenty-four-hour rooming-in I had originally sought to no avail. So I waited for my official release until the next day when Len himself could do it; he had cut his weekend short so that he could attend to his patient.

On Sunday morning Len strode into my room.

"Now *you* tell me what happened. Dr. S. told me, and Dr. K. told me. I'm having trouble understanding how things could have gotten so fouled up."

I recounted my adventures of Thursday night and Friday. Len looked pained, then said something crude about Dr. S.'s medical acuity.

Then he shrugged. "Ah well. It's over. I don't suppose it matters now, but I would have had you come in Thursday night, especially with a second child. I don't see how this could have happened! I'm truly sorry. Truly. It will hardly make amends, but of course I won't charge you any . . . obstetrical fees." He laughed and I didn't. "You could sort of say the whole thing's on me!" It occurred to me that he was probably taking preemptive action to ward off a malpractice suit.

"Well. Len." I hoped I was sounding gracious, amused, generous, rather than self-righteous and bitchy. "Just do all of us a favor: the next time a woman tells you that she's going to have her baby, pay more attention to her than to the calendar. Anyway, I forgive you your error," I added facetiously. "I forgive you for making me feel like a dimwit and a nut. You're right. It's all over."

"Friends?" he said.

"Friends," I said, thinking about saving the thousand dollars.

Monday morning I was back in the playground, wheeling the baby carriage slowly as Alexandra—not yet two—toddled along, holding onto its side for support. Zachary was so big he already looked four months old. Alexandra was thrilled with her new brother. ("Look!" she'd exclaimed, leaning over the side of his cradle the day before. "He has five fingers!" She counted the pearly little kernels on his feet. "Five toes too!" she chortled, as pleased as if she'd invented him herself.)

Michael and I and Zachary were the neighborhood's hot story. Even months later, at some local cocktail party, I would have people relate *our* story to *me* (the identity of the protagonists having been lost in the retellings) with apocryphal embellishments. We achieved a certain celebrity by becoming part of the collective-young-couples' nightmare. It was an object lesson to all those smart, optimistic, self-assured women who rocked their babies and chatted busily in the park: even people who behaved themselves—who fed their children health food and saved sensibly, who were devoted to each other and were intelligent and moderate and practical, people who had every reason to be blessed—could have things go very very wrong.

# SUMMER AND FALL 1970

IT WAS A SUMMER LIKE ALL NEW YORK SUMMERS: hot, tarry and enervating by day; by night exhilarating, friendly and loud, the mood sustained by the steady thrum of salsa.

In all its sameness, the world looked fresh to me. I was new the way the baby was new, and I groped lazily through a warm fog of motherhood, slowed with the ripeness of lactation. Days and nights became a familiar round of pushing a spoon at or proffering a breast to the thrust of small mouths which opened blindly toward me like bells of flowers seeking the sun; transporting small bodies slippery with summer sweat to and from the park; then feeding once more; and bathing, detaching the tiny hands that wound in my hair and clutched at my clothing and hung on my fingers. I loved doing all this; I loved being real and right and normal, knowing where I belonged and what it was that was expected of me. Knowing who I was. The regularity, the certainty, the crowding made me feel secure: I swaddled the children in my caring, and they swaddled me in their need.

There was also immense relief at no longer actually being pregnant, at having the deed done and the reward finally won. While my pregnant friends had bloomed and blushed, I had looked harassed and pinched from constant morning sickness, deformed from the low, heavy, protrusive carry my body improvised in the service of gestation. Both my pregnancies had seemed to attack me, feed on me, drain me, and ultimately trick

41

me in both advent and climax; lushness and the satisfaction of savoring myself in the mothering role came in with the milk. There was such pleasure at being in a province I knew better than anyone, where there was no intercessor between myself and my children, or between myself and my body's functioning. That was one of the reasons it took so long for me to call the doctor about the pain in my chest.

I had been toying with the idea of returning to modeling—it seemed such an easy, lucrative, part-time endeavor—so at first I thought the pain was from carrying my portfolio and a heavy makeup bag while I walked around to see photographers. I'm not used to this anymore, I thought. I must be getting old. I guessed that I had pulled a muscle in my neck that connected with something in my back: the pain was deep inside my right shoulder as if the rope of tissue that held my head to my body were fraying at its source. I took hot baths and slept with heating pads and had Michael rub my shoulder, knowing that was what Dr. G., my internist, would suggest if I called him, and wanting to dispense with the obvious. I reminded myself to carry my bags only on the left, but the pain in the shoulder persisted, radiating down my back, curving around the scapula, and hooking into my chest like a thrill of fear. It sometimes seemed to improve, and then would come back, in no sensible relationship to the careful ministrations Michael and I lavished on it.

In September I gave in and saw Dr. G., who advanced a couple of unimaginative hypotheses: "Stop nursing—your breasts are too heavy for your frame and are pulling the muscles of the chest wall," and "What do you expect? Hauling two babies around all day?" In short, it would surely go away. He also tendered some fatherly advice on the management of tension, suggesting I get more rest, get more fun and diversion, and learn to Relax. I should also not give in to it and pamper myself.

I thought Dr. G. was suspicious of me . . . if not of

outright malingering, at least of some minor disintegration of the moral fiber. Dr. G.'s position on physical complaints was reductionistic and pragmatic—even karmic—and his approach was either to convince or cajole one out of them. Or failing that, embarrass one out of them. In this he was like my cool, pinched mother, who didn't approve either of being sick or rewarding it in others, and who had taught me not to rely on the subtle modulations in the body's processes for any cues: hypochondria lurked behind every complaint. My father —even more hardheaded—simply chose not to believe in illness and has been rewarded for his apostasy with a gratifyingly healthy life.

Dr. G. was doing his best; I couldn't blame him for his attitude, which was at any rate familiar. I felt apologetic about adding to the ranks of typically health-obsessed, attention-seeking females who swarmed through his office because only their doctor would listen to them. And I hated to think of myself as typical . . . especially in such a predictable, self-indulgent way. Dr. G. had always been nice to me and not in the least reproachful when some worrisome symptom had miraculously responded to "Take two aspirin and call me in the morning." His stern joviality and vague affection for me were endlessly reassuring.

Also, I had to admit that even *I* was suspicious of me: I had read enough psychology to see myself refracted through his prism and to be remotely shaken by the spectrum of possible neurosis. He would probably attribute my complaints to deeply rooted conflicts about my femininity, particularly since every physical problem I had ever had was so intimately associated with my being female; he would see me as, quite literally, hyster-ical. There was something circular and self-destructive and confusing about the way in which my womb (*hystera,* in Greek)—or symbolically, my femaleness—was not only apparently to *blame* for my being high-strung and anxious, plagued with imaginary organic disorders, but at the same time the *locus* of these disorders. (I dippily came to take refuge in the view that, born a Libra, my

vulnerable point was my reproductive organs.) I sometimes felt like the heraldic beast choking on its own
tail, going around and around, consuming itself in pain,
misdirected attention, and guilt.

Where had I got off the track? How had I evolved
from a naive twelve-year-old who had awakened one
morning with a bad cramp she thought was from something she ate, only to be surprised by the reddish-brown
stain in the crotch of her yellow pajamas, into a woman
so neurotic that she could no longer control the ways
in which her body suffered what was in her head? As
competent as I had made myself in my world, my body
betrayed me again and again. Perhaps I had just never
adjusted.

By the time I was thirteen, the proof of my womanhood laid irregular siege to me in a mensal ordeal I
spent each intervening period recovering from. I
dreaded those first twinges that signaled the resumption
of the assault that then drove me through three white-
knuckle days a month before I could relax into simple
discomfort. My mother and her friends were right: it
really was a curse—messy and smelly and frequently
embarrassing. My mother uncharacteristically tolerated
my moaning and groaning; she already knew that
women carried the major burden, that life as a woman
was hard, and that women paid and paid and paid. It
was only natural one should have to submit to the de-
gradations of the body—it was one more rivet in the
massive structure of "the way things are," and a further
reminder of how little control a woman had over her
life and the particulars that that life dished out.

It was not until college that I learned, with the absolute egotism of self-abnegation, to be disappointed in
myself for these lunatic weaknesses. Cramps were no
excuse for anything, not even for themselves; menstrua-
tion was a perfectly normal, perfectly natural function.
Normal and natural functions should not be disabling in
an otherwise healthy young woman. Didn't I realize the
pain was psychogenic, that I was punishing myself for
my own reluctance to assume fully the legacy and

obligations of my femininity? There was nothing organically wrong with me. (And what about the throwing up, the diarrhea, the pallor, the cold sweat?) Tsk. Our . . . problems . . . can be very . . . powerful. And then hurriedly: it doesn't mean the . . . pain . . . isn't *there*. It does mean it isn't . . . well . . . real. Oh.

I tried to learn to take more responsibility for myself, as suggested by the deceptively motherly-looking school physician. I obediently rummaged through the tangled circuits in my head, suspecting shorts or bad connections, sniffing for burnt-out junction boxes. I wanted to be whole and above suspicion. I *did* like being a woman—but in spite of my efforts to control my "resistance" to the natural course of my body's functioning, I could never make myself remotely regular between my periods, never comfortable during. It was unnatural. *I* was unnatural. The doctors said don't worry, it will straighten out when you get a little older. Then they said, Don't worry, a pregnancy will do it.

Pregnancy certainly did do it, the first one announcing itself with a malaise so profound I feared terminal illness. I called Dr. B. after losing a splendidly inoffensive breakfast.

"I'm sick. I can't see straight, I can't walk straight, and I just threw up. I have a headache too."

"Congratulations. You're pregnant. How long since your last period?"

"Five weeks—the normal amount. I expect anytime from last week till two weeks from now." He missed my sarcasm. After all, it wasn't *his* fault.

"Too early to tell, no point in a pregnancy test yet. Maybe it's the flu. Let's see how you feel tomorrow."

Tomorrow was worse. When I finally went to see him, I watched the top of his head, his shiny dark hair slicked back, floating in the valley of the white drape, as he gave the verdict.

"Well, it looks like a duck, it walks like a duck, and it quacks like a duck. . . ." His smiling face shot up into view between the peaks of my knees. (Was he happy for me, or was he simply looking forward to the big OB fee?) "It must *be* a duck," he concluded.

I should have gotten round and ripe; instead I turned gray and stringy with morning sickness, afternoon sickness, and night sickness. Even water wouldn't stay down. By the third month of both pregnancies I was in the hospital, ostensibly being treated for the "severe hyperemesis gravidarum" that had left me dehydrated and undernourished; I knew without being told that there was an additional reason, that I was being removed from my environment and denied all visitors except Michael, so that the cycle of guilt and inadequacy to which I had fallen prey would be broken: my sense of failure at not being properly, beatifically pregnant made me edgy and tense—exacerbating the nausea—while the nausea and vomitting in turn made me ever more fearful of the loss of control they symbolized.

My hospital admissions were interpretative free-for-alls; every protophysician who wanted to give his mittel-med school psychology a whirl turned up to take my history—("morning sickness is a manifestation of ambivalence toward the pregnancy, a subconscious attempt to expel the fetus"). "Are you sure you really want this baby?" the little pencil-necked interns would inquire slyly, picking their hangnails over my admissions records. I said, "Yes. Yes!" very politely, wondering if they knew something I didn't, if something were showing—a tag end of my "psychological conflicts about my femininity" fluttering past the hem of my well-organized personality like a torn slip—and "Yeses" would rattle through my tranquilized tin-can head like a few dried-up old peas.

They scared me, those doctors. I *did* want babies, so much wanted them, looked forward to them, as if my children were the final segments of a closing circle I could happily tour the rest of my life, moving faster and faster, tighter and tighter, till I was a blur of bliss, turning into rich yellow butter like Sambo's tiger. I had

worked at conceiving babies, taking progesterone shots
to get pregnant with Alexandra, and Clomid (the drug
that made septuplets, and worse) for Zachary. How
*dare* they suggest fears, ambivalence, possible rejection
of the hairless translucent mousie huddled there inside
me! . . . True that the first pregnancy was a consci-
entious response to Michael's losing his student defer-
ment on graduating from business school; also true that
my intention had been to complete the family as quickly
as possible (my own brother and I were twenty-two
months apart and had been great, wonderful friends as
we grew up—something I wanted for my own children). True that fantasies of six children filling a big
old house with noise and laughter and clutter had shrunk
to a more practical and realistic three after Alexandra's
birth, and then further withered to an orderly two with
Zachary's appearance. But the ones I had I loved, I
adored. They made me real. Maybe they were all that
made me real.

So in September I left Dr. G.'s office not exactly convinced, but at least reassured. *Everybody* said it was
hard to have children close together; it put so much
stress on the mother. Dr. G. was a good man and a good
doctor with a fine reputation: I paid him for knowing
the difference between imaginary maladies and real
problems. I wasn't ready to follow his advice and give
up the nursing just yet—my closeness to Zachary meant
too much to me, and the finally normal, abundantly
natural functioning of my body meant too much to
me—but I did make certain always to wear a very
supportive bra, avoided hoisting the children, and was
careful about wrestling the carriage up and down curbs
when fully loaded. I got more rest and worked at a
sunny disposition.

While Alexandra was delicate and wiry, quiet and
quick—a dragonfly of a child—Zachary was a large,
beautiful, phlegmatic baby who retained the same clear,
serene expression he had worn the night he was born,

who patted my full breast absently as he nursed, his gaze playing meditatively over my face as a pianist might let his fingers drift over the keys. I was pleased that the nursing was helping me lose all the weight I had gained during the last months of pregnancy (when I could eat again); I was already back to my prepregnancy weight and still losing, something that was never easy for me to do—my weight had been the source of a constant struggle since I had begun modeling during my junior year of college, when it became convenient to represent myself as the healthy, athletic type. My relative leanness lent some credence now to Dr. G.'s hypothesis that my breasts were too heavy for my body, so I was not especially surprised when the pain in the chest and shoulder didn't improve. Perhaps it was even a little worse.

In October I unexpectedly resumed menstruating—unexpectedly because a woman who breast-feeds without offering any supplements usually will not begin to flow again until well into the second half of the postpartum year: it is nature's way of preventing a parturitional traffic jam, and is a good, natural contraceptive. I started spotting at the end of September—a scant three months after birth. My periods, always irregular, were even more so, and it seemed that they lasted longer than before. (It wasn't until December, when I began to keep a careful record of on and off days, that I realized I was menstruating lightly more than half the time.) Dr. B. thought my body was perhaps having some trouble regulating itself—but would, soon, as bodies do. He also thought perhaps a small piece of the placenta had been left behind, in which case he would consider doing a D & C—a dilation and curettage, the scraping clean of the walls of the uterus—if the condition didn't correct itself. Irregular bleeding is a not uncommon postpartum complication.

I called Dr. G. back in October. I thought the pain was worse. He wanted to know if I had yet abandoned the nursing, and made a knowing cluck over the phone when I sheepishly replied that I had not. If I weren't going to follow advice . . . well . . . I could almost hear him shrug. I should try to save my strength. Also, was I perhaps a little depressed? Might I be emotionally resistant to the new demands placed on me? I was awfully tired all the time, that was for sure, dragging myself from the park to the grocery store to home, and then dragging around the house like a boat being set by the tide. (Anemic, Len had said, because of nursing. Take these little green iron pills . . .) I supposed I *was* kind of depressed, too, being so tired and all. I felt chastised; I was taking up the doctor's time.

One evening in mid-October, after the children were in bed, I plopped into the big sofa to indulge in a little mindless TV and unfolded my needlework: one of a set of place mats for my mother decorated with flowering branches, their fruit in a tiny Danish cross-stitch. I was hunched over, peering at the linen and meticulously counting threads (the pattern required eye transfer from a master sheet) through the large magnifying glass that hung around my neck on a ribbon. All at once there was a searing pain, as if an arrow had pierced my back in the long, soft part between the right scapula and the spine, exiting my chest just above the right breast. For a moment I was so startled I couldn't breathe; I sat paralyzed, waiting to see what would happen—whether it would get worse (in which case I would die), or subside (in which case there would be time to be genuinely frightened). The place mat slipped off my lap and crumpled onto the floor. I made no move to stop it nor any effort to retrieve it, but sat as still and alert as a dog pointing a bird. I might have been listening for something.

Seconds passed and more seconds. A minute perhaps, and then the phantom arrow was slowly withdrawn with a wrenching twist and a pull, leaving a dull ache like a bleeding wound. I took a careful breath—a mere sip—and then a deeper one. Whatever it was, it was pretty much gone.

Damn my nearsightedness! I should have known better than to have sat there, head to chest, inviting something in my sore shoulder to stretch—and when it could stretch no more, tear—as I had tried to focus on the colorful little Xs that crawled over the fabric in my lap. Ruefully I bent over to pick up the place mat, reaching out cautiously with my left arm, and then my right, to see if I could identify the source of the muscle pull, or pinched nerve, or whatever it was. My heart was still pounding from the shock of the pain. I had to lie down.

While the pain's sharpness had dissipated, the shredded sensation lingered. Now I had really done it. For the first time lying down didn't help, but rather intensified the pressure in my chest, as if a spiny black sea urchin were trapped and writhing in my right lung. Screws of discomfort tightened every time I changed position, which was often, and it hurt to breathe normally. Michael was sympathetic and attentive, rubbing my back until I fell asleep.

He was always so nice to me when I wasn't feeling well.

Much as I didn't want to do it, I made another appointment to see Dr. G. I was sure something was wrong now. But in the couple of weeks I waited to see him, I wavered. The "bad place" had gone away—seemed to have healed. Indeed, I could hardly feel where it was any longer. There was a new "bad place," but it didn't bother me as much; it had come on stealthily, and I had only casually noted it. I was nervous about trying to explain all this: it shot to hell my theory of a muscle pull or a pinched nerve, unless my muscles and nerves were rearranging themselves every ten days or so. The only other thing I had to complain about was my constant fatigue—though I knew what he would say about that; I could save him the trouble. I was just going to have to lay it out and hope he believed me; I had waited this long for the appointment; I couldn't *possibly* be imagining such things; he was the doctor; he would know something about my mysterious affliction.

My resolve, my impulse to insist, faltered once I had been examined and found myself sitting across from Dr. G. in his tastefully decorated office. I smelled patronization coming on. He hadn't looked impressed with my recital of symptoms, had only smiled and nodded, listened to my chest, thumped me, and kneaded me here and there. We did blood pressure, pulse, temperature, finger stick. Except for my persistent slight anemia, it looked as if I had a chronic case of active imagination. I squirmed like a bug on a pin, crossing and uncrossing my legs, as Dr. G. rocked back in his big leather chair and regarded me thoughtfully. He let the weight of the moment settle over me like a fine film of soot; it was clear what he thought of my elusive pain. But when he spoke his tone was kind.

"How are you feeling about your life right now? In general, I mean."

I was caught off guard. I was expecting more advice, perhaps a little character-building chastisement.

"Uhh . . . fine. Why?"

Dr. G. swiveled around and looked out the window that faced Park Avenue. The blinds were discreetly tilted, but looking up through them one could see bars of mobile gray sky dashed with bare branches. The susurration of the afternoon traffic was punctuated by an occasional horn blast and the squeezed sound of fast stops when the light changed. He tapped his finger tips together.

"I mean," he said, pausing elliptically, "are you happy?"

Happy? Wasn't I half of a practically perfect couple? Didn't I have two gorgeous children, bright and sunny as a spring morning? A renovated eight-room co-op on Riverside Drive that looked south and west over the Hudson? A very handsome, well-educated, impressively employed husband who . . . well . . . looked after me? Wasn't I a lucky girl? Still doing a little modeling, taking courses to keep my mind agile, taking care of my family? Why shouldn't I be happy?

"Of course I'm . . . fine," I said again.

"Let me be direct with you, hon." I flinched at the "hon"—as much from ambivalence about my fuzzy pleasure at the affectionate familiarity that made me feel small and protected and properly female, as in annoyance. "You have called me or been here no less than four times this fall. You are complaining about a pain that has no apparent organic basis. I would order a chest X-ray except that I see no logical reason for doing so: your chest sounds clear, and there's no evidence of muscle damage, though of course that wouldn't show on an X-ray anyway. All I can tell you about the chest and shoulder pain is to watch straining that area. Now as for the anemia—we understand, I think, what's causing that." (We? I thought. We? I must have become a group project.) "You have been losing blood because your menstrual cycle has not yet adjusted itself, and of course, nursing your baby is a big drain on your system—it has to be your choice to give that up. But it's not so unusual for any young woman with children only twenty-one months apart to be a little anemic, and certainly tired. Are you eating well enough?"

I nodded. I was in my health food period. Our refrigerator was crammed with wonderfully fresh organic vegetables, raw nuts, unpasteurized milk and juices, homemade whole grain bread and yogurt. My children even teethed on dog biscuits—which were, after all, subject to the same FDA standards people food was, and much healthier than the zwieback that disintegrated with fifteen minutes of moist mouthing. I could not be faulted in my attention to nourishment.

"The reason I'm asking you this," Dr. G. continued, "is that I want you to think whether this persistent chest thing mightn't be telling you something else. I'm not prying when I ask about whether you're happy; I'm just trying to help you out. I am your doctor, and we have to work together and play detective a little with this thing. Quite frankly, my guess is that there are areas of your life you are having trouble facing—I think you are coping with any number of adjustments and perhaps disappointments—and the result is a funny pain in your chest and shoulder that flits around and is sometimes here and sometimes there and sometimes not anywhere at all." He was warming up.

"But I can feel exactly where it is," I broke in. "Even when it moves and goes somewhere else." (It was a weak finish.) I tapped my chest above the right breast. "It's usually right about here, but sometimes I feel it straight through, in the corresponding place on my back." I reached around awkwardly to point, as if the verbal description alone were not convincing. "Sometimes it's a little lower, here, under my ribs." I jabbed myself illustratively in the right side, taking courage from the mapping procedure. "Once I even felt it on the left side," I went on hopefully, "and it has this quite definite pattern: it hits like a spike being driven in, and it's very sharp for about five minutes . . . maybe even half an hour. Then it gradually goes away until after about five days or so I can hardly feel it, even though it's still there, a little. Then within another week, it's like I get another one, and I start all over again." It sounded very lame as I listened to myself; I wasn't being convincing. Dr. G. was twirling his pen between the thumb and forefinger of both hands, waiting patiently.

"You must try to help me. And yourself," said Dr. G. It was as if I hadn't said anything at all. "You must be willing to recognize this for what it is. Now, I'm not a magician, and one can never be sure, but I can tell you this. There seems to be no organic basis for your complaints, so it is only responsible to entertain the possibility of an underlying emotional cause. Does it seem to you that this ever happens when you have any particular reason to be upset, or stressed, or especially tired? If you would turn your attention to that, I suspect you will find some interesting coincidences." He raised his eyebrows with undisguised pleasure at his own diagnosis. "As I said before, you have no other symptoms that would lead me to suspect any physical problem at all: no cough, no suspicious lung sounds. Your heart is strong and fine, and you're young, with no history of any related symptoms. We mustn't forget that our body can play very funny tricks on us sometimes. . . ."

"But it's not my imagination! I can feel it!" I knew I was being defensive, protesting too much, contributing to the evidence against me. I wanted the chest pain to go away, but I was also worried that it might; then I would have demonstrated I was as neurotic as he thought I was. And my voice was trembling with a hint of the very hysteria I was denying. It would be awful to cry now: I would have to be more canny. I arranged my face into an expression of openness and vulnerability.

"Don't misunderstand," Dr. G. went on. "I'm not saying the pain isn't *there*. I'm saying there is no good *reason* for it to be there. As far as I can tell you are a perfectly healthy twenty-six-year-old who is a little depressed and probably running herself into the ground unnecessarily. You're very busy and under a lot of stress. I don't know any way to get to the bottom of this without considering every possibility, and this is one of the possibilities we must consider." His voice eased into a lilt, a singsong, as if he were comforting a child. "Sometimes if we look very hard *into* ourselves, hon, we find there are things working below the surface that we are putting a lot of energy into not seeing. And that costs something emotionally and psychologically; you may be paying a price you're not even aware of." He abandoned the recitative and reassumed his kindly, Father Knows Best voice, at the same time letting the chair flip him forward so he was leaning across the desk toward me. "I'm your doctor and you must trust my judgment. That's what I'm here for. Now we have to work together to find out what this is and get you back on the track."

I hung my head and looked at the pattern of folds in my skirt. I felt scolded; who was he to have opinions about my private life, even if he *was* my doctor? I was coping pretty damn well, and I didn't want trouble, didn't want this man tap-tap-tapping around my life as if he were looking for a reflex.

It was true that things weren't precisely as I'd imagined they would be, but whose adult life was? Part of growing up was taking that into account and getting control of it. I had made my adjustments, my peace with myself. I was no different from anyone else—a little problem here, a little problem there: we learned to smooth things over, keep things going. We did what we could, did the best with what we had, what we were given. I had poured myself into my marriage and into my children, and if the water ran deep and turbulent . . . well . . . whose business was it anyway? It would calm with time and devotion as its surface had calmed with determination—a sheet of gray silk drawn over the churn of the currents. That was being civilized. And mature. And sensible. And I didn't want anybody tossing rocks in, shattering its glassiness. I felt close to crying, something I refused to do here, now.

Swallowing hard, I raised my head and looked at him coolly. "As you say, anything's possible. I'm probably just too tense. I've always been tense."

"Perhaps if you were to find some diversion that would get you out of the house every day, hon. And please, try to relax a bit, take it easy. You've got quite a lot on your hands, you know. I mean, we can't be surprised sometimes that these things take their toll. And think about what I said. If you want to come back and just talk, we can do that too. Or I can give you the names of a couple of good men you could explore some of this with. Problems don't simply go away by themselves," he added cryptically as he reached for his prescription pad.

Dr. G. is one of the rare doctors who has legible handwriting—a large, handsome, cursive script. Even upside down I could read the word "Librium."

"I'm not ordering you to take these," he said as he wrote, "but I honestly think they'll help. Take them according to instructions when you feel you need them."

He tore the prescription off his pad and rising, handed it to me. I folded it neatly in half and tucked it into the side pocket of my bag as if it were a dirty picture.

"Well, I'm relieved nothing really seems to be the matter," I chirped, anxious now to get out of there, into the sharp, damp twilight.

"Try to get more rest, hon," he said, walking me to the door, "and think about what I said. You'll find things will straighten out of their own accord if you can address some of this. And I'm always available if you need to talk." His smile was warm. Maybe things would be all right. My depressions would lift, and my tensions would evaporate. I was a little crazy, but I was safe.

# JANUARY 1971

RIVERSIDE DRIVE SEEMS LIKE THE COLDEST PLACE ON earth in the winter; the wind comes off the Hudson with the deafening force of the Seventh Avenue Express going through a local station. Our bedroom faced due west, and even with storm windows, our shades often stood straight out into the room, blown horizontal. One learned to ignore the wailing the wind made—and to separate out similar human sounds—but it took practice.

I had always been a good, but light, sleeper, awakening at the slightest sound. I was especially sensitive to anything that might have been a child's cry. This particular night, something dug me out of a dream and flung me into consciousness; I found myself suddenly wide awake, without knowing quite how I'd got that way, staring at the agitated shadows on the ceiling. I did a quick inventory, as if gathering the contents of a spilled sewing box, winding the threads of time, place, person onto the right spools (I am me; I am here, in my own bed; the room is cold; I have children: might one of them be crying?; where is Michael? Oh, I remember, California, on business. . . .) as the blood pounded in my temples and the bends of fast surfacing from the depths of sleep made my scalp and fingertips tingle, my stomach and neck cramp. Between the thuds in my head, I tried to determine whether I had heard a child, knowing that in the strange time warp of night it can seem many minutes between one holler and the next, although the actual time is only as long as it takes a baby to refill its lungs. I waited as the pounding slowed, reluctant to get out of bed in the cold, even—selfishly—to see whether the children were both covered, something I ritually awakened to do during the night. There was absolute quiet above the sighing and moaning of the wind.

But why then was I so wide awake? I focused my attention on my breasts; perhaps a dream had made my milk let down, and Zachary, with the uncanny percipience of the nursing infant, "knew" and had awakened. But I didn't feel the familiar pressing sensation toward the nipple that signaled the contraction of the tiny muscles that control the milk ducts. And I was dry.

I listened again, feeling somehow . . . called, even though I could hear nothing. The conviction that I was needed or wanted built until it was so strong I decided to get up anyway and check the children, braving the cold, just to be sure. I felt too sensitized not to have been awakened by *something*. Groaning silently, dreading putting my bare feet on the frigid wood floor, I sat up in bed, tossed back the many layers of blankets (I was always cold), and swung my legs around, leaning forward to push myself up off the low bed.

At the moment I pushed, something terrible happened: I didn't know what, except it felt as if the right side of my chest had been blown away. The pain was so immense that my mouth gaped like a speared fish's, and my eyes widened till I could feel the lids stretch and thought my eyeballs would pop out from the pressure in my head and roll across the floor like sodden marbles. My left hand flew to my chest, as if it could hold it together, and my body curled to the right, contorting the way a trout does when it hits the boiling water. I was making funny "unh . . . unh . . ." sounds as I tried to keep my balance on the bed. The "unh" sounds bled out of me until there was no breath to make them anymore.

As my empty lungs automatically began to refill, I realized I couldn't breathe. It felt as though the night air were bouncing in and out of them and wouldn't

stick; each jerk of reflexive filling brought a spastic recoil that shut them down again. Splatters of sparks were
going off on the floor, which I could see through a tele-
scope of black velvet. I fell forward onto my left shoulder and lay there with my cheek pressed against the
splintery, acrid old wood.

I'm going to die, I thought. I will lie here and die,
and the children will shriek in their cribs for the two
days until Michael gets back, when maybe they will
have died too.

There seemed to be a lot of time to think, as the first
panic passed. I wondered how long I could live without
air; couldn't one go almost five minutes without brain
damage? Maybe the steel bands that had crushed my
right side would loosen in five minutes. Relax, I told
myself, calmly going limp in obedience to my own di-
rectives: you'll lose less oxygen and give yourself extra
time. Now, I explained to myself, this is how we shall
manage this. I will pretend to be a yogi, being buried
alive, able to breathe so shallowly I can survive with
almost no oxygen. I can be that yogi. I will breathe
without breathing. I will let my very pores breathe for
me. Relax, I reminded myself soothingly. I found that,
lying there, a little of the pressure was relieved and I
could take the shallowest of breaths, so shallow I wasn't
sure I was breathing at all. My lungs struggled to fill,
but I kept them to the merest nicks of breath; I wasn't
going to die after all.

I didn't want to move, didn't know what a change of
position might bring on. The telephone was right above
me, but I couldn't reach it, so I grabbed the cord and
tugged; the phone hit the floor with a ringing of bells
and the rubbery clatter of plastic. It had a lighted dial,
but I didn't need a light; I knew where O was.

"Operator," said the woman at the other end nasally.
"What can I do for you?"

"Operator," I said, trying out my ability to speak,
and finding that I could only manage a whisper. "Operator . . ."

"Speak up," the operator said sharply. "You'll have to speak up. I can't hear you."

"Operator," I started again. "Please. Listen. I can't talk any louder. . . ."

"What?" she said.

Oh, God, I thought. Please. Please New York Telephone, just for once, be patient and efficient.

"Something's happened. Please. I need help. Call my doctor." I gave his name. "You'll have to find the number," I said. "I don't have it."

"Is this an emergency?" she said.

Ordinarily I could have been very sarcastic, but I was willing to beg, promise anything, humble myself.

". . . Because I can call the police," she went on. "Do you need an ambulance?"

"No, no ambulance." I didn't want to overreact, make another scene as I had in June. "Just call the doctor." I gave her his name and number and mine, and carefully put the receiver back on the righted cradle.

In the five minutes it took Dr. G. to return the call (the middle of the night is one of the rare times one can usually locate one's doctor), I managed to pull myself back up on the bed. The pain was still bad enough that I was wrenched grotesquely—afraid to straighten up, with my right arm pulled in tight, the hand a slack claw—but I could breathe a little more easily. I sat in the chill, listening to the wind, and waited for the phone to ring. I'd forgotten about the children.

"What seems to be the matter?" asked Dr. G. when I answered.

"I don't know." That was the truth. "I can't breathe. I'm in incredible pain." I began to cry.

"Now don't just go to pieces. That won't solve anything. Tell me what happened."

"I was asleep, and I woke up for no reason, and when I got up to see if the children were all right, I had a kind of heart attack. I fell on the floor. I couldn't breathe." The crying was making me hiccup and now my nose was running.

"Did you lose consciousness?"

"No, I just kind of fell. It hurt so much. I didn't know what had happened."

"Where's your husband?"

"He's not here, he's in California. I'm all alone with the children. That's partly why I'm so scared."

There was the most infinitesimal pause.

"I see. Has he been gone long?"

"He just left today. He'll be back in a couple of days."

"How are you feeling now?" he said gently.

Actually, I was suddenly much better. The pain seemed to be almost entirely gone, as if someone had cut that steel band riveted through my chest and it had fallen off. I straightened up. It *was* gone, leaving only kind of a sore spot. I started crying harder. I knew Dr. G. could hear; I was so embarrassed; I must seem so crazy.

"Better, I think." I was waffling. How could I tell him it had gone *away*? After waking him up in the middle of the night?

"Do you have any phenobarbital in the house? For the children?"

"Yes, I think so," I said.

"This is what I want you to do, hon. I want you to go and get it, okay, and I want you to take a big slug of it, okay? I am going to stay on the phone while you do that. Do you understand me?"

"Yes," I sniffed, laying the phone on the bed and getting up. As I walked in the dark toward the children's bathroom, I tried to think how to handle this. I just couldn't bring myself to admit that as soon as he had called, the pain had fled, disappeared, evaporated. It sounded too silly. I checked the children, who were sound asleep, as I walked through their rooms, knowing I was stalling, and went through the charade of getting the bottle, even carrying it back to the phone with me, as if he could see what I was doing. I drank a little right from the bottle so I could say I had and picked up the phone.

"Have you taken the phenobarb?"

I nodded dumbly like a child, even though he couldn't see me.

"Feel better?" he asked. I nodded again. "Are you there?" he prompted.

"Oh, sorry, yes, much better. I think I'm all right now. Yes, all right."

"Good!" he said heartily. "Now I want you to get a good night's sleep, okay? And you call me in the morning to tell me how you're feeling."

"Thanks," I said. "I'm sorry I woke you up. Really sorry. I was just so scared.

"Don't worry about it, hon, okay? Just take care of yourself. I'll talk to you in the morning. . . ." He said "morning" like the woman on *Romper Room*, drawn out, in a perfect descending fifth.

I curled up in bed in a fetal position, lying on my right side, with my left arm across my chest, the hand on the opposite shoulder, and fell asleep instantly.

I was a little afraid to call Dr. G. in the morning. I had never taken the Librium, or indeed the rest of his advice; my life was just as busy and I continued to nurse Zachary. It was nobody's fault but my own if I couldn't follow his orders or wouldn't respond to his prescriptions. And the next morning, as the wind riffled the stony Hudson, and the branches of the iced trees in Riverside Park clacked and rattled, I wasn't sure my "attack" had happened at all. I had frightened myself; Michael wasn't there; it was complications of panic, hysteria. There was little trace of the obliterative and mysterious pain, and what was left was indistinguishable from the low-level discomfort I had had since July. I should try to figure out what had happened though: what was real and what was not; what was to worry about and what wasn't. I was procrastinating about "checking in."

I thought about how I had felt. My experience seemed somehow familiar and finally, after puttering around with the children's breakfasts, I could identify

why: I remembered reading an article in the *Ladies'
Home Journal* on the medical complications associated
with the use of the oral contraceptive. One case history
had stuck in my mind, in which a young mother of
three experienced chest pains that eventually became
debilitating. I couldn't remember how the doctors had
treated her chest pains, or even how they had diagnosed
them—how they were labeled—but I did recall the end
of the story, which affected me greatly. This young
woman's mother had come to help her care for her children and her house, and was sitting with her daughter
as she rested on the sofa. Needing something, the
woman with the chest problems arose and started across
her living room, when suddenly she stopped. Her
mother watched as a strange look came over the young
woman's face. She clapped her hands to her chest, saying, "Oh God! What have I done to myself?" and collapsed, dying there on her own living-room rug. Her
mother was powerless to help her.

Maybe what I had was something like that; I had
had the same reaction myself the previous night: Oh
God, what have I done to myself? I rummaged through
the stacks of paper I kept, chronicling everything from
the best inns in Bavaria to how to repair a bicycle,
searching for the article. (I knew I had cut it out, but
I was much better at clipping things than organizing
them.) I was disappointed I couldn't find it, finally, but
cast around for the words I thought I remembered that
described the condition that had caused the young
mother's death: I was pretty sure of "pulmonary," less
sure of . . . what? "Thrombosis?" Maybe that was it.
Maybe "pulmonary thrombosis" was what she had had.
It didn't sound quite right, but I felt confident Dr. G.
would know what I was talking about, that he would be
grateful for my input. Maybe he hadn't thought of pulmonary thrombosis yet.

With my meager knowledge at the ready—a five-
pound test line trawling for sharks—I called Dr. G. I
was so sure I was going to be helpful with my own

diagnosis; I finally had some kind of label for what I thought I was experiencing. It certainly made it sound more important, more real.

Dr. G. wasn't impressed, although he did sound harassed: he was quite clearly busy. He wanted to know whether my "pain" had come back, whether it still hurt, if I was all right. He was about to hang up on me, having satisfied himself on some score known only to him, when I pushed through his good-bye.

"Uh . . . I wonder something. Something I read, actually. Well, what I mean to say is . . ." I paused and then blurted out my offering, casting it on the altar of his indifference, sacrificing myself to his potential ridicule. "Do you think it could be . . ." I struggled for the accurate term, still unsure I had it right, "pulmonary thrombosis?" (What was I *talking* about? I didn't even know what that *meant*!)

"Pulmonary thrombosis?" The telephone may have emphasized the derision in his tone. "Pulmonary *thrombosis*? Where *ever* did you get that from?"

"I told you. I read it in a magazine. It sounded just like what happened to me. And this woman died."

"Dear, dear. And what magazine was *this*?"

Instantly, I was contrite, I wanted to take it all back; this was sounding perfectly ridiculous. Now I had to tell him where I'd read it: death sandwiched in between the crewel pillows and the cream-cheese loaves.

"The *Ladies' Home Journal*," I hesitantly apologized. I wasn't sure whether he was going to laugh out loud or scold me.

"The *Ladies' Home Journal*," he repeated, as if *he* were answering *me*. He sounded angry. "When *will* you women learn? If you want to go to the *Ladies' Home Journal* for your medical care, you don't need me, now do you? I think I know enough about your case to make a judgment about such things. And those goddamn magazines," he continued, "they're so irresponsible, scaring women the way they do. They publish something like that and half a million women decide to go off the Pill and get pregnant, or some damn fool thing. The problems with the Pill have been blown all out of proportion by people who misunderstand the statistics. Anyway, you aren't even *on* birth control pills. You haven't been on them for years." He was right. Of course her case was different from mine. Except that the symptoms were the same.

"Why don't you just leave the diagnoses to me?" he admonished. "*I* am the doctor. I have everything under control."

# SPRING 1971

———◆———

THANK HEAVENS SOMEONE WAS IN CONTROL, BECAUSE I was clearly losing my grip . . . though it wasn't clear whether I was losing my grip because I was ill, or ill because I was losing my grip.

Anyway, it didn't matter: I didn't care anymore. I didn't have the energy. As winter thickened into spring, it took the most astonishing level of willpower just to get out of bed; I craved sleep with the pathetic urgency of lust, longing only to surrender myself to its seductive morass—spongy with dreams—where there was no responsibility, no guilt, no disappointments, no contradictions. Depression seeped into each day like rain into a basement, getting darker and deeper and more stagnant, backing up into evening and tomorrow and next week.

I had lost my Libran balance. Wings in, head down, I was in a steep dive toward some murky bottom I couldn't see.

Despite my constant fatigue, I couldn't sleep—I who had always fallen into unconsciousness as if from a high place. Insomnia was a new experience: the leaden night, the thin torn morning hours, the steady wash of respiration punctuated by the crackle and ping of radiators. I wove in and out of sleep, writhing through wrung-out nightmares and waking to the pain in my chest that vibrated there like a vicious kitten, clawing at me as I lay on my side, subsiding into a loose bubbly black purring when I turned onto stomach or back.

Once awake, I found it impossible not to think, not to examine what was happening to me—and why. I palpated my life as if it were a distended abdomen, trying to locate the source of disease, and was finally forced to relinquish the pretense of sleep and retreat to the big Voltaire chair in the corner of the bedroom. (I could breathe more easily sitting up), where I sat, wrapped in my grandmother's quilt from the bottom of the bed, hugging my knees and rocking like a catatonic, thinking, thinking, thinking, until I wore myself out and napped—brow to knee—only to be snapped awake again by some elastic dream so the thinking could go on, squeaking and banging in the cage of the skull like a hamster on a treadmill.

Night after night, yo-yoing between alpha and delta, I sat and thought—digging into the fissures that had fractured my seamless life—and watched Michael sleep his peculiar frozen sleep in the flickering amber of the arc lights on the street. I watched him because he was so serene, so sure, so intact; I watched him because he was the axis of my life ("Man is woman's religion; woman is man's shrine," he had once written me); I watched him because he was my cabala.

His posture was so thoroughly characteristic; he lay on his back, as narrowly and economically arranged as the marble effigy of a medieval king poised on the lid of his own sarcophagus: limbs attenuated (feet pointed and crossed, parallel arms bound to his sides by some filament of sleep), peaceful head angled oddly from the body so one postulated a fall and a broken neck, or a nocturnal query to which he awaited an answer in vain—so unlike my twisted, childlike sprawl. He was self-contained and self-sufficient, whereas I, even in the deepest chasms of slumber, scrabbled insensibly toward human contact and animal warmth, plastering myself to Michael's cool length shamelessly, winding my limbs around him like pale sinewy vines.

Our sleeping was remarkably like the rest of our secret lives together: Michael calm and centered, me frantic and clinging and sloppily damp with need. Michael said I was like an alcoholic, pouring in all the attention and affection I could consume and never getting enough. Michael said I had a problem; Michael thought I ought to "go get cured." Michael suspected me of nymphomania.

What was the *matter* with me? What was the matter with *me*? I was greedy and immature, romantic and insecure. Why couldn't I be normal, be satisfied with what other women seemed to be satisfied with? What right had I to be unhappy, with all I had . . . with all I was? How dare I? The devotion of a good man, the magnificent comfort of a family of my bosom, should have been all I needed or wanted.

I had tried. I had tried to be a good wife, a good mother, a good person, but although I seemed to fool everyone else on this score, I knew I had failed at what I had most wanted to be: nearly perfect at everything. In my five years of married life I had gone from "unstable" (Michael's judgment) and nervous to full-time crazy, becoming less capable, less competent . . . more undone. . . . Private shame for my weakness drove me underground (into the children's bathroom as it happened) where, alone at night, I could cry behind a series of heavy doors without waking Michael and exposing myself to his disdain, howling at the white tiles as I progressively lost control and perspective, sobbing and gurgling into yards of toilet paper I never bothered to detach from the roll, loathing myself for all this neurotic need coming to the surface like scum, betraying its presence, betraying Michael, betraying our marriage.

I was rotting from the inside out.

In 1966, when I had married Michael, I fancied myself a woman of the world embarking on my finest adventure—an accomplished, intellectually gifted, self-reliant person of character who had the further good fortune of an interesting face and the ambition to do something with it by becoming a model. That June I was in full bloom: I graduated respectably from Barnard, was on three magazine covers in a row, and got married (twice: a Jewish ceremony in New York, a loosely Christian one back home, so that Michael and I could satisfy both our principles and our traditions). The weddings were cascades of lily of the valley, showers of candlelight, kaleidoscopes of dancers in white dresses and black tie. We were the golden couple, blessed and reblessed by fortuitous circumstance and admirable purpose.

But I cried myself to sleep on my wedding night, burying my face in the foamy white nightgown—bought by my mother to commemorate a virginity existing only in her stubborn optimism—where it lay washed up against the headboard of the hotel bed like a breaking wave. Michael had dutifully and peremptorily made love to me and then had sunk immediately into an exhausted sleep, leaving me feeling more alone, more abandoned, than I could ever remember. For now I was his. Now I was real and important only when he made me that way. It seemed after all that that was what it meant to be a "real wife": to have given over your beingness and the right to validate you, transferring it from your family to your husband. (The minister had said to my father: "Who gives this woman to be taken in marriage?" and my father answered, "Her mother and I do." And I could even remember the time when the words were just "I do" . . . from the father. Given from the father, who loves and protects and shapes, unto the husband, who will from this time forth love and protect and shape.)

Certainly I was tired, brought down by the strain of two ceremonies and the traveling and the inevitable familial tensions that arise on such occasions, but I felt a special and horrifying letdown there in that room with the champagne going flat and the roses dropping their petals and my new husband economically and sensibly asleep. I don't know what I expected, but it was important to me that this was the first time I had been sexually legitimate. I wanted to feel transcendent and instead I felt like a nuisance; it seemed that the very ritual that released me to be most truly and joyfully myself ironically marked some collapse of desire in Michael, some inhibiting and shackling of what we had shared with so much anxiety and anticipation before we were married. Michael never appeared to love me or want me as much again—now that he had me—as he had when I was not yet his.

If only I could have forgotten that night; if only I could have pressed it in the heavy wedding books with the rest of the flattened memories; if only it hadn't seemed so portentous. But the memory stayed sharp and bitter, it wasn't softened and abrogated by what followed; and what had hollowed out a place somewhere in the middle of me, making me feel empty and bereft, caught and grew there until what should have been the center of my life became a vacuum. I knew it was the result of my having missed some major truth associated with the event of my marriage.

But I was disinclined to do any significant dissections on its frail structure, sheathed as it was with good intentions. Marriage was forever—at least mine would be—because I abhorred divorce, abhorred my parents' collective divorces (four, if you counted their divorce from each other as only one). My marriage would work because I had planned it that way, carefully thinking everything out down to the smallest details—a triumph of rationality over passion.

I smugly thought myself wise, temperate, and foresighted, having never seen much good come of passion. Passion meant highs, but it more often meant lows, and from all I had seen and experienced, the law of diminishing returns set in quickly in any relationship based on passion. ("Love! Love!" my mother would say in a tone of voice that suggested supplication and weariness. "Don't count on it.") And we had the usual collection of family homilies, apparently handed down through generations of women: "Don't trust men! They're only interested in one thing . . . and when they get it . . ." (here the eyebrows were raised and the head shaken); and, "You won't love at eighteen what you love at sixteen . . . You won't love at twenty what you love at eighteen" (fill in the blanks in an infinite progression). On love and money, finger wagging: "When the wolf comes in at the back door, love goes out the front." And finally, from my dowager grandmother, with her flowered hats, her fox neckpieces, and her impressive bulk that suggested an extravagant float in the Rose Bowl Parade: "Kissing won't last, but cooking will!"

I had, in many ways, my grandmother's temperament, so on the whole I thought it not unlikely that she was right, that a good recipe was far more dependable and probably more staisfying than romantic love. Passion was convulsive, tumultuous; it was sweaty grapplings, people panting on each other and trading their germs, the ultimate archetypal contest for control between male and female. Passion was an old and tired practical joke played over and over for which one inevitably fell, which always made a fool of one.

But what does one know at twenty-one or twenty-two—or maybe ever—about passion? About love? Even about sex? . . . beyond what one stumbles through blindly and learns in messy, furtive experimentation? What *I* knew was pragmatic and ambiguous and fraught with anxiety: like most guilt-ridden "nice girls" who grew up in the fifties, I was terrified of being bad, immoral. And I was terrified of being used: in the fifties and sixties it was easy to get used—or fancy yourself used—in the halting gavotte of male-female relations, danced to a melody we all pretended we knew. At the same time I loved the excitement, the romance of sex; I loved the feeling of specialness and the certitude of a focus narrowed—for those wonderful moments—just to me. There was, at any rate, almost no excuse for being sexual.

True Love was the only justification and apologia for carnal involvement (and even this not until the sixties); nothing else short of a florid psychopathology was either comprehensible or forgivable. I myself fell into True Love for the first time in high school (it was like taking a header down a flight of stairs), but my bright, stubborn, difficult boyfriend and I decided—having fully absorbed our parents' prohibitions against explicitly sexual expressions of affection—that a moral triumph over all those dour grown-ups lay in *my* (technical) chastity and *his* courtesy. He was unrelentingly courteous; he was also a splendidly creative lover, dumping me over the brink of orgasm for the first time in the milky hours after a New Year's Eve dance when I was seventeen, on the tweed sofa in my living room. Until I experienced it, I had no idea such a sensation actually existed outside of the series of confusing euphemisms assigned to it in trashy literature. I was sure I had died—or was about to: I couldn't breathe for long moments after it had happened, and fancied death a not unsuitable punishment for my transgression against the sanctity of church, school, and my mother's sofa.

By the next year—my first year in the wild, unfettered, politically suspect East at Barnard—I was in love with a Yale swimmer whom I adored to a distraction sparked by a dash of newly acquired New York sophistication. I was egregiously slow; while I was still agonizing over "how far to go" with some friends as backward as I, my dormmates were discussing the proper execution of acts I considered so unnatural that I felt as I had when I was ten and my mother had explained gently to me what it was one did to conceive a child, making me gag in revulsion and disbelief—staring at her all the while with eyes suddenly relieved of their scales of naïveté—and swear to myself that I should never allow such degradation to be inflicted on me. One does, as a matter of course, change one's mind: by the time I was pinned—engaged to be engaged—in my second semester of college, my virginity had become a burden I was anxious to unload.

As usual I chose carefully, waiting till a weekend that was so far beyond the time I should have gotten my ever-tardy period that there was no possibility of its being mid-cycle. (I could manage only one new experience at a time: I would leave contraception to the second such encounter . . . if indeed there was one.) So it was in a creaky bed in the tacky Hotel Taft in New Haven that I gave my Yalie the "ultimate gift"—as my mother was fond of saying—that I had to give. He and I had composed a well-rehearsed fugue of concupiscence which required his tonic tussle to my dominant refusal: "C'mon. Please. I'll be careful. I won't hurt you." Then, hopefully: "I brought a . . . thing. . . ." Me: "No. We can't. I want to, truly, but it isn't right. I'll get pregnant . . ." (pause, punctuated by sounds of struggle) ". . . *Don't!* I'm not *kidding.*"

That day in January in our rented love-nest smelling of ancient cigarette butts and legions of dirty feet, I unexpectedly failed to refuse . . . which left him no choice but to go through with the act and relieve me of my burden, while I wondered why I didn't bleed, and whatever had happened to the hymen I had protected for so long? I also allowed myself to consider the possibility that outside our very door lurked the hotel detective, waiting for the right moment to burst in and arrest us for fornication—*in flagrante*—so that we could further humiliate each other and ourselves (to say nothing of our parents) by being tossed out of our respective Ivy League schools.

Coitus turned out to be no momentous happening—certainly nothing to have waited for and worried about for so long. It was an aesthetic as well as an erotic disappointment, an operational adjustment with little to be said for it except that it removed a bit farther the primary arena of indelicate sexual activity. But I had lost my virtue forever; nothing separated me now from the pathetic little townies who were commonly referred to as "pigs." And to what? To a penetration by an ugly, knobby stem of tumescent flesh that was somehow, unbelievably, a part of the person I loved so much.

I loathed myself—especially that part of myself that dared to crave such unseemly violation.

It all wasn't worth it. I was always and ever afraid of getting pregnant in spite of taking a feverish number of precautions (all at once for good measure and just in

case): Mother had said—and I had believed her—that
if I ever got pregnant, I was on my own . . . and out
for good. It also wasn't worth it because my relationship with the swimmer did not outlast more than a few
perfunctory couplings. When he left me—needing to
"find himself" (which I read as escape)—I responded
with a pseudopregnancy, a parasite of grief. Because I
had already found *my*self, with him, and I had wanted
nothing more or less than to be with him forever.

Once having given myself, having compromised my
purity, I felt worthless, vulnerable. A true Episcopalian
Midwesterner, I had always had something of a hy-
draulic relationship to the Divine: I had sinned and I
would have to pay for it; I would be punished for what
I had done—what I had betrayed—until I had learned
to put things in proper perspective. My penance would
be humiliation and deprivation—the humiliation of sexual inadequacy and the forfeit of pleasure during coitus
because I was what I thought of and the manuals then
described as frigid; the humiliation of being driven
again and again into sexual expression that was essentially joyless and guilt-making and uncomfortable if not
downright painful—an act of generosity to some needy
young man who never knew what it cost me.

Until Michael rescued me, his wanting me an em-
blem of forgiveness. I met him in a class my junior
year: tall and slender, with perfect posture and the col-
oring my grandmother called Black Irish—dark curly
hair, green eyes, and the clearest ivory skin rouged with
a slight flush—he was breathtakingly handsome, impressively intelligent, and had beautiful manners. People tended to label him "sweet" because of his slow liq-
uid smile and dreamy look, and he *was* sweet. Sweet
and kind. Such a contrast to my lather, my intricate intensity.

Michael was exactly what I thought I needed, with
his vaguely hygienic air and cool detachment. I was
tired of being hustled and tired of being tempted to de-
grade myself: the men hung around me like flies. His
sanitary spirituality was the perfect foil for my grubby,

sodden corporeality. As he was fond of saying (and I was fond of conceding), "Man is infinite; woman is finite."

That was why I married him. I was sullied and he would clean me. I was broken and he would mend me. He required more of me than I ever required of myself, and the cathartic fire of his acceptance and approbation would redeem me and raise me and make me what I had aimed at and missed. He became my safe place, my light aginst the dark, my talisman to thrust at my lowering God as evidence of my immaculate motives.

And I loved him, loved him with all the love I had to give, all the love I could imagine conferring on another human being, because he was what I was not, because he rang with a crystalline clearness I knew was damped forever for me. The irony was this: as unsure as I was of how I felt when I married him, as much as I had originally had to convince myself of my undying love and my need to be married, now, now after five years of marriage, I was still in love, more in love, painfully in need of love. The more I wanted, the more I had to give, the less he needed or had to spare.

So what now was I to do with this voracious, ungrateful part of myself? A part I didn't want and had no vocabulary to name (because all the ways of saying it were only testimony to my inadequacy)? A malignant scrub that sprang up in darkness and damp like fungus and threatened to infect my life? How was I supposed to stop wanting what I had long ago denied: the sheen of lust on the forehead and shoulders, the pounding of the heart, the weakness in the knees, and the tremor in the thighs? I couldn't make myself stop wanting it, couldn't exorcise the demon that hissed and spit in silent resentment when my husband turned his back on me, when he neglected to touch me, when he responded with anger to my awkward attempts at seduction. In my naïveté—though not in my innocence—I had gratuitously gifted him with the power to define my womanhood, and I no longer felt like a woman, but like some sexless elderly relative deserving of politeness and respect, or like some extravagant and markedly inefficient but decorative device for the well-appointed home. I was invisible. Dispensable. And worst of all, inconsiderable.

When I said desperately, "Michael, I love you, I love you," I wanted to see my breath cloud the mirror of his beautiful face, I wanted him to reach through his glassy indifference and pull me to him so my ears would burn with the words of furious desire I wished him to mumble into them. I wanted to crack the smooth shell of his self-regard and make him look at me, touch me, respond to me, want me. Instead his features darkened, his mouth turned down. "You shouldn't have beer with dinner," he would say. "It makes you silly. You are degrading yourself." (He didn't have to say "again.") "Please, please," I would whisper, so the current au pair wouldn't hear, "Make love to me." In front of the kitchen sink I would fall on my knees and fumble with his belt, saying, "Please, please," over and over because I *had* had the beer and it *had* made me silly. "It won't take long, I promise," I'd say, my fingers trembling. And then he would step back, so that I lost my balance and had to catch myself against the refrigerator. "Now stop it. You are ridiculous. You turn my stomach when you're this way." And he would be gone, gone to write, or think, or read *The New York Review of Books,* leaving me slumped next to the freezer, wondering what I had done, how I had failed, where I had lost him.

Where I had lost myself.

One day when I was pregnant with Zachary, I had confronted him again with my frustrations, the unsatisfactory nature of our intimacies, reassuring him with a rush of panic that everything else was fine, worked fine. (I wanted him to change, not leave me.) I tried to explain how difficult it was for me—how trying I found it—for him never to show interest in my *womanliness* (to be distinguished from never showing interest in sex). He snorted suspiciously, reminding me of my own problems with sexuality—my exorbitant and seemingly unending need—and suggested I examine myself more carefully before judging his responses. He reminded me that I was not looking exactly tempting in my current fecund state. He reminded me that we had never been interested in many of the same things, and sex on my schedule just happened to be one of them. He felt perfectly normal and was relatively content as far as the marriage was concerned: I had better seek my own solution. And he reminded me again of his advice that I go see someone and get this need "fixed."

"I'll tell you what's going to happen," I had said measuredly, working up my courage. "You will push me into having an affair. I need to be wanted. I need to feel loved. . . ."

"I do love you," he interrupted sullenly.

"Yes, yes, I know" (we had been through all this before), "but don't you *see*? Not in a way I . . . understand . . . quite . . ."

Michael looked at me as if he were studying a specimen. "Do what you want," he said finally. The response threw me. I had used my trump card to goad him and he had overtrumped.

"But it's *not* what I want! I'm married to *you!* I want it from *you!* We only have sex . . . in bed. . . . Do you know what I mean? There's the mechanics and nothing else. I want to feel wanted even when we *don't* have sex, I want to feel *involved*. It's as if I'm in this desert, dying of thirst, and there is this lovely oasis full of lush palms, and I can hear the water running, but there is this high fence all around—not so high I can't see what's on the other side, but too high to climb, and it keeps me out, so I'm always thirsty." A phrase from a toast at our wedding came back to me: a friend of Michael's had wished us this and wished us that, and then ended his valediction with "enough to eat, enough to drink, for thirst is a dangerous thing." I paused, remembering this, and said, "That's what I feel like."

". . . Then do what you *have* to do," he said. "I don't care."

I hadn't expected it to turn out this way. I sat and

waited for him to take it back, but he was deep in *The Village Voice.*

"You leave me little choice," I said and got up, intending never to mention it again.

I didn't, but he did. Months later, some time after Zachary's birth, I was in the bathroom, occupied with my evening *toilette,* when he said suddenly from the bed where he was lying reading, "Well, I guess you never had that little affair you threatened."

Inasmuch as he hadn't asked a question, I was not inclined to volunteer an answer.

"Whatever happened to that affair you were going to have?" he said more loudly and precisely.

"What affair?"

"You know what I mean," he replied, exasperated with my obtuseness (which I was more often criticizing *him* for). "That affair you threatened you were going to have. You know."

"Oh. That." I went back to brushing my hair, while he waited a decent few seconds to see whether I intended to answer him.

"Well, so much for your frustrations," he said in a satisfied tone. "I didn't *think* you'd carry through with it."

I couldn't stand the smugness in his voice.

"How do you know I didn't?" I was standing in the bathroom door, my hand on the chipped jamb with its myriad tiny rainbows of generations of paint. I looked right at him, though it took every fiber of nerve I had.

He returned the look.

"Did you?" he demanded. *"Did you?"* he said again, more loudly, because I had turned back into the bathroom.

I snatched the door open.

"Yes. Yes, I did. I did it. You don't know me as well as you think you do, you know. You think I'm afraid of everything. . . ."

"Well, how was it?" he said in a slimy kind of voice.

"Okay. Just okay. Not terrific. But I did it. And I'd

do it again if I had to." (The last part was the only part I thought was probably a lie.)

"Who?" he said.

"Nick." Nick was a male model I had known for years—longer than Michael—with whom I occasionally had lunch. I knew Michael thought he was gay.

"How many times?"

"Twice," I said stoutly, realizing that that hardly qualified me, after all this time, for *belle de jour*.

"Twice?" The way Michael said the word, it sounded as though it were stapled to his tongue. He looked at me for a long time until I could no longer meet his gaze and shut the bathroom door.

We never discussed it again.

But what wasn't said between us—the confession had lacked absolution—swam around like a spirochete on a black slide. I had again cheapened myself, destroyed the sanctity of our marriage. Nick managed to stay my (nonsexual) friend throughout, patiently listening to me obsess; what I couldn't tell him was that after my great "experiment" with him, I felt even less a woman, rather than more. It wasn't because of *him*, because with the right woman I was sure he would have been a wonderful sex partner. It was *I* who had been inadequate, who had lain as stiff as a log, who had cried because of my inability to participate with any enthusiasm. I was frightened when he came at me, his cock swaying in the air as if it were suspended by an invisible wire; frightened when he had rolled my sweater above my breasts and laid himself there between them, wanting me to take him in my mouth; frightened when he hovered over me, his trembling weight suspended precariously as he panted and dripped sweat into my eyes; and finally repulsed when he came into my hair (a poor compromise) where it was spread on the bed. I couldn't wait to be clean of him and rid of the implicit reproach of his presence. "I'm sorry. I'm sorry," I said repeatedly. "I don't think I'm very good at this." And I shook for hours afterward, then was depressed and guilt-ridden as I fed the children, sautéed the veal scallops, and crawled into bed by myself (as usual) because I went to bed earlier than Michael did.

Michael had once said, "If I give you enough rope, you will hang yourself."

That was why it was increasingly easy to believe that the shortness of breath, the pain in the chest, the incessant bleeding, were the products of a symbolizing mind: I bled out my womanhood in staccato, violet-brown blots in the bed and in my underwear; I struggled against that noose that choked off my breath, knowing it would continue to tighten as long as I had failed to come to terms with the appropriate and natural limitations of my life.

And then there was God—the Great Organizer for whom no sin was a hidden sin, for whom no sin went unpunished. The Great Organizer had this time organized a sickness for me. As a warning.

My "illness" was taking on mythic proportions.

Anything was possible, as Dr. G. had said.

That was the main reason I hadn't flounced out of Dr. G.'s office when he implied that since my body had been scrutinized without result I should have my head examined. Because I knew he had seen through me and he knew that I knew that he had seen through me: the shrouds around my marriage—like the curtains around a hospital bed—were sufficient to mask only part of the pain, leaving the rest to squeeze under and over and around the edges. It never occurred to me to change doctors: if the ones I had were smart enough to see through me, they were smart enough to deal with me. Anyway, the thought of climbing onto a new Dr. B.'s examining table to hook my feet in the stirrups and expose my most secret, most shameful, most violable parts, or letting a new Dr. G. with the internist's impulse to psychosomatic interpretation do further readings on the entrails of my mind, was more than I could face. I could hardly get out of bed in the morning; how then could I get new doctors and start with them all over again, complaining, apologizing, convincing?

They were right about me; they were all right about me, Michael and the doctors. I craved their support, their attention, and I wanted them to take responsibility for me because I could no longer take it for myself. Michael was strong, loving, and supportive in direct and inverse proportion to my being weak, demanding, and pathetic: now that I was sick, depressed, and helpless I was consequently and paradoxically happier than I had been for a long time. The doctors were solicitous, but it was clear I was tolerable only as long as I was recognizable. My acquiescence made me familiarly and acceptably female. So when the doctors went with crazy, and Michael went with sick and crazy, I went with what was easiest, homed in on the expedient. I needed them. I needed them all. I didn't want to be abandoned to my own thunderous roil of emotion . . . or worse, to the Great Organizer.

Capitulation is the most basic affirmation of female identity.

These were the things I thought as I sat through the night hours, rocking against my knees, as Michael slept on, marble-yellow in the night. These were the things I thought as I wilted through the days. This was what I thought as I looked at myself and saw the cold pallor of craziness and paranoia that had leached out what maternal bloom I had managed to muster in the last months of the pregnancy and the first months of nursing.

Len had tried to help once, years ago, a scant six weeks after my wedding, when I found myself in his office, chain-smoking shakily when I wasn't shredding damp tissues in my lap. I had wanted to be reassured— to find out if I *was* normal, to find out why I *wasn't* normal, to find out how it was that I felt so empty and panicky and alone. Len had insisted that absolute blame has no place in the working out of problems between two people. ("What's normal is what's normal for the two of you." He also said, "This marriage won't last six months if you don't get help. And it may not last six months if you do.")

But I didn't want help. I didn't need help. I needed character. Character and determination and some of the flat gritty Midwesternism that was capable of breeding a blinded faith in one's ability to accomplish whatever one set one's mind to.

I didn't want advice because it was hard for me to admit to myself that I might have been wrong. I didn't want recriminations.

I didn't want to get up in the morning.

I didn't want to be bothered with anything.

In the middle of that spring, when there was only a reflexive sleeping and waking, and when the long list of things I didn't want finally included my confusing and confused life, I went to the psychiatric clinic at the nearest hospital to tell somebody whose job it was to listen that something in me was dying. Or maybe I was killing myself. Or about to kill myself.

The clinic wasn't impressed. The stern, gray-haired social worker had heard it all before. Did my husband beat me? Did he drink? Did *I* drink? Really, it seemed I had little to complain about. She asked me what kind of fantasies I had had about killing myself and I realized that I hadn't even thought *that* out: I had conceived of suicide less as an act than as a kind of acquiescence.

People who don't really know whether they are going to take pills or jump off a roof, people who can't even say exactly what it is that makes them so miserable, are "chronics" rather than "criticals." There is no rush for a chronic because she is so likely to go on being . . . chronic; it is her penchant for misery that is her problem rather than her problem that is her problem. After checking her watch and informing me that they were taking no new cases at the hospital, the social worker suggested a couple of low-fee mental health clinics on Central Park West.

I called one immediately for an intake interview and

waited patiently for my rescue: soon someone would help me. At my appointment a couple of weeks later, I began with my concerns about losing my mind (my metaphorical illness that refused to succumb to all my attempts at Good-think), the havoc I was wreaking on my marriage, my lack of understanding of my role as a woman. The female doctor who was willing to do patient evaluation half a day a week for no money nodded sympathetically and said the clinic would call to assign me to a therapist.

I never heard from them again. I assumed that I was not an interesting enough batch of symptoms and behaviors, imagining myself passed around the table in a manila folder while each therapist shook her/his head vaguely and declined one more case of hysterical conversion and loamy, garden-variety misery.

It seemed I was neither crazy enough nor sane enough to be taken seriously.

This all happened in March. By the beginning of April, I felt so sick and so desperate I no longer had even the necessary energy to contemplate killing myself. The pain in my chest was as heavy as a stone; the brilliant drizzle of fresh blood—not the brownish menstrual sludge one would have expected—was real, apt, threatening. Pride was irrelevant. I went back to Dr. G. one more time.

Dr. G. sighed a great sigh when he saw me. I sat in his office—pale, puffy, and hangdog—and cried, leaning slightly to the right so the heaving of my chest wouldn't dislodge the pain and set it rolling. I told him about my visit to the psychiatric unit and my fear I was losing my mind. I told him about not being able to sleep anymore. I told him again about the bleeding, on which I had begun to focus as the only material evidence in my favor: a trickle of nuttiness is dismissable, but blood commands a certain respect. My weight—usually about 125—had slipped to less than 110 even though I was still nursing Zachary, and my clothes flapped around me like the luff of angry sails.

I trailed Dr. G. into the examining room and sat on the end of his black Naugahyde table, undoing my blouse and slipping it off my shoulders so that I was accessible to the stethoscope that hovered in the air behind me like a snake readying itself for a strike. Dr. G. listened and listened to my chest, saying, "Take a deep breath. Keep breathing. That's it," as I looked listlessly around the fluorescently beige room. The purring that was so much with me at night predictably refused to make itself evident, so I mentioned it without much conviction.

Walking from behind me into my range of vision, Dr. G. took off his stethoscope, rolled it around his hand, and stuffed it in his pocket. He stood for a moment, pursing his lips and gazing at me steadily, waiting for me to look up.

"I want you to have some X-rays, hon."

I stirred from my stupor. "X-rays?" I said slowly. "X-rays? Here?"

"No, not here. There's a radiologist—a friend of mine—a few blocks away. You can walk over there and get them taken, and then walk the films back to me when you're done. I'll call him and get him to fit you in. Go right now. I'll wait for you."

The radiologist was a distracted-looking man with neat gray hair. I stood this way and that—arms akimbo—while the machines hummed and thudded, and then sat and waited until he brought the dripping negatives into his big office and shoved them into the clips on the wall-to-wall light box. There was my chest, the ribs curved delicately together like praying hands wound with the gauze of tissue. Rocking back and forth on his heels, the doctor beat a minute tattoo against the films with the end of his ball-point pen as he peered at the first, the second, the third, the fourth, and then back at the first. Tap-tippety-tap-tap against each picture. I thought he would say something, but he didn't.

"What do you see?" I ventured finally.

Tap-tap. And then the pen went back into the breast

pocket of his white coat, glinting at me with its shiny steel top.

"Well. There are some . . . changes. . . ."

"Changes?" Changes? From what to what?

He snapped the pen back out and bounced it against the first tenebrous rectangle of celluloid. "Here. Here."

I didn't see anything—the whole business looked like a satellite photo of bad weather to me. Should I have been worried about the white webby parts or the blacker, clearer places? I tried to look knowledgeable, and stood up next to the doctor to examine the films more closely. I still couldn't tell what it was he was looking at. As I brushed his sleeve, the doctor looked at me with slight distaste as if I had made an unwelcome advance, and edged toward the door.

"Please sit down for a moment. I want to call Dr. G. I won't be long." He went into a lab and shut the door while I retreated to the chair and contemplated my translucent self from there.

He was back, as he had said, in a moment. He pulled the now-dry X-rays out of their clips and put them in a manila envelope that was large enough to mail a small child. I stood as he held it out to me.

"Dr. G. is waiting for you at his office, so go directly there. He will explain everything to you."

"Thank you," I murmured, shaking his hand, genuinely grateful.

He smiled with unexpected warmth. "You're welcome," he said.

I practically skipped back to Dr. G.'s along Park Avenue. I wasn't! I wasn't crazy! I really was sick! Thank God! It was an unusually warm day for April, so I took off my light jacket and tied it around my waist. I felt important, with my impressive package. I felt substantial, with my real sickness.

I felt more alive than I had since the fall.

Dr. G. met me in the anteroom of his office, now— long past office hours—empty.

"I'm sorry it took so long," I apologized. "I came right back."

"No matter, hon," he said, separating me from my prize, and retreating with it to his own light box. I began to follow, but he waved me into the waiting room.

He came back without my X-rays.

"What is it?" I asked, propelling myself out of a chair.

"There are changes . . ." he said.

I knew that already. "What kind of changes?"

"Changes we associate with pleurisy."

"What exactly is pleurisy?" It was one of those conditions you think you understand until you find you have it and realize you have only the vaguest idea of what it really is. I had had it filed somewhere between diphtheria and tuberculosis.

"Technically, it's an inflammation of the pleura—the membranous sac around the lungs that keeps them from rubbing against the chest wall as they expand and contract. Pleurisy can be quite painful in the way you describe because the lungs lose the cushion of fluid against which they move inside the sac. So they rub. And the friction causes pain; it can also cause the buzzing sensation you describe. . . ."

"But what does pleurisy come from? What does it mean? Do you catch it or develop it?" It sounded more like a symptom than a cause.

"It depends," said Dr. G. cautiously. "It can be a number of things . . . but we don't have to get into all the possibilities." He finished hurriedly: "Suffice it to say that in your case I suspect a kind of low-level, long-term infection that could well turn into a full-blown pneumonia if it's not treated. I'm going to prescribe an antibiotic for you; be sure to take it until all the pills are gone. There's enough for ten days." I nodded my head, absorbing and sorting all this new information: pleurisy, pneumonia, antibiotics.

Bending over a magazine table in his anteroom, Dr. G. wrote out a prescription in his large, ornate hand, gave it to me, and then steered me toward the door.

"I'll expect to hear from you when the pills are gone," he said solicitously. "Let me know how you are. I think this'll do the trick."

I stood and watched as he shut the door softly. The sunset had turned the city sky a bloody orange.

I waited a reasonable two weeks for the predicted flood of cure that would sweep me along into health and optimism. I thought *maybe* the chest pain had diminished slightly, but it was hard to tell; it occurred to me that having fought so long for this illness I was reluctant to relinquish it: antibiotics may be good for disease, but they don't take the imagination. I decided to try concentrating on reversal for another couple of weeks before opening myself to Dr. G.'s diagnosis of terminal uncooperativeness. In the meantime, I had developed a nasty case of monilia—a particularly unpleasant vaginal yeast infection that is one common sequela of a heavy dose of antibiotics. First the itching drove me nuts. Then it drove me to Len. It was either go mad with genital pruritis, or face Len and his threat of D & C.

I had been hoping that nature would take its proper course and stem the bleeding, on the theory that almost anything—left alone long enough—will correct itself and go away. Now, displayed on Len's examining table, I could hardly hide the fact that I was still bleeding. Predictably, Len pressed for his D & C to remove any vestiges of tissue left clinging to the uterine wall postpartum, where they provoked a steady, debilitating, drip-drip of blood. I would enter the hospital in the morning and be out by the evening, Len said. A simple, safe procedure, he reassured me.

Like falling off a log, said a neighbor who had recently had one herself.

I had the D & C in May. Len and my neighbor were right, there was nothing to it: in and out the same day. You go to sleep and you wake up an hour later, modestly covered, all nicely scraped and put in order. There was no pain; I was left only with a vague gnawing sensation nesting low in the gut, forcing me to wonder obsessively about what I would have felt had I been conscious, what my body went through while my mind took a ride on the T-zone special. The wondering led me to associated speculations, so that finally the most unpleasant aspect of the experience was what happened in my imagination, in my graphic recreation of that "simple procedure": the medical school class leering up between my legs while I was racked up there like a chicken waiting to be trussed; the awful fibery rasp made by curette when the uterine wall is clean; the indignity of being so utterly present and yet not there at all, the indignity of being forever an entry in some post-adolescent stranger's salacious data-bank that he (they were all hes—the people in the white coats—to me then) drew on for masturbatory interludes while studying . . . or worse, being the big, anonymous, sloppy cunt—torn and then awkwardly healed after childbirth, dark, turgid, wet-breathed—that was an archetypal object of mirth and scorn even after these children became "real doctors."

It is terrible to become an object even to yourself.

# JUNE 1971

———◆———

RECENTLY I WAS SURPRISED TO FIND THAT WHAT I remembered best about Epiphany Hospital (the place, not the experience), was the floors. Say "hospital" to most people and you will evoke in them an olfactory rather than a visual memory: that cloying blend of antiseptic, of overcooked gray meals and autoclaved toast, and the peculiar heavy odor of warm, sweet decay—like a corsage kicked under the bed after the prom, forgotten and left to rot—shared by every setting in which people are sick together. But hospitals as a category are distinguished by their smell; Epiphany is further distinguished by its floors: floors of white-and-black marble (checkered, compass-rosed, striped, tessellated), speckled terrazzo like the broken shells of wild birds, and worn, liver-colored linoleum.

I had forgotten the floors—although I would have recognized them anywhere, I had looked at them so often while I was there for tests—until recently, when I had occasion to visit Epiphany on the wildly improbable off chance that the administration of the hospital could somehow be peresuaded to release my medical records to me. In typical New York fashion, I was watching where I was putting my feet as much as where I was going, following crumbs of directions tossed at me by laconic guards—crumbs that kept getting eaten up in half-stairways to locked doors and unstaffed, cage-like elevators—when I was suddenly transported into the past, mesmerized by the floors and the long-since repressed associations they prompted. It wasn't just the setting: I was standing in an impressive rotunda of classical proportions giving onto a chapel at its southern tangent and transected by a complex series of hallways drawn out from the rotunda like the radii of a spider web. I knew the rotunda, even knew the chapel (where I had prayed—awkwardly—having forgotten how to cajole God) . . . but it was the floors that jolted me, the floors that took me back to myself in a wheelchair that June, being rolled noiselessly through the corridors, of myself playing an obsessive, childish game of Where Am I? I would close my eyes, and ride, waiting until I was sufficiently disoriented before reopening them, and then, shielding with my hands any advantage from peripheral vision, try to guess which building of the hospital complex—and which part of which building—I was in, using the floors as my sole cue. In addition to being diverting, the game had the advantage of protecting me from people's looks . . . especially those of other patients. I could at the same time pretend I was not seen and avoid looking myself; there isn't, after all, much one can observe with dignity from a sitting position: the ample bodies of nurse's aides, the yeasty bloat stretching tight their blue uniforms, a button nestled in the dimple made by their navels; the battered wainscoting, which someone had thought first to paint one color and then another, so that it changed like mood around a corner; one's feet, in their silly, furry slippers, placed precisely on the footrest of the wheelchair. It was easiest—and most socially acceptable in that tightest-knit of communities—to practice a patient's humility and ride with the head down and forward, letting the hair fall like heavy silk curtains on either side of the face. Only children and the senile rode proudly and in splendor, gazing around perkily as if they were perched in a landau on a sunny day in the Bois de Boulogne.

I mention all this because it is odd what memory selects to preserve, odd what surfaces. Until I saw the floors again, I had forgotten who-I-was-in-that-place— a different person from who-I-was-somewhere-else—

meaning that when I was frightened, and bored, and
ashamed (when, in short, I was a Patient), my betrayal
of myself was made final and complete.

I cannot recall now how it was that I finally got put
in the hospital that first time (not counting the D & C)
in June 1971, which is strange if only because there is
so much of the stay itself I remember with a brutal clarity. Somehow, I suppose, the inconsistencies of my case
overrode Dr. G.'s resistance to reinforcing my hypochondria. I do recall that further batches of chest X-
rays were not encouraging: the sinister dark blotches of
increased lucency were still there; more had joined
them. The pleurisy, or the incipient pneumonia (or
both), was tenacious.

When Dr. G. admitted me that June it was for
"tests"—tests of what, tests for what, was not made
clear, in the hospital spirit of "everything a patient
knows can hurt her . . . and cause trouble for her
doctor; don't get them imagining more horrors than
they have already conjured. . . ." I was treated, rather,
as if I needed to be taught a lesson, to be shamed out of
the inconveniently annoying symptoms that refused to
respond to proper and conservative treatment. Dr. G.
and I were working up to a prickly adversary relationship; and while I may have been oversensitive, I interpreted scorn in his thin smile and hearty "We'll have
this problem cleared up in no time, hon." I was still
afraid of his opinion of me; my sanity was on the line. I
prayed to be really sick: disease and destruction before
madness.

I looked forward to being in the hospital, looked forward to being in a place where people were supposed to
feel sorry *for* you rather than suspicious *of* you, where I
would be taken care of, where someone else would be
in charge. I wanted to get out of the house and the
roles that I lived in; I wanted to bury myself in the
chaste blankness of someone else's clean sheets. It made
going in those grand old Catholic-hospital scrollwork
doors like stepping through the Looking Glass, where

everything that threatened me went away, where it was all right to be eccentric, and sick, and do nothing, and disappear. Maybe I would be able to think here; maybe I would try to straighten myself out. Or I might not think. I took books, and jigsaw puzzles, but spent most of the time staring at the ceiling.

I should have missed the children but I didn't. They were so finely sewn into the confusion of my life that it was nearly impossible to separate those threads saturated with my love for them from the rest of the fabric. I was concerned for them and about them, but I didn't miss them. It was a sublimely narcissistic sabbatical from responsibility . . . including responsibility for myself, which I gave over easily to those who knew me best, and knew what was best for me: Michael and my doctors.

This calm surface of solipsism was broken only once—the first night in the hospital—when I bathed in the tiny faded bathroom and my milk let down: it was the time of day I ordinarily set aside for nursing Zachary, now almost one year old. The milk oozed and dripped, then ran fast into the hot bathwater where it made cloudy spirals over my thighs. It made me cry. I cried for its pathetic nacreous blueness, for its diminished volume, for Zachary, who was weaned so unfairly and abruptly. (Dr. G. had finally won.) And I cried for myself, for the last evidence, spilling into the tub, of my absolute worth. Zachary would manage, of course. He wouldn't even miss me, wouldn't remember in two or three days—a sanguine, affectionate, smiling baby who trustingly, willingly, went to anyone, whom anyone could please.

While I blotted the children from my conscious thought, I dreamt of them . . . dreamt of them and Michael. They were bad dreams—unusual for me even in the worst of times. They were bad, and they were unfairly distorted with anxiety and resentment and frustration, but they came relentlessly, plowing through propriety and denial like an army of bulldozers. There was one in which I watched, horrified, as the babies rolled down the slope of a lovely lawn, rolled into the busy street that fronted it, bouncing softly like beach balls, with breathless little plopping sounds. They lay on the white pavement next to each other, looking bewildered. I was above them, on a landscaped terrace gay with striped awnings and stone urns foaming with geraniums. Bright-lipped ladies and slick gentlemen inclined their heads toward each other; one could just hear their soft murmurs punctuated by the tinkle of glasses. Perhaps there was even a violin. They watched with detached interest, as if at a sporting match, as I screamed soundlessly, batting the air and trying to run to snatch my babies from the road—empty for the moment, but unquestionably heavily trafficked. But there was to be no running; I could not even move. My feet were rooted to the grassy hill. No one came to help. There was a hollow rumble and a yellow semi rounded a curve in the distance: the children still lay in the road like turned turtles, waving little arms and legs as if to flag the truck down. And then the road was humming with traffic, it was over, there was nothing to be done.

And another, involving Michael: he is standing at the door of our old green Volvo, which is parked in a low-ceilinged, dank garage lit by a single naked light bulb. I am standing about twenty feet from the car, behind a pillar. The children are in the car, their faces hovering on the other side of its closed windows like moths trying to escape a summer night. Michael opens the car door a little, and then slams it. It makes the decisive metallic sound I associate with well-engineered, well-constructed cars, which echoes through the garage: SLAM SLAM slam. Michael opens the door once more, as if inviting me to get in the car with the children (who look frightened), but I am moving too slowly to get there and in before he shuts it again. As we confront each other, the children watch through the car window. Suddenly from behind the car spring flames. The children don't see them, but Michael does, and I do. Again he opens the car door a tiny bit and then slams it (SLAM SLAM slam). The children begin to cry, and the little faces are joined by pairs of hands spread on the window like pink starfish. Their mouths are open, but I can't hear them (because of that well-engineered Volvo). Michael looks determined and grim. Once again he opens the door a crack and slams it. I am screaming and screaming, trying to get to the children, clawing at the piller and then at the floor, feeling the concrete tear away my nails. My screaming seems to satisfy something in Michael; he moves to stand in front of the car window, blocking the melting faces and flattened palms from my view, stretching his arms sideways as if he were being crucified between the fenders. I wake up, pleading, as he turns his face from me and the flames crackle and stink.

In spite of my dreams I slept most of the seventeen days I was in Epiphany, or lost myself in reveries. Sleep, or the appearance of sleep, was effective camouflage, discouraging conversation with any one of a succession of roommates who asked embarrassing questions about what a *healthy young person* was doing in the hospital. I had had and would have no operation; I had no scar to exhibit, no accident to recount. I had only one doctor, rather than a "team." "Having tests" sounded hypochondriacal and self-indulgent: the tests weren't even *interesting*. In short, I had nothing to contribute to the patient community; I recognized myself as the conversational wallflower who turned up occasionally at my grandmother's bridge parties, where "the girls" cross-ruffed each other's tales of death, bankruptcy, and wayward husbands.

Nothing was explained to me about what was being looked for, what was suspected. I was given no outline of the diagnostic strategy being pursued and was encouraged to understand that pressing for answers was somehow an invasion of medical rights and territory. This attitude toward a patient's natural and reasonable curiosity about what was being done to her and about her was a strong incentive for me simply to opt out and give over to the hospital routine entirely, wore down

any residual stubbornness the way a heavy rain erodes
a denuded hillside. I was X-rayed from every angle;
my blood was assayed—spun, cooked, cultured, and
discarded. I spent hours in the cardio-pulmonary lab,
sitting in a stall that looked like a study carrel, breathing irritating, salty-smelling stuff through a tangle of
black hoses. What was this supposed to do? . . . I was
expected to cough. . . . But I didn't *feel* like coughing. . . . Didn't *feel* like coughing? What was I *doing*
here if I didn't feel like coughing? I *must* feel like
coughing! Try!

With concentration I managed a few halfhearted
hacks, but I was bush league compared to the serious
coughers—mostly waxy, gray-stubbled old men sitting
with gnarled hands on knobby knees, bathrobes and
hospital gowns gaping so they looked like a benched
team of unenthusiastic flashers—who produced juicy,
phlegmy rattles. Spit it up! Spit it up! the attendants
dashed around and urged as my fellow coughers
wheezed and snorted and spat and I considered the
probability that if I didn't already have some disease, I
would be likely to acquire one in here. I left these ses-
sions with a nasty taste in my mouth, a sore throat, my
chest tight and aching, and a disgruntled attendant
peering morosely into my paper cup which contained
only a "disappointing" sputum sample. My reputation
for uncooperativeness grew.

Mostly, though, I sat—eyes closed and legs stretched
out, displaying myself to the white morning sun—on a
cantilevered sunporch that commanded a magnificent
view to the east. Then in the afternoon, when the sun
got yellower and the air heavy, I retreated to my room
where I napped fitfully until Michael came to visit.

He came every day, putting his cool hand with its
delicate sensitive fingers over mine, kissing me sweetly
on the mouth, on the forehead, on the cheek—
whichever was most convenient. He sat on the bed—or
on a chair if the nurses were around—telling me about
the children, about work, about what he was thinking
and reading. He had the beginnings of a summer tan,

which always made his eyes even greener and the aris-
tocratic arch of his nose and his high cheekbones more
defined by a gloss of pink. He was loving; he was encouraging. But I wanted ardor, felt its lack especially
acutely here, where it was hot, and smelly, and the air
shimmered with pain and need and fear. I dreamed ardor; I obsessed ardor: through the Looking Glass a girl
can entertain limitless fantasies—so much rest, so much
attention to the body, makes one exquisitely conscious
of it. The heat, the long afternoons, the tossing on the
rough sheets striated by the golden light seeping
through the Venetian blinds, made me think of warm
hands, not cool ones; made me think of kisses not on
the forehead or cheek or even on the mouth, but of
kisses on the neck, behind the ear, between the breasts,
at the back of the knee—slow kisses with a flickering
tongue that would leave a sweet wet trail like the trickle
of nectar. In the heaving of my afternoon naps, my
breasts—still heavy with lactation—moved against my
rib cage in languorous ripples; the skin of my thighs
tingled as one leg slipped over the other. My hair stuck
to my temples in dark whorls. My mouth was con-
stantly dry.

In the afternoons, I dreamt of sex as well as of violence, of being filled with a splashing power like water
into a hollowed-out gourd. I dreamt of being naked, of
being nibbled . . . of being humiliated, exposed, and
ravaged. I was powerless to withdraw, and my dream
men looked (carefully), touched (tentatively), and finally fell on me, mingling their helplessness with mine.

I began to feel like a deep-hued, velvety flower, lost
in a cloud of my own heady perfume. Michael didn't
notice, kept his cool distance as I shuddered and licked
my lips.

Len noticed.

Len, on the staff of a different division of the same
hospital, had taken to dropping by when he had a few
minutes—ostensibly to cheer me up. He was welcome
company—well-read, thoughtful, kind—and willing to

talk to me, enduring my chatter and making me feel that specialness that I sought but so often eluded me. As a doctor, he was free to come and go as he pleased, and he would turn up at his own odd convenience: before surgery early in the morning when everyone was still asleep, at lunchtime prior to visiting hours, but most often at night, when the floor's denizens had scurried back to their beds to check out the evening's TV. Then Len and I stood side by side in the dark on the same veranda I dozed on in the morning, leaning on its rusty rail, from which you could see as far away as the glittering bridges draped over the dark shimmer of water, as far away as the neon in Queens; or we sat in the quiet lobby, at opposite ends of a turquoise plastic porch settee with a frame of iron vines. I tactfully steered clear of medical talk, not wanting to trespass on professional territoriality, nor wanting to drive him away by being tiresome. Instead we talked about literature, about lifework, about people's behavior. Inevitably, we talked about relationships: why people choose as they do, and the demented drive to misery that steers one into unhappy places and then perversely abandons one there, while at the same time one assures that same dilemma by obstinately working—always and ever—to make it right and make it better, shunning the admission of failure and the graceful relinquishing of the contest as if to stop trying were the Devil's own work. I was still comfortable talking about my doubts about my life only to Len, as if his knowing the deepest recesses of my body made him somehow the suitable choice for revelations of the soul. He helped, if only by listening (which he did well); he helped because I felt safe and protected when I talked to him. He was older, he knew so many women and he knew them so intimately; surely he could tell me whether I was strange, psychotic— whether there was any hope for me and the mess I'd made of my life. And he helped me to put names to things I barely understood so that naming, for me, became from that time a significant ritual and essential first step in grappling with any problem.

I was so grateful for his attention. I was so grateful for his generosity. I was so grateful for his solicitude. And inevitably I began to measure distances in myself in terms of my distances from him. For his part, he was affectionately proper: he declined to close the space. He never touched me.

But I wanted to be touched; I wanted forbidden things. My afternoon fantasies were more and more explicit as the faceless lovers became recognizable. Len and I remained circumspect; the rustle of the increasingly highly-charged air between us discreetly went unacknowledged. The nurses and the other patients saw only that he was kind, and that we talked, and that we played a great deal of chess on the magnetic board he brought me one day, marching into my room without notice as usual, and wordlessly flipping open the board on my bed. He set up the pieces, still without so much as a greeting, and plunged into an elegant opening gambit. I was watching his face—rather than planning my own strategy—thinking somehow to unmask him, to unmask myself. He looked up then as if I had said something—which I hadn't—and solemnly held my gaze until I was forced to look down at the board. When I raised my eyes, he was still looking at me. He winked.

"Your move," he whispered.

For the first week and a half in Epiphany, when I was not dreaming or sunning or waiting for Len, I had tests—to "find out what's going on here." Most of them were not very taxing (though I was beginning to develop a desperate aversion to needles); their most trying aspect was the endless waiting and boredom, followed closely by the opacity of the technicians, who were not to be pumped for information, forcing me to resort to devious means to obtain it. Dr. G. was not to be pumped for specific information either, leaving me to piece together what I could from my medical contraband and educated guesses. It was apparent from the noxious-fume exercises that they wanted me to cough up a sample of something—something from my lungs that could not be discerned in the saliva alone (or maybe at all), something that wouldn't be slogging around in the upper reaches of the respiratory tract. Germs they could culture for, so it wasn't germs: that meant they were looking for blood. And if they were looking for blood, they were looking for some evidence of lung damage not directly related to disease. I thought. Results of tests were never discussed with me, but were magically stirred into a concoction of diagnosis that would be presented before my release—I "needed to know nothing" in the interim—so I tried to pay careful attention as they were done, and to strike up a crafty conversation with any technician I could lure into one who might potentially enlighten me.

One test had such clear results that even I—as medically and anatomically unsophisticated as I was—could discern them. This test was a lung scan. In a scan, radioactive dye is injected into a vein, and then carried to the heart, from which it disperses to the rest of the body. In any single scan a particular isotope is chosen for its capacity to be taken up by the part of the body the doctor wants visualized; in my case the area of uptake was the lungs. The half-life of the isotope is just long enough so that pictures can be taken of the "hot" organ when it appears on a small TV screen as a seething cloud of thousands of minute blips—a monochrome pointillistic miniature. If all is as it should be, the organ will appear on the screen as a living, pulsing light-shot replica of its textbook counterpart. If, on the other hand, the perfusion—blood supply—is limited by some obstruction, the organ will take up the radioactive substance unevenly or in patches and will look only like pieces of itself.

I was seated with my back, my front, and then with either side pressed to the scanning device, and by turning my head far around I could see the little green screen and its shower of blips. Even *I* knew that a pair of lungs should look just like that: a pair. My radar, however, showed a twisted oblong—or approximately the shape of a lung—on what corresponded to my left side, but on the right—the side on which I had been experiencing the pain and tightness—was only a stubby round lump with a wedge-shaped bite out of the bottom. The disparity in shape showed up from every angle. I was jubilant; unquestionably something was the matter.

"What could cause an outline like that?" I asked dopily, cannily, counting on the previously established mood of casual camaraderie with a young female technician to yield some useful information.

"Oh," she said absentmindedly, "a tumor, probably."

A tumor. Tumors were serious stuff. People had to respect you if you had a tumor. You were *somebody* with a tumor. Tumors that show up on radar screens cannot possibly be the product of an overactive imagination. A tumor means you are really truly sick.

I trembled with anticipation all afternoon, anxious to confront Dr. G. with the evidence of my sanity, to have him acknowledge that I had been right about something in my chest. A tumor! I had known! Thank God: no more crazy, crazy no more. But when he dashed in at four, white coat flying, he made no mention of the scan. I didn't want to bring it up myself, didn't want to give away my limited advantage in being smarter and more resourceful than he took me for, so I waited until the last moment, as he turned to leave, when I could contain myself no longer, and asked his opinion of the scan . . . he *had* gotten the results, hadn't he?

He had gotten the results. He saw nothing unusual, nothing to worry about.

"But it wasn't *normal*," I said, my voice rising. "There were big *chunks* out of my lung. I saw it *myself*."

He smiled and shook his head with one of those "Are we going to have to go through this again?" looks, and walked up to the bed.

"Hon." He shook his head once more as if I were an incorrigible child who simply could not stay out of trouble. "One test means nothing in these things; there is so much that can go wrong in a scan. They often have to

be redone because they are so inaccurate—they are
what we call a gross test. You have no other indication
of any kind of . . . blockage. We're going to do this
again in a couple of days. In the meantime, let's not
jump to any conclusions."

He wandered off. I felt terrible. I wanted my tumor
back.

It didn't happen that I got my tumor back, but I did
get punished for the wishing: the Great Organizer
again, the Great Organizer who always saw to it that all
scores were evened.

They came to get me one morning without warning,
hustling me off my chair on the sunny veranda where I
lay sleepily surveying the morning city. I stumbled back
to my room, blinking, stretching out of the honeyed stupor induced by the hot sun. A white hospital gown lay
on my bed as if it were guarding my place—my new
totem. I was to get out of my pajamas and put it on.
Doctor's orders. No questions please, but oh, by the
way, we need your signature on this surgical release.

What surgery? I wanted to know. Didn't your doctor
tell you? Just a routine test. The release was a mere
formality but necessary because this would involve a little cutting. And hurry: they want you upstairs immediately.

I put on the scratchy gown; it had faint yellowish
patches—rambling and variegated, like the map of a
coastline—that made me shudder. A stretcher appeared
through the wide door of my room and then backed up
again into the hall like a car jockeying for a parking
place.

"Mrs. C.?" A tall black man with a green shower cap
pulled down over his ears was reading my name off a
roster on an aluminum clipboard, glancing at the number on the door, at me, at my roommate, and down
again at the roster. I nodded my head as his eyes swept
back up to me.

"Okay, let's go," he said. "Get on." He stroked the
stretcher as if it were a woman.

"But I don't need a stretcher!" The stretcher was scary. The stretcher was humiliating. I was perfectly capable of walking anywhere, but hospital rules said wheelchairs for all patients—a source of some conflict with the staff for me the first week. I thought it was probably a very effective way of subtly—or perhaps not so subtly—reminding the patients who was in charge. Or maybe they thought you would take off out the nearest door if they let you walk. Maybe they could only keep track of you by the number on your chair. Or maybe it was just that they needed a way to keep the chart *with* the patient but out of the patient's *hands*. I had finally succumbed to the wheelchair rule, after considerable grumbling. But now a stretcher?

"Why can't I just take a wheelchair like I usually do? This is silly."

"Can't. Get on."

I didn't move.

"Where are we going? Are you sure you've got the right person? I'm not supposed to have any kind of surgery."

He looked back at his clipboard as if there were a picture of me there to compare with the reality in the stiff gown. He looked at the number of the room above the door again.

"Yeah, it's you. C'mon. I'm on a schedule."

Directing hateful black thoughts at Dr. G. for not having told me about this, I tucked under my arm the ubiquitous *New Yorker* that functioned as a security blanket, and feeling perfectly ridiculous with the naked back of me bouncing in the breeze, I padded out into the hall in my bare feet. The stretcher was higher than my bed, so that climbing onto it was a production that reminded me of the cutesy illustrations favored by small-town pediatricians of a toddler (back view) struggling into a bed, one leg hoisted too high for balance and the back flap of the Dr. Denton's partially unbuttoned. The fellow in the shower cap got me nicely arranged and then a floor nurse came by, putting some sort of written order on the taut sheet over my stomach.

She paused at the head of the stretcher where I was fumbling with the magazine, searching for the article I had been reading: because I was lying on my back, the pages fell in my face as I turned them. She was very pretty, with short blond hair, creamy skin, and rosy cheeks. I put down the magazine.

"You'll be going up now," she said softly. "We'll see you in a little while."

"Wait a minute." I caught her hand. "What is this for? Why all the special stuff?"

"Hasn't someone explained this procedure to you?" She looked briefly distressed, and then, recovering herself, smiled reassuringly.

"*Someone* has not only not *explained* it to me, *someone* hasn't even told me what it *is*."

"I see." She seemed to think for a second, and then leaned closer.

"Well," she began, "it's a test—an X-ray kind of test—where they use a radiopaque dye and then take a number of films quickly to record its progress through the system. . . ."

"Like the scan," I interrupted.

"No-o-o, not really like the scan. This is a much more *precise* test. . . ." I guessed she was avoiding being too specific.

"Why the surgical release? What are they planning to . . . cut?"

"They'll cut into a vein in your arm so they can insert a catheter through it directly into the heart. It's only a tiny incision. It's done with local anesthetic and closed with a couple of stitches. Nothing serious, but any kind of surgery—even the most minor—requires a release."

"Ah. Well. That doesn't sound too bad," I said cooperatively.

"No, not bad at all," she echoed cheerily. "The only potentially uncomfortable part is when the dye itself is released. Some people find it a little . . . irritating."

"What does that mean . . . 'a little irritating'?"

"You may get this sort of tickling sensation, a flushed feeling. . . ."

Some hesitation on her part made me watch her carefully. Her description lacked a certain conviction.

"Well, good luck. We'll see you shortly." And she turned and was off down the hall before I could say anything else.

While I was being wheeled upstairs I thought about it. Nothing had yet happened to me that was too awful, or too painful, although I felt like a pincushion from the blood-letting and my throat and chest were sore from the coughing machine. How bad could a test be? After all, they weren't going to cut anything off. Or out.

I had already made friends with the people in X-ray; I said hello and waved my *New Yorker* as I sailed through the waiting room and beyond it and was left next to a blank wall in the corridor, my chart swaying in a little sack attached to the stretcher near my feet. I pretended to read but I was distracted and nervous: the portents were inauspicious. A nurse with a shower cap walked by, glanced at my chart, and leaning over me, waited while I put down the magazine and folded my hands. It looked like a speech.

"Have they told you what to expect?" She was as abominably cheerful as the floor nurse had been. I tried matching her tone, reciting back what I had already been told.

"Well, y-e-e-s, I guess that would be a fair description. . . . But I don't think *I* would describe it as a . . . tickling sensation," she emended. "It can feel sort of like a burning. Like heartburn. Have you ever had heartburn?"

"Terrible. When I was pregnant."

"Well then, you have an idea." She stood up. "I'm just telling you this," she added hastily, apologetically, "so you know what to expect, what it might feel like. Some people feel nothing at all."

That's nice, I thought. And what do *other* people feel? *Heartburn?*

I was wheeled into a room that looked more like an

operating room than an X-ray room—with its tile walls and its hoses and pumps and dials and what I came to think of as utensils—where I was transferred to a shiny black table overhung with jointed contraptions out of a monster movie. "The doctor will be here in a minute," one of the nurses said when I looked around. There were a lot of busy people in the room. Somebody took away my *New Yorker*.

Dr. W., a man I had never met, swept into the room already wearing a surgical mask so that all I could see between his cap and mask were a pair of twinkly blue eyes. As he shook my hand, introducing himself, I liked him immediately and decided to trust him.

"We'll get started as soon as I've checked something," he said, and disappeared behind a glass partition. Nurses and technicians raised and adjusted the surgical masks that had been hanging around their necks as an intern began to fool with my right arm, stretching it out, swabbing me with Betadine and alcohol. "Don't worry," he said matter-of-factly as he worked. "This can be pretty uncomfortable, but if you can hold still so that we don't have to take a second series, it'll all be over in a few minutes."

I just stared at him.

Dr. W. seated himself to my right and arranged my arm on a small padded board that looked like the thing I used to iron sleeves, tucking a napkin all around me as if he were planning to make an especially messy meal of me. I suddenly wanted Dr. W. to like me; it seemed somehow to matter that we could be friends. I tried to joke.

"Is that to catch the blood?" Dr. W. looked up from his arranging and then chuckled.

"You bet. We wouldn't want it all over the floor."

He had folded the napkin so that the crook of my elbow was nestled in a little cloth pothole.

"Can I watch?" I asked.

"Up to you."

I was shaking; the room was very cold. "I'd feel better if I could see what's happening."

"Watch. Be my guest." He pushed some of the cloth out of the way, and then began to make little pricks and probes with a syringe of lidocaine. The skin surface deadened almost instantly and as it deadened he worked deeper until a substantial patch was numb. He explained what he was doing as he went along, reminding me, as he pushed back the tissue, that the vein would be "sacrificed." I thought of the small animals I had dissected in high-school biology—how neatly they were packed inside: not at all gushy as I had been afraid they would be. I wasn't gushy either, but I was bloody, and Dr. W. mopped with little squares of gauze as he worked. I felt nothing when he cut, and only a peculiar tugging sensation when he hooked and lifted the vein—a fat, bleached, gristly worm being pulled from purple mire. When he incised it to insert the catheter so that he could tread it up into my heart, the blood poured smoothly over my elbow—thick, dark, and hot in the cold room—into the intricately folded napkin, running richly like a baby drool.

I took advantage of those minutes of a doctor's undivided attention—a rare treat—by asking questions about the procedure and the conditions for which it was considered diagnostic. The test was an angiogram: wherever the radiopaque dye went, its path would stand out brighter than bone on the X-ray film. Angiograms could be committed on various portions of the anatomy; mine was to be a pulmonary angiogram and would show in great detail the circulation in my heart and lungs, or, as might be the case, the lack of it. (Aha! The scan was not so easily dismissed after all!) The dye would be released under pressure well along the vein (via the catheter) and would go directly into the right atrium of the heart. Then the heart muscle would take over, pumping the dye first into the lungs through the pulmonary arteries—exactly as if it were deoxygenated venous blood—and then, when it returned to the left ventricle, back through the body to the head, limbs, and other organs. A series of pictures would be taken of its progress, and any obstructions in the heart or arteries would be clearly evident.

Did he expect an obstruction? What was he looking for?

Dr. W. glanced up from his mopping and threading. "You never know until you find it, do you?" he said noncommittally. I should have known better than to ask a direct question. I tried a flank attack.

"All *I* can think of that could block circulation would be some kind of tumor," I said provocatively. I narrowed my eyes. "It's a tumor you suspect, isn't it?" I had trapped him: if he evaded me, I would assume tumor, and he knew I would assume tumor. If it could be something else, now was his chance to tell me, or *he* would be responsible for putting hysterical notions in my head. He capitulated gracefully.

"It could be other things. An embolus, for instance."

A small piece of evidence dropped into place. Was *that* the word I had been searching for in January? Was *that* what that woman had died of? I asked Dr. W. to explain "embolus" to me.

An embolus is any kind of foreign matter— sometimes an air bubble but usually a blood clot— carried in the bloodstream from its original coagulation site somewhere in the body and swept through larger and larger veins until it reaches the heart. Sometimes an embolus will "stick" on its trip back to the body's center; more often it finds its way quickly back to the heart, either to be caught in one of its chambers—one cause of heart failure—or to make it through the heart and then get "strained out" by the lungs, where the passages are again smaller—and finally small enough to trap the embolus, where it clogs the vessel and effectively ensures the death of all the tissue fed by that vessel's branches. If an embolus forms in the left heart, the surge of an artery can propel it into the brain where it can cause blindness, "stroke," or even death. (In truth, Dr. W. told me very little of this on that occasion, but what little he volunteered did prompt me to ask what *caused* emboli.) He looked at me for a moment before going back to work.

"In women your age? They've been known to be a complication of birth control pills."

"Oh, well. I haven't taken birth control pills for years."

"Then it doesn't really apply to you, does it?"

I was silent as he gave some final instructions to one of the technicians. He was having difficulty deciding how many cc's of dye I could tolerate, and the two of them tossed numbers at each other briefly. They decided on the higher one. I squirmed on the table; it was as hard as a slab of ice.

"You will feel the dye," he said, stepping back to observe his handiwork, "as I push it in, and then I'm going to run for it. Behind that partition," he added, indicating the lead-sheathed enclosure. "You won't be able to see me during the angiogram, but I can see *you* . . . and hear you if you . . . need me." Through the thick glass I could make out a wedge of efficient-looking machines crusted with blinking lights. "No matter what—now listen to me—you *must not move*. Don't even breathe. You may want to, but don't. There will be a helluva racket as the X-ray plates flip over, and you will feel a heavy vibration, but it's nothing to worry about. Are you ready?"

"Will you know right away if there's anything there?"

"As soon as the films are developed. We do that immediately to make sure they come out."

"Will you tell me what they show?"

He smiled. At least it appeared that he smiled: his mask crumpled and his eyes wrinkled.

"You know I can't do that. Dr. G. will discuss the results with you later."

"I don't mean 'discuss the results.' I mean" (and here I lowered my voice conspiratorially so that he had to incline his head toward me) "couldn't you simply tell me whether you found *something* there? It would be such a relief just to know whether there is something there or not."

He shook his head ever so slightly. I was aware that the nurse standing on the other side of me was watching us as if interested in his handling of a patient who wanted to know more than she had a right to. He squeezed my hand in reassurance and turned away.

"If you're ready, then, we'll get this over with. Now remember, *no moving.*" He picked up the veterinary-sized syringe filled with dye where it had been laid next to my arm. The thin plastic tube on the end of it burrowed into the small ugly gash in the crook of my elbow. The skin of my arm was bluish.

"Wait." I caught his sleeve. "Just one more thing. I don't think I've gotten a straight story from anyone. How . . . uncomfortable . . . is this really going to be?"

"What do you want to hear?"

"Please. I have to know. Don't surprise me."

He cocked his head and his eyes glittered. A single drop of perspiration rolled from under his paper cap.

"I think," he said, "it would be fair to say it will be somewhere in the neighborhood of"—he sought a word—"excruciating. . . . Satisfied?"

I nodded and licked my lips, and letting go of his sleeve, grabbed the edge of the table with my free hand.

"Here we go!" he said, and released the dye. As he had promised, he ran for it. I felt for a moment as if I were in the front car of a roller coaster, poised at the top of the first grand hill, waiting for the moment that the last car would creep over the apex so that the machine could begin its maniac plunge.

Feel the dye? *Feel* the *dye?* It tore through my upper arm like napalm and was gobbled by my heart where it stopped an instant, as if hesitant about which way to go—which pulmonary artery to illuminate—like a frenetic rat lost in a maze. I was just beginning to construct the thought, This isn't so awful, when I felt it shoot back out, all directions at once. It was piggyback fireworks—the kind that explode and explode again and again. There was in the same instant a slamming, enormous pain on the right side of my chest that made my body stiffen and bend up off the table, my back arching like a bow strung too tightly. As the table whirred and the X-ray plates clacked like a freight train, I tried to say "Stop! *Stop!* I can't take it!" but my mouth had popped open and my tongue flew around in it like a hunting buzzard. My lips stretched back over my teeth like heavy elastic and would not form words.

"Don't move!" they were hollering at me. "Don't breathe. Hold it hold it hold it," they chanted, watching their dials.

In another moment the dye had pooled in the center of my chest again. Oh, God, it's through, I thought, just before it detonated once more. This time the sensations were . . . vertical: the dye, with little diminishment of force, seared through my neck to my head, and down through my body to my groin and legs. In my skull my brain exploded, gray cell by gray cell, like tiny light bulbs burning out, each with a minuscule *pock!* and incendiary flash. My vision blurred and I thought I was going to pass out as showers of fire fell around me in the darkened room. My body was as rigid as a corpse. The X-rays went wham wham wham as the table shook.

The burning continued, rolling up and down my body in waves, but I knew I must be finished because the table stopped vibrating. "You can breathe now," someone said loudly as people charged from behind their barrier and did pulse-taking kinds of things of which I was only dimly aware. A nurse wiped my forehead with a towel. The rigidity went out of my body: someone had done the tablecloth trick with my bones, leaving me only with trembling flesh on the shiny black table. I consciously closed my mouth, which still gaped soundlessly at the murky ceiling.

"Are you okay? How do you feel?"

I didn't trust myself to say anything. Luscious tears

filled my eyes and spilled, running down the sides of
my face and curling into my ears. They came and they
came, as if the angiogram had forced all the water in
my body to the surface where it ran like a thaw-swollen
stream.

"Are you feeling all right?" a nurse said again, canted
over me.

When I opened my mouth to answer like a good girl,
a racking sob tumbled out, so I closed it quickly. I
looked at her and nodded.

"It will ease off quickly now," she said soothingly. I
nodded again and let the tears fall.

"You did very well," said Dr. W., patting my arm. "I
think we got a good series." He was getting ready to
pull out the catheter and take the couple of stitches the
incision required. When I could trust myself to talk, I
asked for a tissue, and then said angrily, "I *didn't* do
well. All I did was hold still as best I could. That test is
*terrible. Terrible!* I'll bet it could kill a person."

"It affects people differently. It gives some people a
charge."

"I'll bet. Did you ever kill anybody with it?"

"Sometimes older people don't tolerate it too well;
every once in a great while you lose somebody, but
we're pretty careful about whom we administer it to:
we like strong, healthy specimens. Like you. One old
lady," he chuckled, "sat straight up after we finished
and said, 'WOW! My husband never could do that for
me.'" He laughed and I responded with a weak smile
as he finished tying off the sutures. They looked like
little cat whiskers. I shook with the cold and the shock.

"We'll have you out of here right away. I just want to
take a look at what we got." He vanished for some minutes, and when he came back, he walked directly to the
stretcher I had been transferred to. I knew now why
they had insisted on it.

"Those birth control pills," he said. "When did you
say you stopped taking them?"

I grabbed his hand and looked up into his face
which I could see now because he had taken his mask

off. He had a W. C. Fields nose and a handlebar mustache.

"Thank you," I said, knowing he hadn't asked a question but answered one.

The angiogram shook me up: it shook my physically, leaving me drained and placid; it shook me emotionally, leaving me weepy. While a positive test of any kind—in view of my long struggle to justify myself as a non-neurotic, ordinarily (as opposed to extraordinarily) sick human being who happened to be a woman—evoked a kind of smug satisfaction, this was no fair trade-off. I wanted no more vindicating positive tests—or any tests—as agonizing as the angiogram. Up until now I had had some dismal moments, had run the usual gamut of pain (for which I had a low threshold: I was always the princess who couldn't tolerate the pea)—including childbirth—but I had never known pain so great that I was uncertain as to whether I could survive it, whether my body and brain would pause in midshudder and stall, like a plane at too high an altitude. On the way back to my room, subdued now and bored with *The New Yorker*, I realized I belonged to a new tribe, had been initiated into a new realm of sensation, and was forever after slightly altered. The boundaries of imagination had been pushed back into territory inhabited by the barbaroid: I had the rawest possible material for fresh fears and would always now know myself to be more vulnerable than even I ever thought possible.

I considered pleasure and pain, considered the thin line (for which I had new appreciation) that divides intense physical stimulation—or intense physical response—into what feels good—what we enjoy and want more of—and what feels bad and annihilating. The angiogram was a splendid example of "good" shading into "bad"—if Dr. W. was to be believed—along with too much tickling, or getting drunk, or being touched after orgasm: the sensations it produced were not unlike those I had had once—in college—when a friend thrust an amyl nitrite capsule—a popper—under my nose and urged me to take a deep breath. Not knowing what to expect—having had no prior experience that inclined me to be cautious in sniffing substances I knew nothing about—and furthermore being historically something of a dunderhead when it came to taking a dare, I inhaled and felt the same violent, magnesium-flash spattering—a product of the vasodilatory capacity of the drug, used for angina victims—that the angiogram had induced. But the popper, on the whole, would have to be classified as "fun"—a high—mimicking, with its delectable flushing and prickling and pounding of the heart, the absolute heights of excitement that accompany tremendous sexual tension. The angiogram, on the other hand, crossed the threshold into pain, into loss of control, and then kept going into terror until one wondered that one found oneself intact rather than stuck in small bits to every surface of the room, torn apart in unidentifiable globs of suffering.

And there was the emotional toll, brought to the surface by the physical stress the way wood grain is brought up by dark stain. I was afraid of pain. Pain was for evil people; pain was for punishment.

While I had had dying fantasies, and while there was a complicated "wanting out" whose purpose was beautifully served by more and more symptoms, I had not counted on *inflicted* pain—to be distinguished from the pain my own body sprouted. What I did to myself was my own business; what someone did *to* me was another matter entirely, worthy of fear and respect. The deaths, the sicknesses, I had envisioned for myself involved a more remote draining away, as I drained away in dreams I had occasionally in which I was a spectator at—as well as participant in—my own demise, in which the breath dribbled in single molecules from between my fetchingly parted lips, that slowly did life leave me . . . in which the light was stolen from my eyes as smoothly and reluctantly as if life itself were an opalescent cloth dragged tenderly across my body and face, leaving me finally naked, staring, eyes focussed on the back wall of the universe. Sickness was Jenny in *Love*

*Story*, Beth in *Little Women*, Marguerite Gauthier; sickness was getting weaker and lovelier and more translucent, feverish spots of color riding high on the cheekbone; sickness was being appreciated, and being begged for forgiveness: sickness was filigreed with protestations of undying love.

I hadn't counted on blood—unless it was decently contained in a plastic syringe. I hadn't counted on stitches like cat whiskers, and the humiliation of a mouth open, a tongue protruding in mute agony, a body arched and open as if lost in the crippling throes of passion, while strangers looked on and took measure of me with these intimacies. I hadn't foreseen being violated, or having people know me as I was unlikely ever to know myself.

Suffering was a concept I had washed in primary colors; somehow I had missed the shadings. It was the clear, saturated hue of not feeling loved, of being trapped and accepting it. It had the clean lines of a grid where one hung, twisted and mewing. Suffering was the eerie, murderous slippage between psyche and soma—between mind and body—that could nudge into motion a landslide of helplessness that buried everything in its path. But the suffering I had known had lacked resonance, because it had no complement in the body that gave it volume and weight. Or that gave it time . . . memory.

There was real suffering in the hospital, but until now it hadn't quite registered. I heard people calling in the night (usually old women who moaned and complained so that the rest of us couldn't sleep, or gabbled nonsense to themselves, requiring the nurses to look in often and straighten their bedclothes as if they were frightened children and murmur, "Yes, yes, dear, now go to sleep. Everything will be all right."). Some of them keened through the day, curled into their beds like clenched fists, shades drawn, the still air mounded in their rooms like dung. One must be touched by it and live with it, I guessed, to understand it.

Then there was my roommate, a young woman not

much older than myself, who exhibited her suffering as if it were a work of art. This was the other extreme, exciting in me contempt for women's stereotypically labile complaints. She was brought in by wheelchair at the end of my first week in the hospital—small and pale, with short messy no-color hair, delivered from Intensive Care, having had, the week before, open-heart surgery to correct a congenital defect. She was sullen, difficult, and thoroughly unpleasant to share a room with. Attempts at the usual courtesies and encouragements were sourly deflected: I couldn't expect her to be very gracious—she had other things on her mind, like her pain and her misery—but she complained ceaselessly—complained of what she had been through, of the inattentiveness of the day staff, of the ineptitude of her private duty night nurse, of the cruel indifference of her mother and sister and friends (she was unmarried)—in a tiny, bitter whistle of a voice. After a couple of days of sympathetic and patient effort, I stopped trying and gave full rein to the death-dealing thoughts she aroused (They should have cut her heart *out*, I thought meanly to myself). She rasped and groaned all night, choking dramatically, cursing fate, and reminding me as I lay awake that I had no idea what she was going through: something equally as terrible should happen to me so I would know what it was like. Now I would have to think this out all over again, try to understand her experience—although, having no coronary defect, I would never have that most terrifying of surgeries, when the heart is stopped, and cut into, and opened out like a bloody flower, and then (God willing) started again. I had no suffering to contribute, no adequate retort; I could only watch and listen warily—disliking her immensely all the while for her blaming, and her coughing, and her pain—and compare what I saw to what I already knew.

I was still shaken when I got back to my room. The little incision on the inside of my elbow throbbed, my lungs felt fried, and I had a bad headache. I quietly crawled into bed, ignoring my roommate's afternoon cacophony, feeling exhausted, scared, and wanting to be left alone. I was just drifting off into a nap when a loud male voice barked out my name as if it were the announcement of a bus stop, making me jerk and go blank with fear for a split second. I opened my eyes slowly and turned my head to the approach of a burly intern who had his face screwed up into what I took to be his idea of a no-nonsense expression.

"I need a blood sample. Sit up, please."

I got up hesitantly, feeling a little bewildered as one often does when awakened out of the first few moments of sleep.

"C'mon, I haven't got all day," he said needlessly as I groped my way upright. I gave him as disdainful a look as I dared, inasmuch as he was the one with the weapon, and bared my left arm, expecting the worst. Which I got. Taking me roughly by the arm, he pushed the needle through the thin skin of the forearm—the vein in the elbow had clearly been overused—but when he popped the vacuum tube onto the syringe, there was no blood flow.

"Damn!" he said, pulling the needle out and shoving it in again, working it around like a pig rooting for truffles. I began to feel odd and light-headed. He was hurting me, and I was in no mood to be hurt. Both of us looked at the syringe. Nothing.

He snapped off the rubber tubing tourniquet and tied it again tighter; it caught the tender skin of my upper arm and pinched. "Couldn't you loosen this a little?" I asked.

"How do you expect me to get the blood specimen if I loosen it?" he snarled. His ego was on the line. He jabbed me again, angrily. Still nothing.

Then, uncontrollably, tears started up in my eyes and rolled over my face, meeting in two lines at my chin. He didn't notice the tears, but when I began shaking he looked up.

"For Chrissake, Mrs. C., get hold of yourself!" I

shrank back from him and pulled my arm away just as he was preparing to stab me a fourth time.

"Please come back later. I just had this angiogram and it upset me. I'm not feeling too well. Couldn't this be done later?" (And by someone else, I added to myself.)

"I'm here to take it now because we need it now. And I have other things to do than to come all the way back here just for a sample of your blood. Now pull yourself together. You're acting like a baby. I'll get it this time." I thought he was probably determined to get it if he had to use a hatchet and a rubber bag.

"Please let one of the nurses do it." I was holding my arm against my body, unwilling to relinquish it to him. "I can't stand being poked and poked and poked." But my judgment had been compromised; it was clearly the wrong thing to say: he was like a maddened bull in his determination to prove his adequacy as a bloodletter. Call a *nurse*? I was sure he would have sooner cut off his cock.

He didn't answer but took my arm decisively, his lips set in a thin line. How far did my rights go? Not far, I guessed. Could I refuse to be stuck again? They would just send another sadist, instead of one of the wonders from the IV team, who could take four vials of blood—each with their identifying color on the stopper—without missing a beat in the conversation and without pain. I chose a spot on the wall above his head to concentrate on and pretended I was no longer sitting on the edge of my bed on the eighth floor of Epiphany Hospital.

Somehow, by some Divine Grace, the clod found and pierced a vein—much to our mutual relief—drew the blood, and was gone. We hadn't said another word to each other. The inside of my arm was all shades of purple and green for a week after, giving the IV team something to cluck over.

Final interim diagnosis: multiple pulmonary emboli—even though I wasn't coughing up the blood I was supposed to; even though my blood chemistries had been unchanged; even though Dr. G. said that "something about it just wasn't right, the symptoms didn't add up." The scan had, after all, been accurate, and the angiogram had "revealed a definite pulmonary embolus in the upper right lobe obstructing the arterial circulation." There was also marked enlargement of the right side of the heart, and I had developed a murmur.

I cared less for the details of the diagnosis than I did for having been right. Having been right all along. And now that the problem had been pinned down it could be taken care of: I was started on the anticoagulant Coumadin—ironically the same drug taken by my roommate—which was expected not only to prevent further embolic episodes but to help dissolve the embolism they had definitely found.

The Coumadin therapy was touchy business, requiring careful reading of clotting time and blood protein factors so that the right dosage could be established. I still sunned and dreamt while they fooled with the dosage, and now I spent time feeling vindicated. I was warned not to take aspirin while on the Coumadin—which I would continue as an outpatient—as it could cause internal bleeding, and to watch myself, as I was likely to bruise easily. Lovely, I thought. I was already bloated and doughy from the hospital food and the lack of exercise (although I *had* collected a respectable tan); I would look great with green, blue, and yellow crops of contusions.

Seventeen days after I entered Epiphany they let me go home.

# SUMMER 1971

NOW I WOULD GET BETTER. EVERYBODY SAID SO, INSISTing on optimism. A diagnosis had been made, medication had been prescribed. The doctors were finally, mercifully, solicitous, anxious to know how I felt, where I hurt. Consultants were acquired: a hematologist who was supposed to be determining the source of and/or explanation for my mysterious symptomless emboli; a tall, graying, worried-looking lung specialist who was to monitor my pulmonary and cardiac functions. I saw them both each week when I rode my bicycle to Epiphany to have my clotting time checked so that the dose of Coumadin could be adjusted, and to have a chest X-ray. My problems with shortness of breath (officially dyspnea) seemed to be exacerbated by the exercise, but in spite of the gasping and spitting and dizziness I was determined to transcend the creeping limitations that crowded my independence and selfesteem. I didn't want to be a baby.

"Don't give in to it!" my mother cautioned during the one phone call she made to me while I was in the hospital. ("I assumed you'd let me *know* if it was anything *serious*," she said, defending her right to neglect me. "You have enough people looking after you there. Long-distance calls are not *free*, after all. . . .") "I know you! You can be your own worst enemy. Get right back in the swing of things," she said, "because this is *not* the time to start feeling sorry for yourself. Thank your lucky stars it's not something worse."

My mother-in-law—in predictable contast to my own

121

mother—thought I should take it easy, thought I didn't
look too well yet, thought (to Michael, to his father, to
her friends . . . not to me) that it *might* be "something worse," something like . . . *cancer*—a typical
Jewish-mother-type hypothesis that was bluntly and explicitly rejected by Dr. G.

As far as I was concerned, my mother-in-law had
earned the right to entertain any possibility she liked.
She had taken over my family immediately, easily, efficiently. The children were brown, giggly, and well-fed
from their three weeks in "the country" (as my in-laws
chose to refer to their suburban half acre), and I received daily progress reports on eating habits, bowel
movements, and the slightest waver in disposition.
Grammy was loving, Grammy was needed, and
Grammy was doing precisely what Grammy did best—
with the kind of earnest enthusiasm and total sense of
mission that had always eluded me. Grammy, in fact,
did it all better than I ever could have, and her competence made me feel even more vaporous and fragile with
my weakness and fatigue, my shortness of breath, my
loathsome, rotted-fruit bruising on hips, arms, and legs,
my loathsome softness. Being sick made me feel defensive, apologetic, and isolated: when Michael and I
drove up to my in-laws' house to celebrate Zachary's
first birthday and then reclaim the children, I felt dis-
mayed and out of place—an intruder in this intimate,
ideal family circle of mother, father, devoted son, and
miraculous grandchildren. My earlier paranoid suspi-
cions were confirmed: I was a superfluity, a living redundancy. Grammy had become Mother: the children
went to her first, ate up what she said to eat up, seemed
hardly to recognize me.

But perhaps that wasn't so strange: I barely recognized myself. I was home and I felt lost; I was on my
way to recovery and I felt sicker; I had had all this time
and leisure to think things out and I was more confused
than ever. Something in me—something in my deepest
parts—was shifting and separating as ineluctably as the

drift of continents . . . then as unexpectedly grinding together to remake—to re-form—my topography. I was an alien in my own country; perhaps I had always been.

The odd dislocations of time and space—the through-the-looking-glass sensation of the hospital—stayed with me: I felt deranged, deracinated, dangerous. It may have been the sluice of summer heat and the fluid white light of July which always had an effect on me, making me feel sluggish, sumptuous, and stoned; it may have been the Coumadin and my thinned, sour blood, or the abrupt reorganizations of my defensively bromidic routines. It may have been fear: in spite of the anti-coagulation, I was throwing emboli every ten days to two weeks—I could feel them, knowing now what the shafts of pain were—and had additionally discovered that emboli could be fatal . . . frequently *were* fatal.

Or it may have been guilt.

I don't remember precisely when I began my affair with Len. I don't remember how I covered my tracks, what friend I was supposed to be visiting late at night. I don't remember the details of the seduction process—which I let Len manage—or even how I felt about what was happening. I do remember that the move from Len's examining table to Len's bed required little effort or change of (moral) position. I was less sure of what I was doing than I was of what I wanted: I had an enormous, inexplicable craving on the order of those that had prompted my popcorn and watermelon binges when I was pregnant. What impulses I was capable of identifying (or chose to identify) were narrow; I wanted Len to cajole me, convince me, rescue me: I didn't so much decide to get involved as I acceded to my own need for it. As Peter Yates wrote in a short story: "She didn't say yes, but she didn't say no. . . . She was helpless and he was helping her."

He did help. He helped because in addition to the same self-assurance and aggressiveness I had found attractive in Nick, Len was further obligated not to humiliate me: it was part of the tacit bargain. The "sex part" came easily, for modesty was not an issue (how could it be with a man who spent all day every day looking at and touching women's genitals?). And Len could hardly dare to be disappointed with me as a sexual partner; he of all people already knew my fears, my inadequacies, and my secrets, as he already knew my body. His role was implicit in our series of transactions of seduction: he was to be my mentor, protector, and interpreter, in charge of all the parts of me I could neither control nor understand. I expected him to harness my body and its works—its neuroticism, its sensitivity, and its capacity for self-destruction.

I expected him to save me as I had once hoped Michael might save me.

We made love certainly no more than half a dozen times that summer—either on his canopied, king-sized bed, or on the couch in his study. (The wife and kids were frolicking by the pool in Connecticut.) He would take me to a nice dinner somewhere—during which I would quite deliberately and methodically drink enough to render me blurred, supple, and receptive ("I don't care what they say," Len had remarked about some drug-taking friends, "Quaaludes, Seconal, grass, even heroin . . . Nothing beats alcohol for a high.")—and then we would go back to his apartment and I would give myself to the experience of him.

Alcohol loosened me up, lowered my inhibitions, and washed the focus of sensation from my fingertips and nipples and clitoris to my throat and gut, sending tidal rips of satisfaction through my body that were totally and wondrously distinct from the anxious nerveless ruffle that lovemaking ordinarily stirred.

With Len I felt—for the first time—responsivity during (and owing to) the act of intercourse itself; for the first time I sought penetration for the pleasure it gave me rather than for the altruism of an alliterative return of favor. For the first time I didn't feel weird and crippled and inadequate and began to think myself educable. And for the first time male power, male rigidity and stamina, aroused me rather than frightened me—rather than implying some debt ripe to be paid—looping through the intensity of my desire and binding it to his. Len was nearsighted, jowly, and slightly overweight. He was petulant and arrogant. But Len was also potent, instrumental, wise. In his gentle, broad-fingered hands, I unfurled like a sea anemone.

"You're very beautiful," he said to me once as I crouched over him. I kissed him—thanking, denying—and then slowly and absentmindedly rolled upright so that I was sitting clear astride, so that my hair swung back and forth as I rose and fell over him—intent, distracted—until he knitted his fingers into the long dark tangle and pulled me roughly down toward his chest. "Very beautiful," he insisted.

"No." I couldn't bear for him to say that; I didn't want idle compliments. He couldn't be quite serious, and I wanted him to be serious . . . I wanted him to see *me*, not his idea of me (or worse, my lost image of myself). I was quite definite about it. "No."

"Oh, yes," he said, giving my hair a little tug of chastisement so that my eyelashes almost touched his lips. "Oh, yes, you are. And don't ever think different." He let my hair go and I swayed backward like a reed. He caught my two wrists and held them out, looking at my body. "Only a woman who knows she is beautiful is willing to show herself the way you do. Like that. To me."

I thought about what Len had said for a very long time after and decided that as much as I would have liked to believe him, it was I who had been right, rather than he. Once, perhaps, I would have been classified as beautiful, but even at the height of my modeling success I felt that it was somehow the combination of my energy, my "unusual look," and skillful makeup that succeeded where "natural beauty" failed. I wasn't unattractive but neither was I any beauty. And now, since

Alexandra's birth, I had been in my sensible-young-matron mode: clean-scrubbed face, glasses instead of contact lenses, long straight hair held back off my face by a no-nonsense tortoiseshell barrette, jean skirts, knee socks. My body had borne two children nursed two children—and looked it: I had just this year resigned myself to a modest two-piece bathing suit with a flower print and little pleated skirt, folding the black-and-white French bikini into an inoffensive little packet and sticking it into the back of my scarf drawer.

I wasn't beautiful. But at the same time I knew that Len hadn't indulged me with reflexive flattery. I *could* believe that at that moment—surging over him with my head back and a flush creeping over my shoulders, trembling like new grass—at that moment, yes (as he said), maybe I was beautiful. He saw something—because he wanted to—and he believed it and he wanted me to believe it, and maybe it was there. He found me lovely. In spite of the bruises—saucer-sized contusions of ocher and indigo and mauve—in spite of the pastiness, the wheezing, he found me lovely. He said so.

No one had ever before found me lovely in this way; or if he had, he had neglected to tell me so. The way all brides are beautiful, the way all babies are cute . . . in the same way every woman is lovely, ought to be lovely, if there is someone to see it. It made me feel sane in a new way.

The summer nights folded back and forth over each other like a card trick in fast hands. If this was what it was like through the Looking Glass, maybe I was never coming back.

I wanted to think I was getting better, but the evidence was against it, and by August the general level of anxiety had escalated along with the incidence of the emboli. I felt no small ambivalence about these developments, and the concerns aroused by the continued deterioration of my health were mitigated by the perverted pleasure I felt at each new attack, each vindication. The doctors' increasing nervousness and diagnostic repositioning made me feel elated and freed.

"Humph," said Dr. L., the pulmonary specialist, as I sat in his busy office near the hospital. "Can you tell me where the pain is currently located?"

I could tell him quite precisely, as it happened, as if it were a lesion on the surface that could be seen and felt. I moved my fingers tentatively over the pectoral muscle, prodding gently, breathing more deeply than I usually did so that the expanded lung would push the pain out toward my fingers like a splintered point of bone. "Right here," I reported, having found the spot in the hollow below the clavicle. I made little massaging motions as if I could coax the pain back into the deeper parts of my body that felt less acutely. "Why? What's there?" Dr. L. had swiveled around in his chair and was holding the latest X-ray up to the light of the window.

"What's there is an infarct about the size of a dime," he said. (An infarct, I discovered when I got home to my *Webster's New World Dictionary*, is "an area of dying or dead tissue resulting from obstruction of the blood vessels normally supplying [that part of the anatomy]." At the time, it seemed an impertinence to ask what an infarct was. I knew what an infarct *felt* like, which had more relevance.)

"What do you . . . do . . . about infarcts?"

Dr. L. Frisbeed the X-ray onto his desk. It skidded across the top and I watched, fascinated, as it stopped just short of the edge.

"There's not an awful lot we can do about one that's there that we're not doing already," said Dr. L. (I assumed he was referring to the anticoagulation.) "What we have to think about now is how to arrest this process, how to stop the emboli and the damage they are causing. (To say nothing of the damage they *could* do, I thought.)

"We have two choices, really. One is to cut off the route of access of these emboli: that means a vena cava ligation. The other choice is to get to these clots at their source, which from all signs is somewhere around the ovaries . . . probably the ovarian veins themselves. At any rate, I think we're going to consider a laparotomy so that we can take a look at what's going on."

I had never had an operation. Again I felt that eerie combination of exhilaration and dread. *They* were serious. That meant *I* was serious.

"What do you think? . . . Ah, what do you think? . . ."

"I can't really say yet," Dr. L. interrupted, standing up. "I must talk to Dr. G. and Dr. B. On the one hand, a vena cava ligation is a pretty drastic measure; on the other, we have your reproductive capacity to consider. . . . But of course our first and primary interest is your health."

It was Len who called me later that week.

"Hi," I said warmly. This was, after all, my lover as well as my doctor.

"Hi," he said grimly. "Listen, I want you to come in to the office." His tone was measured.

"Couldn't we just have dinner?" I said playfully.

"No. I want you here . . ."

"Want to lash me to the stirrups?" I teased.

"C'mon. Cut it." I sobered quickly. Suddenly my fingers hurt from holding the phone too tightly. "We need to talk and I want to see you to talk to you. I have met with Dr. G. and Dr. L. The time has come to make some decisions and I think you and I should go over the options."

The next day we went over the options, which amounted to no option. The doctors were unanimous in the supposition that the emboli were originating in thrombosed ovarian veins, damaged during pregnancy and childbirth. The diagnosis fit what few symptoms I had (I still had no blood in the no sputum that went with the no cough—all classic symptoms of pulmonary emboli) and seemed reasonable in light of the long episodes of vaginal bleeding and my fairly recent delivery. I wanted to know how one treated thrombosed ovarian veins.

"You don't treat them," said Len. "You excise them—take them out."

I shrugged; I guessed he would take out what he had to. He didn't say anything for a long moment, seemingly engrossed in the exercise of turning his pen from end to end against the blotter.

"We may have to do a hysterectomy," he said abruptly. I recoiled in the chair as if he had hit me.

"Why? Why? I don't understand! Why a hysterectomy? . . . That would mean I couldn't have any more children," I added unnecessarily. I made a move as if to get up, to come toward him—I didn't know why, whether I wanted him to commute the sentence, to forgive me, to comfort me—but he responded with an almost indiscernible drawing-back: we were doctor and patient, and this meeting was all business.

"Because," he continued in his measured tone, "the ovarian veins are not only tightly wrapped around the ovaries—making it almost impossible to remove them without damaging the ovaries themselves—but they are responsible for the circulation to them. Once we interfere with the ovarian blood supply, we . . . compromise . . . their function as egg producers. Now I sincerely hope that we find some badly thrombosed veins on *one* ovary so that we can leave the other and leave the uterus—which, you understand, is totally useless *without* the ovaries and would simply become a source of problems in the future—or if worse comes to worst, leave you with enough of one or both ovaries that we wouldn't throw you into a precipitous and premature menopause."

"I don't understand."

"You would be sterile but not menopausal. Fortunately, the body can adjust to a lot of trauma: even a *piece* of *one* ovary can preserve your hormonal balance. We wouldn't want to deprive you of *all* estrogen support at the age of . . . twenty-six?"

"Almost twenty-seven," I whispered.

"At any rate," he went on hastily, probably spurred by the look on my face, "we'll be doing everything we can to avoid . . . sacrificing . . . your uterus, and I feel fairly confident we can spare some ovarian function, if not all of it. . . ."

"We?" I said as if I were just waking up. "Who's we? I want you! You're going to do the surgery, aren't you? Please! I wouldn't let anybody else touch me! I wouldn't let anybody else do it!" I knew I sounded shrill but I didn't care.

"Of course I will, if you want me to. I'm your doctor."

"You'll be with me, you'll stay with me, right?" (Blubber, blubber. Was this me?)

"I'll be with you. Don't worry." Len sounded enormously reassuring. His dark brown eyes were soft. "When I said 'we' I meant us, all of your doctors. One or two of them will unquestionably scrub and be in on any decision. We all have your best interests at heart. . . ." Diminuendo. Full rest. He looked down, as if he were embarrassed. Two measures of rest . . . four. (Perhaps he was trying to gauge my full reaction.) Attack; crescendo.

"Well, you didn't want any more children, did you?" he blurted. "You have told me that you didn't. And now you won't have to worry about contraception, which has always been a problem. . . ."

"Yes. Ha. I did say that, didn't I?" I tried to appreciate the irony, maybe even work up to a hollow laugh. The curse of the curse: lifted. The mess, the bother, the worry about getting pregnant, the cramps, the mood dumps. The perfect solution! And a fast way to lose—what?—three pounds? Yes, I said it, didn't I? But did I mean it? Could I have ever meant for such an idle wish to be taken seriously? Did I mean for *this* to happen? There was something murderous and perverted about it.

Len plunged on reassuringly. "We'll do a bikini-line incision. That means you won't even see the scar—it will be buried in pubic hair. Recovery is quick these days; you'll be back to normal in no time. So what do you say? Let's schedule this and get it over with. Stephani?"

I was busy counting the sins of commission and omission that had brought this on me, struck by the O. Henry twist: the man who in this world knew my body and its network of responses best—the man who made love to me—would now make healing violence to me as the instrument of the punishment I was to suffer for the very acts I had committed with him. He had taught me, he had opened me; but that was just a preface for more profound, more poignant intimacies.

Yes, let's get it over with, I thought. Let's take it out, get rid of it. Please relieve me of the dozens of small deaths that are consuming me; give me precious ease where there is only dis-ease, pain for guilt. There was a purity, an inevitability about what was happening to me, its roots curling far down into my past and my sins and my psyche and my karma. My transgressions had accumulated until their weight no long admitted a congenial erosion: I had to prepare myself instead for a magnificent landslide of retribution. One certainly got precisely what one deserved, and now all that was left to me was the dignity with which I accepted the balancing of the scales.

Len interrupted my reverie. "You know, we really have no choice," he said well-meaningly.

I was beginning to see that.

I was back in Epiphany in August. That's when they did it. As usual—as expected—nothing went . . . as expected. The Demerol they gave me on the morning of the surgery—to "relax" me—made me dizzy, made me nauseated, and then made me throw up. The throwing up predictably made me anxious and upset, and this, together with a foul-up in the OR schedule (I was to go down—or was it up?—at 7:00 A.M.; at 10:00 A.M. I was still sitting in my bed, hungry, arms folded, and scowling), conspired to make me a nervous wreck by the time they came to fetch me.

Once fetched, I was filed into a tiny blank cell in the operating suite, where I tried to lie on my stretcher obediently and good-naturedly until "they" were ready for me. However, as the last giddy effects of the Demerol wore off, I realized with some alarm that this floor was kept considerably colder than were the patient floors. I dread cold almost as much as I do nausea, and I had been shipped out with only a hospital gown and a thin sheet covering me. I didn't like cold, I didn't like throwing up, I didn't like being hungry, and I especially didn't like being abandoned at a time like this. Anger gives me energy: I soon found myself pacing barefoot around the closet I was in like a caged animal, the sheet wrapped around me for warmth, thinking the evilest thoughts about the hospital's callousness, its doctor-orientation as opposed to patient-orientation. I could have waited in my room! where I would have been warm! and Michael could have sat with me so that I didn't have to be frightened alone! They could have given me the Demerol later rather than earlier; certainly they knew that the schedule had been changed!

After many many minutes I allowed myself a tantrum and accidentally/on purpose picked up the rhythm of my pacing, hitting the stretcher (so that it, in turn, hit the wall) on every third or fourth circuit. Presently, of course, a steely-looking nurse pounded in to see what was going on.

"What *are* you doing?" She exploded. "Get *back* onto that stretcher where you belong. You are *not* supposed to be up!"

"I'm cold," I said sullenly. "I'm tired of waiting. I would prefer to wait in my room until you get your operating schedule straightened out. Better yet, schedule me for *tomorrow*. I don't want this operation any more today. It's too late. I rescind my consent."

"Don't be ridiculous," she snapped. "Why, I've never *seen* such a display. Really!"

I changed my tack, collapsing immediately in the face of irate authority. "But couldn't I have a blanket? I'm so *cold*."

"There are no blankets on this floor." Her voice turned harder to match her hard eyes. "I'm busy. I don't even know why I'm *talking* to you!"

"But when are they coming for me?" It was my best kindergarten whine.

"When they're ready for you," she snapped again. "Now lie down. I don't want to find you up again. Why, I'm re*sponsible* for you while you're on this floor." She snorted and wheeled out the door, pulling it shut behind her. I got back onto the stretcher, completely cowed and fighting back the tears, shaking with cold and anger.

"I'm sorry," Len apologized when he dashed into the operating room into which I'd finally been transferred. "It's just been one of those mornings . . ." I looked at the clock on the wall: it was one in the afternoon. The room itself was small—almost intimate—and seemed more like a little, misplaced piece of a clinic waiting room than a properly impressive theater of gore and blades. There were windows, and a light overhead which was not lit; in it I could see my reflection: my lips were blue. The cold had eventually done what the Demerol had failed to do—I felt drowsy and thick and careless. I barely responded when an intern couldn't find a vein to get the IV started and had to call a resident. I kept saying to myself, Soon this will be over. I can wait. I'll wake up in a few hours and it will be done and over and I will have paid up and life will go on. . . .

Len looked strange and vulnerable in his surgical greens, and I had trouble integrating my conflicting images of him—the suited, tied, white-coated, and polished Len and the intimate and open man with mussed hair I had come to know recently. This Len in his surgical garb was a disquieting combination of the two: professional, arrogant, competent, but with his hair out of place (perhaps from doffing his green cap), powerful arms bare to the shoulder, and the wide V of his shirt exposing his neck and a wedge of hairy chest. Nobody here knows what I know, I thought to myself as I watched the muscles in his upper arm swell and twist as he kneaded his hands together while talking to the anesthesiologist.

Len came over to the operating table and rested his hands on the edge, leaning forward over me. "How are you doing?" he asked gently.

"I'm still mad," I pouted.

"That's okay. You have a right. Are you still so cold?"

"I don't know. I guess not. I think I'm numb."

"Everything will be all right," he said, taking my hand and holding it between both of his. I was startled that he was willing to be so openly affectionate in front of other people—his colleagues. I was worried he would compromise himself; only later did it occur to me that it was probably not unusual for a surgeon to indulge in some valedictory laying on of hands prior to assaulting his patient with a scalpel. Only later did it occur to me that it was probably as much for him as for me.

"Don't you have to scrub?" I said, looking around worriedly.

He tightened his grip. "I will. As soon as you're out. I'll stay here with you till you're out."

I felt an immense wave of gratitude. As long as he was holding my hand, I would be okay—no panic, no shaking, no fear even. He was an excellent doctor—the best; I had asked around: he had a formidable reputation as a surgeon. He would take good care of me. He wouldn't let anything happen to me. Perhaps after all it was less an irony than a blessing that it was my lover, who was going to carve into me, who would be quite literally up to his elbows in me; perhaps it was one small gift in all this, that I wasn't being deserted to someone who didn't know me or care about me. Or care *for* me. Who better to violate me than this man? (Len told me later, during one of our nightly talks, that as he stood over me at the operating table during the surgery, gloved hands deep in the viscera as he felt for the pear-shaped womb, he was quite suddenly and unexpectedly overwhelmed with an intensely graphic image of our lovemaking so palpable and immediate that he withdrew his hands and stepped back, letting the resident take over. I have ever since wanted to believe that this was in fact so.)

Len smiled reassuringly and held my hand tighter. For a moment I felt dazzled. "We're going to start the Pentothal now. You can count backwards from ten." He chuckled. "You won't get to one."

"I don't want to count," I said, looking up at him. And then the room began to shimmer, as if the dense cold air had turned to water and I was at the bottom of a green-tiled pool. Lights and faces swam over me like bright flat fish. I tried to focus on Len's eyes behind his glasses.

"Sweet dreams," he said. It was the last thing I heard.

When I awakened in the recovery room the pain was horrid: I was drowning in it and couldn't get my breath. When I heard someone call my name, it was like a lifeline thrown to me to tow me to a safe shore. I tried to focus. If only I could focus, I would float up out of the dream of pain, out of a nightmare of slicing and searing and disembowelment. If I could just focus on the voice I would wake up from my nightmare.

And then I remembered where I was: nightmare into nightmare. I tried to open my eyes but it seemed they were sewn shut. Then one eyelid—only one—cracked open; I wrenched my head back and forth on my neck as if that somehow might help me to see—the way I had shaken a baby doll when I was little to make her rolling eyes unstick. (What a tiny thing to control! Only an eyelid!) Then the other eye popped open and I was startled to see Dr. G.'s face only a few inches from mine—a large mobile mask, fuzzy around the edges, talking at me while my head still rocked from side to side.

"Stephani," he said sternly, "it's all over now . . .

we're all through . . . can you hear me? Answer me if you can hear me." I thought I said yes but what I heard myself do was moan. The whiteness of his coat hurt my eyes, so I shut them again.

"Open your eyes," he ordered. "Can you hear me?"

Very slowly I looked at him again, concentrating on keeping my eyes open . . . but concentrating was like trying to climb a glass wall. I wanted to feel my stomach to see what they had done, to see what shape the terrible pain that was squatting on me had assumed, but my arms wouldn't move.

Everything hurt so much, was colored with agony: I had been dipped in it like an Easter egg. And what was Dr. G. doing here? Where was Len? Oh, yes, I had forgotten: Dr. G. was in charge of my case. Len, as he (Dr. G.) had hastened to assure me, was merely the plumber. An expert plumber, but nevertheless a plumber . . . in the hierarchy of hospitals in which the gynecologist is one (spare) cut above the pear-shaped psychiatrist, but well below the internist who is himself inferior to the imperious surgeon. Len simply did the bidding of those above him in the hierarchy.

"Yes, I can hear you," I said with the greatest effort. It seemed to take forever to form the words and push them out.

"We got it," Dr. G. said. "You have nothing to worry about anymore. We located the difficulty and we got it. The surgery went beautifully."

I nodded, fighting my way through the haze of pain and nausea and anesthesia. I had to ask Dr. G. a question before he left. I searched for the words, arranging them like Scrabble letters on a tray in my mind before laying them out on the playing board, and then read them off carefully so I would not be misunderstood.

"What . . . did you . . . did they . . . do? How much . . . did they . . . have to . . . take?"

Dr. G. looked serious and sad for a moment, and then shook his head. "We had to take everything, hon," he said softly, still very close to my face. Maybe it was a secret and nobody else in the recovery room was supposed to know.

"What's . . . every . . . thing?"

"Both ovaries, the Fallopian tubes, the uterus. The cervix, of course. There was nothing else we could do. The ovarian veins were badly thrombosed—on both ovaries, though the left one was worse—and there was no way of cleaning that up without removing everything. It's better this way. We couldn't take the chance of leaving anything that might cause trouble later."

I felt as though I were in an echo chamber, still back on the "everything." Everything? Leaving nothing? . . . My God, they had done it. I was castrated. Not just no longer capable of having babies, but castrated. Somehow I was sure they would leave an ovary, or at least part of an ovary.

Everything. I turned my face away and closed my eyes again, abandoning myself to the pain. Feel it, I thought. Feel what it's like to have all your womanly parts gone. Feel what it's like to be punished.

Michael came every day, staying as long as he could. Len came every night and sat with me for more hours, drawing the curtain around the bed in my semiprivate room so that we could be quiet together in the crepuscular glow of my roommate's bedside lamp while he held my hand, absent-mindedly tracing the veins on the inside of my wrist with his fingertips. There was nothing to say, even if I had felt well enough to talk, so I allowed myself simply to be comforted by his presence.

I was much sicker than I had counted on; the surgery had been more extensive than anyone had counted on. The incision was not of the nearly-invisible variety that had been promised, but a long gruesome gash that went from above the navel to within half an inch of the natural bifurcation of the genitalia. It caused me considerable discomfort, though I began to wonder—after a week of pentazocine injections in the buttocks and thighs—whether the painkiller wasn't worse than the pain. Len told me that he and Dr. H.—the chief of surgery at Epiphany, who had scrubbed in as Dr. G.'s "representative"—had wanted clear visualization all the way back to the kidneys, requiring more viewing space than a low, horizontal incision would have allowed. ("We couldn't take any chances," said Dr. H. when I saw him.)

But I had more to worry about than how the incision looked. I had begun to vomit in the recovery room after the surgery and hadn't stopped. I strained and cried, holding my split belly with both arms as I retched again and again into a kidney-shaped basin, afraid I would tear open and spill my paralyzed intestines into the sheets. Once the peristaltic action starts again, the vomiting will stop, Dr. G. assured me. But my body was in revolt against the insults perpetrated against it, and my intestines refused to move even the sparse contents of my stomach along in an orderly fashion.

"We've got a problem here," Dr. G. announced on the third day after the operation as he strode in, followed by a nurse carrying a stainless-steel tray with a towel discreetly folded over it. Trailing close behind was a nurse's aide wheeling a small, efficient-looking machine on a trolley. I felt too ill to be curious about which of my many problems he was alluding to. Dr. G. took the tray from the nurse, sat on the edge of the bed, and turned back the towel, revealing a clear plastic tube about the size of a gas siphon nestled among other paraphernalia. A tube? I was already catheterized, so it couldn't be that . . . but how many places are there to put a tube?

Dr. G. explained to me about the nasogastric tube as he unsheathed it from its sterile packaging and balanced it in his hand.

"Is this really necessary?" I asked with distaste as I looked over the machine that came with it. (Why was this happening to me? Why were things never "as usual"?)

"I'm afraid so," said Dr. G. "Every time you vomit

you put the healing process in jeopardy—to say nothing of the discomfort you cause yourself. This will keep your stomach empty until peristalsis begins."

He stood up so that the long end of the tube danced over me like water forced from a spigot until he captured it and smeared it with a lubricating jelly. He tilted my head back and threaded the tube into my right nostril, making me sneeze and then cough as it slid down the nasal passage into my throat. I began to gag and felt as if I were choking, raising my hands to push him away.

"Swallow! Swallow!" he urged as he pushed. I swallowed, and the thing slithered down my throat as he fed it in slowly and steadily all the way to my stomach—which was apparently a long way down. It was a most unpleasant sensation; I was repulsed.

The tube was taped to my face and then attached to the machine, which ground away like a minute Volkswagen, slurping and sucking as the bile and stomach slime marched through it in a cloudy yellow column. I fell back on the pillow: just the thought of the thing was thoroughly exhausting: yellow stomach juice inching out my nose into this machine, yellow urine running into a bag hooked over the side of the bed. I was disgusting, knotted in all this plastic tubing, pumping fluid. I didn't know how either Michael or Len could stand the sight of me, or the smell of me.

Humiliation is an important aspect of the inevitable regression that accompanies sickness and pain. Like a baby, I wanted only to be patted or held, needed only my most basic functions tended to. Like a baby, I required little of company but that they be there, keeping watch for demons and doctors. I dozed and hurt, hurt and dozed, waking to find that the day had turned to dark, that someone had come, or someone had gone.

Once, coming out of a dream as if from under a rock—pushing up, fighting my way with a kind of panic back to consciousness through a crust of drug dopiness—I felt all at once suffused with a calm, as if I had stepped from a cold dark room into the sunlight. I lay for a long time without opening my eyes, savoring the sense of being protected, lifted, before realizing that the sense of well-being was traceable to the distinct (but until this moment, unnoticed) weight of someone's hand on my arm. The hand hadn't moved for the whole time I was awake—which was considerable—part of the reason, no doubt, it had taken me so long to identify it as the source of my comfort. I turned my head languidly and opened my eyes to see a nurse from the floor—a nurse I had liked but never particularly noticed because she was so quiet and self-effacing. She was tall and sturdy, with long dark hair like mine, and she was standing there next to my bed—very still—with her hand on my arm. Her touch was like a benediction.

"How long have you been here?"

Her sweet smile broadened. "Awhile," she said.

"I knew it. I could—feel you. You can't imagine what you have just done for me." Even *I* couldn't imagine, but it was something powerful and wonderful and half-remembered. "I thought maybe you were an angel," I added, not at all concerned about the extravagance of my association because I was quite serious. "Really, it felt like the touch of an angel." My voice sounded funny with the tube down my now very sore throat; my tongue was coarse with dryness and my lips cracked and bleeding: I was not allowed anything by mouth, even water.

"You were having a bad time. I heard you." So simple. I suddenly understood what nursing could be and often wasn't, thinking of the night nurse—a small, angry Filipino woman who was rough and hollered at the patients and had a tendency to get medications mixed up, who layered humiliation on humiliation with her treatment of the wretched refuse of her teeming floor.

"Don't leave just yet," I begged. She had lifted her hand from my arm. It rose like smoke to her face as she tucked a wisp of hair under her cap. "What's your name?"

"Nellie."

What an odd name, I thought. A name that belongs to another century.

"Nellie. Nellie, thank you. You helped me so much, you'll never know. Every nurse should be like you."

It took me two long, difficult weeks to get out of the hospital; the original stay had been set for five days. I seemed to lack the strength—the resources—to reverse the deterioration of the prior year. It was hard to stay awake, get up, sit in a chair. I felt like a zombie.

Michael was cheerful and loving. The children were thriving "in the country." I should wait for my strength to come back and everything would be fine; Grammy would keep the children until the beginning of their respective schools so that I could recover. Chicken soup (now that I could eat) imported from the provinces, sunshine, rest; time, of course, time would cure everything.

Holding my hand lightly, Michael had said to me that we would start all over. He would try if I would try. We had both had a bad scare.

I wanted to try. Here was my one clear chance to rewrite the script, make a clean beginning. My debts were paid. I would be different now. Worthy. Relearn my roles. I had been tempered in the refiner's fire.

Months later Michael told me of meeting Len in the hospital stairwell a couple of days after the surgery. (I had tensed, not knowing what was to come next, what sort of confrontation there had been. But it wasn't faithlessness Michael was seeking confirmation of, it was cure.)

Len had been evasive, looking at his hands and turning them over, then back again, slowly.

"I can't say," he had said to Michael. "I just don't know. It really didn't look that bad—the thrombosis, I mean. But I'll tell you this. I don't think we got it.

That's my personal opinion. Whatever it is, we didn't get it."

Len had turned to go. "We couldn't take any chances, though, you see."

# FALL 1971

---

TIME. I'D ALREADY LOST SO MUCH, WASTED SO MUCH
. . . and there was so much to do . . . everything to
be made up for. I could beat this and was determined to
recover in record time as testimony to my strength and
sanity and admirable character. If it took an ordinary
woman six months to recover from a radical hysterectomy it would take me three, two . . . six weeks. If I
just tried hard enough.

Trying required ignoring the resistance of my body
to being hurried into well-being; it remained maddeningly feeble, defiantly bloated and sore, making me
move—in sleep as in waking—with the same obsessive
and tender caution as I had in the last clumsy months
of my pregnancies. Even turning over in bed demanded
patience and ingenuity, while ambulation was a sorry
affair of shuffling and puffing as I felt my way along
walls and banisters like the very old or near-blind:
slowly and grotesquely, squinting against the pain.

Trying also required ignoring the evidence in the
mirror: I looked dreadful. My hair was parched instead
of silky, my face drawn and waxy, suspended above my
body's ruin. I was used to seeing a taut angularity—a
forthright set to the shoulders and a determined place-
ment of the long bones of the thigh in the hip socket;
now my arms and legs had become spindly and
vulnerable-looking. And because the pull of the scar
coaxed the shoulders forward while the belly pro-
truded—tight, hot, and swollen from the long vertical
incision that curved sinuously around the navel like a

143

scythe—because my skin had devolved from being merely pale to looking amphibian in both quality and color (where, that is, I was not yet stained with dark bruising), I reminded myself of one of the frightened, scurrying creatures festering on a Boschian landscape.

Disgusting, I thought to myself, inspecting the damage in the mirror. Repulsive, I reiterated, as I looked down with a queer giant's perspective to where my belly popped out and sagged, all misshapen with the cramping of the cut muscles. I looked like buttocks front and back—the same both ways.

The trick was to bear the punishment with good faith, to transcend it, to see it as a test—to recognize furthermore that the affliction was also a deliverance, an easy way back from the fenny delirium of lust that had stirred me all summer, that had made me rare and lovely. I was through with loveliness now—by choice and by circumstance—and I was ready to be useful and true, plain as the palm of a hand. The snarl of pleasure and daring that had engaged me had come undone and delivered me back to Michael, chaste and penitent. I wanted everything different—or perhaps back the way it had been (I couldn't remember)—wanted it sweet and dreamy and eurythmic, like Michael himself. My affair with Len was over; now I was a woman only a husband could love.

Poor Michael.

I tried to spare him the sight of me—my deformities, my rot. I wanted to give him every advantage in his campaign of effort; I wanted to give him every opportunity to want me and love me, validate me, sanctify me. It wasn't sex I was interested in—it had in any case been forbidden to us for a period of at least six weeks—but I desperately wanted holding, caressing, loving, reassurance. From Michael. Only from Michael. And surely he would come around, when I was less . . . repulsive; he had said he would try. For the moment, our enforced celibacy complemented all that had been stellar in our marriage as well as much that had been askew, for it granted us a blessed peace with and in each other, a grace that protected us both from a familiar, easy contempt—him for me, and me for myself.

Later we would straighten out our problems; for the moment, sex was one more thing—along with the children, and cooking dinner every night, and guilt—that I didn't have to face right now while I was recovering. Doctor's orders.

"Doctor's orders!" I protested to Len the night we had dinner together, shortly before the children were to come home. I had been avoiding him, but one dinner— a drink and a little quiet talk, as we had had in the hospital—seemed safe enough, courteous even, considering the time he had spent with me—such kind, gentle, unselfish time. I had come to his apartment quite innocently—for once: he himself had insisted on my continence for this period!—and anyway one did not molest pregnant women, senile women, damaged women. "Doctor's orders!" I repeated indignantly, pushing Len away. "No sex for six weeks. Remember?"

"Ha!" said Len. "I've just removed the restrictions. I made them and I can change them. You'll recover much faster with a little use. I prescribe a large dose of cock, QED." He kissed my breast through my T-shirt, wrestling me supine on the sofa. "Don't worry," he said, "I'll be very careful."

I felt a wave of panic. I had not planned on this. Our interlude had been just that—an interlude—and it was over now, lost, like childhood. Atavistic. Magical. Gone. The woman I had been was gone too. I no longer had anything to give Len.

"You'll hurt me," I whimpered. I didn't mean just by his penetration of me.

Len took me by the shoulders and shook me a little, looking at me sternly, paternally.

"I wouldn't hurt you. You know I wouldn't hurt you," he said. "I want to make love to you."

"I don't feel like it," I said irritably, almost inaudibly. But he wasn't listening, and his breath came faster as he nuzzled in my neck, putting one arm around me—supporting my back—and the other hand up under my shirt. Street sounds gusted in the open window; I could have screamed, or made some embarrassing fuss, but that would have been silly, excessive, infantile. Dark, panting, and heavy, head down, rummaging at me like a thick, salivating animal, Len reminded me of something oppressive and depraved, something my mind didn't want to concede—some betrayal clotted into the corners of my life, congealed in patches up the walls that contained me.

"I need you," he said, his words running together. "I want to make love to you. We're going to make love." He was working at the tie of my wrap skirt; I hadn't been able to get into any slacks since the operation, with my abdomen swollen to the size of a four- or five-month pregnancy.

He wanted me. He needed me. If only men knew how powerful a de-inhibitor need is! How much more powerful than simple desire! Women much more readily respond to what is needed than what is wanted. How could one deny one's impulse to nurture? An impulse so rooted in me that it inevitably overrode every fear, every misgiving, every resolution: whenever I had said no to a man I became all women saying no—all women who had ever said no—the archetype of rejection and denial, all withholding, all selfishness. To be real—to be affirmed—was to be rich, warm, and explosive: an artery, a breast, a belly, a cunt, ready to be tapped or touched. There was an endlessness about women that was denied to men—or perhaps a circularity—that they envied and coveted. It was so pathetic of them, really. Rooting around, begging. But it was shabby to deny a man access, to deny him what it was so easy to give.

It was partly my fault. I had shared in this, raised expectations: it was my obligation to recognize and minister to these needs I had incubated in him like some virus. I suppose Len had the right to expect something from me—succor for succor—after all the time he had spent with me in the hospital. I owed him something; it looked as if I owed him a lay.

The sofa in the study was in fact a sofa bed, which Len unpleated. I sat on the edge and folded my hands, feeling sacrificial, resigned, resentful, and afraid that I might begin bleeding again and stain the mattress for his wife to see. I shouldn't have come here. I should have known. Or guessed.

There were no sheets, and the mattress buttons pressed into my back when Len took my T-shirt off. Lying on my back I didn't look so bad—everything just spread a little like a broken egg. How could he want me this way? I didn't understand it, but then, there was a lot I didn't understand. The sanitary napkin that I wore to protect my clothes against the sudden gushes of blood that sprang from somewhere inside me—the old-fashioned elastic contraption that held it on—were shed and dropped onto the Persian rug.

Len was gentle, as he had promised. He probed clinically at first; I could feel how much the vagina had shortened since surgery. "Coming right along," said Len, touching here and there. "A damn good job, if I do say so myself. The cervical wound has healed nicely." It sounded absurd, here, with the two of us naked, amidst all the urgency.

Then we made love. Or rather, he made love to me while I lay half across him on my back—a position he had arranged for minimal penetration—holding my breath, afraid that each soft thrust would tear something, rip me at the seams. As Len grunted and ground his way through what seemed to be his pleasure, I stared at the ceiling with its dappled ellipses of rosy light from the discreetly shaded lamps, impatient for this to be over. I couldn't wait to unwind myself and let the sweat and steamy breath evaporate in the September window-breeze. I couldn't wait to stand up and let the semen run down my legs and out of me: I wanted him out and I could get him out. I could clean myself completely of a man now, now that I had no cervix, no tubes, no access to my workings and churnings—a sad sack, purse-string-sutured at one end; a sausage casing, closed and resistant. I needed to keep nothing in me, ever again, of a man. I could empty him into the toilet, wipe him with tissues, excrete him. I was impregnable.

He could take me but he couldn't have me.


I tried to put everything back to normal during September, as if I were setting a table with a proper place for each aspect of my life. I was well-equipped with my new resolve and my new chance: I would register for a master's program; I would get a job; and when I wasn't working, I would stay at home and be a good, attentive wife and mother. There must be some way of making amends, some way of working myself back to where I might have been had I not slipped and slid on a path muddied with insecurity and romanticism. As someone observed: pain concentrates the mind wonderfully. I concentrated. I was willing to forgive if I would be forgiven. I would learn to give more and want less.

Mother love came in rushes, like the hot flashes I had that burst on me so powerfully and unexpectedly, rising from chest to neck to mouth and eyes as if I were a thermometer in which a prickly red column climbed in response to fever. Mother love made my heart pound and my temples ache, battering its way through the stolid dumbness of my Calvinistic reorderings. My children had been well cared for, but without a mother; a Grammy and a Grampy and a Poppy were not the same—even taken all together!—as a Mommy. (I needed to believe that desperately, desperately afraid that I was dispensable, that they managed quite well without me.) In the end, it was the children who suffered the most.

The children—so different from each other—had unsurprisingly reacted differently to my absence. Alexandra was the more distressed; she had grown quiet as I watched her through the small observation window in the door of her new Montessori classroom—a tiny three-year-old huddled silently on a mattress in the corner of the sunny, cheerful classroom, unmoved by the gaiety and clamor, uninterested in the alluring array of equipment, sucking her fingers and watching the other children at play, with her eyes darting here and there like little forest animals flushed into flight. She'll be fine, her teachers—warm and experienced, with children of their own—assured me. We'll watch for trouble and we'll talk. Often. Shall I come in and sit with her for a while? I wanted to know, longing to gather her up in my arms and rock her and tell her over and over that I wouldn't leave her ever again. Ever. The teachers had to push me out the door every day the first week. Go, go, they said. Don't worry. We know how to handle it. It will pass.

Zachary, seemingly so much more resilient at one than Alexandra at three, had already developed characteristic coping techniques, taking the disjunctions in his small world in his stride . . . as if he had a stride. He was still in diapers and he had learned neither to walk nor even to crawl, having invented instead a curious sitting hitch that was unpleasantly reminiscent of the hopeless men on Upper Broadway who, missing legs, inched themselves along on little platforms with roller skates precariously nailed to the bottom, locomoting by means of gloved knuckles scraping and dragging in the street. Nevertheless, he was quite an accomplished hitcher—a dear little shmoo with all his ballast in the bottom like an inflatable toy weighted with sand—curious, friendly, and easy. Zachary was more used to being without me, never looking back when I left, adapting brilliantly to a new caretaker or a new environment, like the experimental infant school at Barnard he was invited to join, where the toddlers fingerpainted with chocolate pudding, pounded Play-Doh of spectacularly improbable colors, and generally had a grand time. He seemed so unjustifiably and insistently content that for a time I feared brain damage.

They would be all right, I told myself. They will be fine, the teachers comforted me, as soon as they see that their world is once again stable and intact. A little time; it would take a little time, but that was to be expected.

My duty to them and myself now was to get things back to normal as quickly as possible.

It was time to get a job; this seemed a good way for me to build strength and distract myself from the tendency to feel worn and beaten and sorry for myself. What's more, the hospital interludes had seriously compromised our family's financial security. I had had twenty-one days medical coverage—for somebody who had never been in the hospital and didn't foresee such an eventuality, it was much, much more than enough—which had been largely used up during my first siege; we had had precious little concept of how fast money goes during an illness. Our savings were depleted just at the time our general living expenses were going up, with the children in school and my recent admission to part-time study for a master's degree in graduate school. I had always intended to contribute: now was the time. The children were a little older; I was through nursing Zachary. A job would be good for me and good for my family.

With Len's help, I found a situation that seemed almost ideal, with good money and a night shift that allowed me to take a course or two toward my degree and be with the children during the day. It bothered me little that I would be working in an abortion clinic, doing counseling and procedure-room nursing. I was not trained, but they would train me. I got high marks for life experience.

It was while working in the clinic that I began to see myself as a woman among women, as a secret sharer.

Intellectually, I had been committed for years to the right of each woman to determine the fate of her body, and the fate of anything her body supported . . . as long as her body supported it. I had devoted time and contributed money to the freedom of choice movement;

here at last was an opportunity to combine academic interests, practical needs, and moral and social responsibility.

I had worked out my arguments to myself carefully, logically, as if I were doing a brief. There were two issues: the moral and the legal. Beyond the issues, there was brutal reality. Morality I left to the philosophers, the theologians, and the individual: morality is a slippery issue for even the most profound and sophisticated thinker, and it has, of course, only situational specificity. I was more interested in the legal aspects: state control, individual freedom, legal definitions, and where they all intersected. After doing some research, I satisfied myself that in the eyes of our *legal* system, a fetus was not a person (it could not inherit, for instance, and it was not counted in a census), and therefore not entitled to the rights of a person under the Constitution. As long as the fetus was a biological parasite on the body of the mother, the mother's rights took precedence over—took *precedence* over, although they did not obliterate—the rights of the fetus. A fetus that could sustain its own life without the mother *was* a person, entitled to a person's constitutional rights and a person's constitutional guarantee of protection. It satisfied me as an elegant mathematical proof would have satisfied me.

Then there was the brutal reality. Fancy debate was a luxury at the clinic. These women—young and middle-aged, single and married, black and white— these desperate women who flew in furtively from Denver, from Mobile, from Columbus—or took the train from Scarsdale or Flushing—were rarely interested in morality, were interested in legality only to the extent that they were prevented from seeking abortions closer to home. (New York State at that time had just passed the first abortion-on-demand law, and while that certainly did not imply that you could ask and get, it did mean that there was now always somewhere to go.) They were interested in one thing only—terminating their pregnancies—and it was clear that they intended

to do so with us or without us. If not for the legaliza-
tion—and clinics like ours as well as doctors who were
willing—very, very few of them would have been able
to persuade a sympathetic physician in some hometown
to do the procedure safely and discreetly: most of them
would end up on a kitchen table somewhere, biting on a
towel to keep from screaming as their pregnancies were
scraped out of them onto greasy newspapers; of having
Lysol pumped into the uterus to induce "spontaneous"
abortion; or taking God knows what because somebody
promised it would bring on a period. These women
were not candidates for the enthusiasms of the social
workers employed by the adoption agencies, though
they might possibly (the unmarried ones)—just *possibly*—be persuaded to carry to term by some lawyer
with a handful of bills and an equally desperate child-
less couple waiting in the suburban shadows to claim
the blond, blue-eyed baby they would never have themselves.

So it didn't bother me. We were saving lives, not taking them. I saw little guilt among the patients (to be
distinguished from sadness and regret), and I felt none,
though many of the other counselors were tortured with
dreams of babies and blood, sometimes so bad that they
had to quit work.

Which is not to say I wasn't troubled by the thought-
lessness and carelessness that were usually responsible
for the unwanted pregnancy. Better an abortion,
though, I thought, than an unwanted child. Because
where was the government's interest in this child from
the time it was born until it reached majority? Who
would love it, pay for it, see that it had the right kind of
life? Was the government about to buy clothes for the
other kids in the family? Pay for their college? These
women were going to terminate their pregnancies anyway—they had been doing it for centuries: abortion,
not contraception, is still the most common method of
birth control in the world—so they might as well do it
here, in supportive surroundings, at reasonable rates,
with competent doctors.

Though I myself had never had an abortion—the only one of the female staff, I think, who had not—I could identify with the women who slunk and staggered—emotionally exhausted—into our facility—a converted garage, a factory of deliverance—their pathetic little overnight bags, printed with posies, bumping their sides. I could easily remember how afraid I myself had been when I had thought—for that month my freshman year—I might be pregnant, the nightmares about slimy alleys in New Jersey, the surly detached voice on the phone when I—typically—made "preliminary inquiries." I knew what it felt like to have the cervix dilated—though these women would have local anesthesia, which I had not, to ease the forcing open of the tight, stubborn ring of muscle that protects the uterus. (I had had an IUD inserted before Michael and I took our long honeymoon in Europe. "This may hurt a little," Len had warned. "Hold on. I'll make it as fast as I can." And then he had done something to me so dreadful, so hideously piercing, that I screamed in pain before I even registered how much it hurt. I had crumpled on the table cramping, couldn't move for fifteen minutes. It was as if a bottle had been rammed up me and then broken into thick dull shards.)

I too had been gelid with fear on more than one occasion, as these women were when they arrived, pale and shaking—whatever the weather—choking out names, addresses, and appointment times to the receptionist. The administration had tried to make the clinic cheerful and welcoming, but such a place can never be cheerful and welcoming, with its bright lights and efficiency, smelling ominously of antiseptic, air freshener, and menstrual blood. The apprehension in the waiting room was a tangible presence and took up as much room as the friends, boyfriends, and husbands.

I counseled about better contraception, probed for guilt and the threat of psychotic break, outlined the procedure. What was done was done; this was no time for scolding. In the future they would either take responsibility for themselves and their sexual activity or

they wouldn't. It seemed to me that the abortion itself
was punishment enough.

I stayed with them during the procedure to assist the
doctor and to give the patients support—keep them
calm and cooperative. (The patients were conscious
during the abortion; anesthesia was local rather than
general.) When I wasn't handing the doctor instruments, or turning on "the machine," I talked to the
women and held their hands as their pregnancies were
sucked out of them; I shuddered with them and for
them because I too had lain under impersonal lights
and spread my legs over cold metal to strangers; I too
had had things—rough fingers, speculae, surgical instruments—shoved in me—up me—invading places so
deep I couldn't imagine where they buried themselves. I
had felt fear and pain and guilt, had felt abandoned and
confused. And then I began to feel something else,
something unaccustomed and monstrous. Something in-
vigorating. Something potent.

It was anger. Not a small, specific, needling anger,
but a great torrent of rage, breaking up niceness, tracta-
bility, ladylike behavior, like a hot spring under opaque
winter ice. It was precisely because these women
*weren't* me—because *they* were the patients and I no
longer was—that I had the luxury of burning with resentment at the way they were frequently treated. I
wasn't one of them, but I could have been. It could
have been I who was subjected to the humiliation, the
patronization, the outright cruelty that characterized
some of the doctors. It could have been I who was be-
littled, ignored, and dismissed. I was angry for these
women who were in no position to be angry for themselves, and it loosed a terrible knot somewhere between
my stomach and my throat. I felt the rage because they
could not—would not dare to. Much later I figured out
that I also felt the rage because in other circumstances,
when my fear, my habit, my need obstructed it, *I* did
not dare to.

There were times when the clinic had the air of an
armed camp: the counseling and nursing staff (many of

whom were undisguisedly members of the radical fringe of the women's movement) squaring off against those doctors who were perceived to be afflicted with lack of understanding and compassion at best, or to be brutal and intolerant at worst.

We all had one particular unfavorite. He was rarely on my shift, and the few times he had been, I had somehow missed being paired with him for a procedure. The counselors weren't above dealing doctors if they could and felt they had to ("I know you're next, but I just *have* to have Dr. X. for this woman; she's really freaked out, and she'll have a stroke if she ends up with Dr. Y." . . . and so on), but for the most part we had no choice about whom we worked with. I had heard about this doctor, but I had never seen him in action—until one night when he was on, and I was on, and I got him.

Prior to the abortion, the doctor always did a pelvic exam on the patient to determine how far advanced her pregnancy was—to make certain it was less than twelve weeks, the limit for ambulatory abortion. For this undertaking, this particular doctor assumed his—I later heard—characteristic (offensive) posture: while he had one hand on her belly, and one in the vagina so that between the two hands he could palpate the uterus (this part was usual), he had also hoisted one knee onto the table extension—between her legs—as if he needed leverage to plumb her body. The position made him look both sinister and contemptuous, as if he were braced to stuff one more article of clothing into a laundry bag already full to the bursting. I was aghast, and could think only to interpose myself between him and her in such a way that I cut off her view of him—how in the *world* would she react to an attitude of such implicit violence?! I kept my eyes on her not only out of concern for her, but because I couldn't bear to look at him. As he dug into her with all the concentration of a little boy making the long central tunnel in a sand castle, her eyes rolled, and grabbing my hand, she caught her breath audibly and straightened her legs, pushing herself toward the head of the table, away from his examining hand.

"Move down to the end of the table," he said, addressing her pelvis, never once looking directly at her. I helped her scoot down and he plunged in again, screwing up his eyes in what I could only interpret as a calculated demonstration of acute medical attention. The girl—she was still in her teens—was holding onto the sides of the tables as if it were a surfboard caught in the curl and she was preparing herself for a wipeout. He cranked at her like a Roto-Rooter.

"Ow. Ow! OW!" she cried, her eyes wild and now brimming with tears, straightening her legs again, this time pulling her hips clear off the table.

"Move back down!" he commanded, scowling, while I tried to soothe her.

"It hurts," she said to me fretfully. The tendons on the insides of her thighs were straining and quivering. She raised her head off the table to look at the doctor, but her gaze kept sliding away as if there were no visual purchase on him. "You're hurting me," she amended. It was clearly the wrong thing to say.

He took his knee off the table and stood back for a moment as her mouth fell open in the onset of hyperventilation. I continued to hold her hand as disgust washed his face like an ugly light, and then he said to no one in particular, as if she were no more conscious than that same bloated laundry bag, "Christ! These women! You'd think I was actually *hurting* them. . . . A pelvic does *not* hurt; a suction abortion is virtually painless." Then to me: "If you were doing the job you're *paid* to do, and helped them deal with their *guilt*, we would all get through this much more quickly and simply." He yanked off his jellied rubber glove with a viscous snap, tossed it in the general direction of the trash, and stalked out.

My anger flared. What did he know!? What did he know from greasing up and plunging in? . . . Which was probably the way he fucked his wife when he got home. How could he have any pretension to ministering

to women—to human beings—with such an attitude?
Had he never been hurt? Frightened? Oh! To see just
*one* man—just *one* doctor—in here! pants down; wrinkled white feet hanging helplessly, suspended from the
spread knees (why are men's feet always whiter than
women's? . . . must be all those short black nylon
socks . . .); deflated little cock flopping and throbbing with fear! Let a woman with bright cold metal in
hand approach him from below, poking and prodding
his testicles, inserting needles into . . . say, the delicate brown flesh around his anus, telling him it doesn't
hurt, to cooperate, please. Then let him have the tenac-
ulum—the instrument that closed like scissors, but instead of blades sprouted two wicked, needlelike prongs,
which met head-on when it was closed—fixed through
the scrotum (as it was clamped into the cervix so that
the cervix could be pulled down into the vagina, providing better access to the uterus—a "movable organ").
And finally—again for argument's sake—(now that the
local anesthetic was working!) have graduated steel
rods rammed into his anus—up his ass—to force open
what nature intended to remain closed—except in the lit-
eral discharge of its functions—thicker and thicker rods
until his asshole gaped like an idiot's mouth, minute
convulsive tremors rippling around and around it like
jolts of electricity! Let him have all that done, and then
let him be patted on the head and told he is a "good
boy"! Let him know, too, what the (woman) doctor
thinks of his fears, his anxieties, as he sweats his bullets.
Why, I have seen a man convulse in agony just at the
sight of another of his sex getting kicked in the balls on
a movie screen!

It was like rape—worse than rape!—because it assaulted a woman's spirit with at least as much thoughtless violence as it assaulted her body.

To have one's pain assigned to neurosis denies its
reality, dehumanizes its bearer, and implies some kind of
genetic inferiority, some categorical moral torpor. It is
organized medicine's most exquisite, gratuitous torture.

*   *   *

I still wasn't getting any better; I felt like an old car with the headlights falling out, the fenders loose, the seats sprung, rattling through autumn, unsure as to what might fall off or break down next. The chest pain continued and was at the same time undeniably worse—lest there be a chance I forget that I was sick in some mysterious, significant way—and breathing had become a full-time occupation: it was impossible to take a deep breath—my lungs felt full of stones—and even the shallow scoops of air to which I confined myself ached like razor cuts.

The emboli continued to boil up from wherever they began—again in spite of the anticoagulation. I was quite sure about each one; at last, at last, the doctors were giving my own testimony some credence, asking me instead of telling me, and finally abandoning their jolly fictions in the interest of enlisting my help.

Only Dr. L., the pulmonary specialist, clung to his little white lies to "protect" me, not knowing, perhaps, how anxious he made me by challenging my sanity, just when I had finally reclaimed it. I only found out much later, while reading about my case in a medical journal, that the embolus I threw in the hospital—while being treated with Heparin, a powerful anticoagulant—was a real event, rather than (1) phantom, a hysterical reaction to the stress of surgery, or (2) (grudgingly) gas under the diaphragm—a not uncommon sequela of surgery. I was quite certain by then that I knew an embolus when I felt one, so Dr. L.'s firm disavowal made me wonder halfheartedly but compulsively whether I was again losing any capacity to distinguish real from unreal, whether panic and hysteria had become a Lamarckian adaptation.

In October, by the time my heart murmur ("a snapping of the valve," said Dr. G.) was becoming more than an incidental curiosity, the doctors' composite attitude had shifted, slithering from the original disdain and dismissal, right through the calm center of partnership, validation, and support (Do not pass Go . . . Do not collect $200), to a churlish peevishness, a stern disgruntlement, as if I had somehow engineered this illness to embarrass them. They appeared short-tempered as they discussed my "lack of progress." I felt chastised, even punished, for failing to cooperate. I'm right back where I started, I thought, except that now the illness is real: we've identified the problem, but now we have nobody to take reponsibility for it. It reminded me of something my mother used to recite at me: "You've made your bed, now you must lie in it." I had been determined to be sick against all my doctors' judgment and advice . . . and now—you see!—I had got what I wanted. Sickness. Operations. Attention. Affirmation. I had, it seemed, asked for it.

For all I knew, Len—who had always been somewhat more sympathetic—felt the same, but I didn't know: since that night in September I had avoided him. Or maybe he had avoided me.

I deserved good news for my birthday in mid-October, but I didn't get it. Instead, Dr. G., clucking and shaking his head, warned me darkly that the very next embolus would force them to do a "lifesaving procedure." (I had tried to forget how easy it was to die of an embolus.) They simply couldn't allow this to go on, he said. How touchy to have an undiagnosed patient currently under treatment die on you, I filled in, silently.

This lifesaving procedure—this vena cava ligation— would be accomplished through an incision that went front to back over the hip (so much for the dowdy two-piece bathing suit; I hadn't liked it anyway). The inferior vena cava is the large vein—about the diameter of a thumb—that is the primary conduit for the blood returning to the heart and lungs from the lower extremities. The proposed intervention—the tying-off of this large vein—would prevent any emboli—still assumed to be coming from the pelvic region—from making their way into the heart because the smaller veins (that would eventually take over the function of the inferior vena cava as collateral circulation developed) would be

far too small to accommodate the clots. There were
drawbacks to having one's life saved in this fashion, the
principal one being the effect on the vascular system of
having that tremendous volume of blood shifted off the
main highway onto a series of rambling country roads.
Sometimes the new, more circuitous routes were unequal to the task of keeping the blood moving; then
veins in the lower half of the body became progressively more distended in an attempt to compensate for
the diminished capacity of the vascular system to deliver the deoxygenated blood back to the heart. That
meant varicose veins—not just of the ankles or calves
or even thighs, but varicose veins of everything below
the rib cage.

My friend Joan, one of the other young mothers in
my building with whom I trudged back and forth to the
park, had once been an occupational therapist in a hospital. She had an old textbook with pictures of people
who had had an inferior vena cava ligation, which in
response to my request she brought along one day on
our way out to the playground. "Are you sure you want
to see this?" she asked with concern before surrender-
ing the book to me. I pored over the medical pictures—
little smudgy black-and-white photographs—feeling
much as I had when I had discovered a copy of *Ideal
Marriage* beneath my mother's nighties, which I read in
uncomprehending, furtive gulps while she was at the
grocery store.

"Here," Joan said, pointing to a picture of a man in
a loincloth who had been photographed in a stance of
self-display that I automatically associated with a freak
show. ("See here! See the deformity!") His body was
lumpy and ropy with gross white varicosities that
snaked up his torso: a blandly morbid Laocoön . . .
only the serpents had got up under his skin where they
writhed and beat with his pulse. It was horrible. If my
collateral circulation failed to develop adequately, I
might look like that. I felt dizzy as I closed the book
and handed it back to her, wishing I had been less

curious and more self-protective. She had, after all, warned me.

From then on I was even more determined to get well, and I wound myself up to a perfect frenzy of demonstration of good health: mind over matter, mind over matter. I would concentrate, deny the emboli, melt them in mid-toss.

It was like an incantation: I will not throw any emboli, I will not throw any emboli. Please God, make me well. I will not throw any emboli.

# NOVEMBER 1971

◆

## PART ONE

I PLOWED ON INTO THE SHORT DAYS OF EARLY NOVEM-
ber thinking my positive thoughts and resolutely rejecting any possibility of failure of the will, praying for
mercy. The holidays were coming—it was no time to be
sick and self-absorbed. I flaunted normality like a ban-
ner.

So I picked the first glorious Saturday afternoon to
discharge an important obligation—an idle promise
that, having been put off and put off again, had begun
to assume the weight of a covenant: taking Alexandra
to Rumpelmayer's for ice cream. "Soon" had finally
become "now."

I was feeling a little stronger, had even gone to the
trouble of putting on makeup and what Alexandra
succinctly described as "big-lady" clothes. Alexandra
herself was a picture: perfect, beautiful, her long, dark-
blond hair tied up in back with a black velvet bow, her
black patent Mary Janes, her miniature Chesterfield
swinging like a bell. Mother and daughter on their way
to Rumpelmayer's for ice cream, like so many other
doting mothers and privileged little girls for generation
after generation of Saturday afternoons.

We could hardly have done better with the weather.
It was one of those astonishingly beautiful midautumn
afternoons when the sunshine intensifies the so-slight-
as-to-be-imagined aroma of burning leaves, when it is
both warm and cold and the air is so clear and strong it
practically cleans your teeth for you. The crowds on

Fifty-seventh Street were noisy and good-natured as they often are at that time of year before the ambiguous mood and forced cheer of the holidays sets in, when everybody feels invigorated and moves purposefully. Colorful midtown duds streamed by. Voices skipped around us and scattered off the buildings like a continuous volley of pebbles on the surface of the brisk air. The vendors, pushing their broken, infernally smoking carts, were doing a lively business in chestnuts and pretzels. Even the litter in front of Bergdorf Goodman looked gay, soaring and swirling brightly in the little eddies of wind, as if trying to make up for not being leaves.

"Hurry, Mommy!" Alexandra urged, dancing around me on her baby-bird legs. She laced her fingers through mine and pulled at me, making me lose my balance. "Oh boy oh boy. *Hurry!*"

"We'll get there, Pussy. Relax." I didn't want to walk too fast; anything speedier than a stroll tended to make me indecently breathless. The cold air stabbed me with each inhalation as it was. Alexandra had spun a few paces ahead of me in her eagerness and excitement, and now, rewinding like a yo-yo, she flung herself against me, burying her face in the pale fur of my coat. "Ice cream," she sighed. I gave her a quick hug and smoothed her hair, took her hand and walked on.

Then there was quite suddenly the funniest smell in the air. I glanced around, thinking that I had perhaps walked into an air current from a building, or the exhaust from one of the city's ever-percolating manholes. I felt oddly alerted, as when one hears one's name called through a fog of sleep, or when one is reminded of something by a fraction of a perception—a faint alarm of recognition I couldn't quite place. Just as suddenly I knew it wasn't a smell at all, but a taste—metallic, brown, insistent—that rode a sudden surge of saliva, forcing me to swallow hard a few times in quick succession to keep from drooling onto the front of my nice coat.

Whatever in the *world*?! I thought to myself, gulping,

and hesitated in the rush of passersby so that somebody ran into me from behind. I turned to excuse myself but instead began to cough explosively, sputtering and spraying.

I reddened with embarrassment, and shaking free of Alexandra's tiny fingers, covered my face and mouth with my hand. The coughing was incredible, irresistible: I had never coughed like that, with an urgency and convulsiveness that could only be compared to the last stages of childbirth. I couldn't get my breath. I gagged. I coughed a strange, harsh, boggy cough that rattled and snarled all the way up from the bottom of my lungs.

My eyes filled with tears as I fought for breath, and through the blur I saw Alexandra looking up at me quizzically. I aimed my purse at her, dropping it into her arms and managing to say, "Pussy: take this," on a strangled exhale. With both hands free, I covered my mouth and face with one, and used the other to brace my belly against the coughing—I thought it might split along the luminous blue incision like a melon—and then stumbled blindly toward Bergdorf's display windows, trying to get myself and Alexandra out of the flow of humanity that jostled and stared. What must these crisp, manicured people think of me, snorting and choking so immodestly?

I groped in my coat pocket for the wad of tissues I always kept there for wiping noses—mine and the children's—and held the whole fat pad to my mouth (my real inclination was to stuff it in), and leaned on my shoulder against Bergdorf's window. I put one hand, the palm slick with saliva, against the cold expanse to steady myself.

All at once I was able to wrap a good hearty breath around what seemed to be some sort of obstruction, and gave a massive heave which I half expected would deposit my innards on the sidewalk. I felt a wave of relief that I had coughed up whatever it was that had been choking me, realizing only in the next moment that there was something in my mouth more substantial than a stringy gobbet of phlegm . . . something large, solid, and raw-tasting. I knew what it was and wished I didn't.

Trying to seem casual—holding the thing on my tongue like a host—I carefully opened one tissue and put the rest back into my pocket. Then, as daintily as I could, I held the tissue to my lips as I had seen my grandmother do in the months before she had died (as I pictured Marguerite Gauthier with her lace handkerchief) and let the grisly chunk drop from my mouth. I folded the tissue nonchalantly without looking into it and, trying to collect myself, held it in my open hand a moment, watching the pattern of little scarlet spots expand and spread together until I held the stamp of a red moth on the white paper.

I turned my back on Alexandra and the stampede of shoppers, preferring the plaster leer of the mannequins, and cautiously opened the tissue. In it lay a bloody bright jewel the size of a nickel, glistening and quivering in the late-afternoon light.

I folded the tissue around it again as if it were a live, vulnerable thing that chilled easily and reached for my bag which Alexandra—standing transfixed—was holding up under her chin, and snapped it open. I tucked the little red-and-white package into my change purse, saying to myself, Don't faint. . . . Go into Bergdorf's and sit down. . . . You are all right. . . . Someone will help you. . . . Don't faint—you have Alexandra to think about—and pushed myself away from the store window leaving a smear of handprint. My chest hurt.

Alexandra laid her face against my coat and looked up at me. "Mommy," she said softly, "there's all red blood stuff around your mouth." And then in the same mock-scolding tone I sometimes used with her, she pulled her little eyebrows together in a playful scowl and said, "What have you been eating?"

I called Michael from Bergdorf's. I thought I was okay for the moment. I thought I should take Alexandra to Rumpelmayer's and finish out our afternoon. (I was sure what would happen now; God only knew when I would have another chance to take her.) Then I would come right home. Didn't he think that would be all right?

"Are you kidding?" he shouted through the phone. "You get back here right away! Right away! What if you coughed up more? What if you passed out? Get right home. I'll call G."

It was all settled by the time I got home. I was to enter Epiphany again that afternoon, "admitted to the hospital at this time because of [my] generally deteriorated state and for possible inferior vena cava ligation." It was while I was speaking to Dr. G. that I had my first wave of hysteria, losing control with the unexpectedness and momentum of a running stumble.

"No, no," I cried, when he spoke of surgery. The tears rushed to my eyes and poured down my cheeks. My nose ran and I didn't bother to wipe it so I had a mustache of mucus. Total regression. "Please, I don't want to," I wailed. "I can't. I'm afraid. I can't." If he was trying to reassure me, I didn't know; I couldn't hear him over the sound of my own sobs, my voice rising like a siren to a scream—"No, please, no please"—as Michael pried the telephone from my fingers and I slumped into the desk chair, crying uncontrollably. Michael put his hand on my shoulder to comfort me as he made arrangements for me to be admitted as he called his parents back from a trip, as he called my mother to come and stay with the children.

It was the first time I had had real hysterics in many years.

As a little girl I had had these extraordinary episodes in which grief—some immense, ineffable grief—came on me like the swift stealthiness of a summer storm, when some little thing would set me off and I would cry and cry and cry, inconsolably. Despair surged through whatever I might have identified at that young age as my soul, breaking off bits with its force and carrying them out so they spilled from my howling mouth and streaming eyes. There was never any comfort for me during those episodes but exhaustion, and I would subside into sleep, hiccuping and sodden.

I cried like that now—unashamedly, loudly, wetly—as spasm after spasm of misery washed over me. What would happen to me? What would become of me? What had I done, why didn't it stop? Nobody seemed to be in control: whatever was happening inside of me was cooking away, bubbling evilly, breaking down the rhythms and substance of my body. I thought the doctors were cutting away at things recklessly; other things were falling off or out of their own accord, coming apart. I had wanted to believe that even if I was confused and medically naive . . . hysterical . . . pessimistic, *somebody* at least knew what to do. All these big strong wise doctors who had known so much about me for so long were supposed to be in *charge* (that being the only consolation for my inevitable humiliation, to my mind). They were supposed to be *helping* me.

I was like a train bent to the track of this mysterious illness, rocketing toward nowhere: soon—very soon—I would simply fly off—jump the track—at one of the sharp turns taken at too high a speed and pile up in a spectacular, shrieking climax. I could see, with my capacity for vivid imagery, the artifacts of my life strewn among the smoking, shuddering, wreckage: my modeling book, pictures of my expensive face stained and streaked; my children, wandering in an aimless daze through the torn metal; Michael, surveying, and then grimly calculating the damage, the coverage.

Finally. I knew. I was dying.

It had not been an ice cream Saturday. And it was the last of the golden, early evening, early November sunshine I was to see for a year: that was out somewhere with my other life. Here, back in one of the old buildings at Epiphany, everything was green, acid, drained of warmth.

I had a tiny little single room, with the bed pushed

parsimoniously into the corner. My view was of dingy brick, soot-soothed windowsills, the blank gray eye of another window. The liver-colored linoleum with its stone-colored gouges. The dormitory-room Formica furniture. The dead-people smell.

I guess—in Dr. G.'s view—I had got a bit more uppity since I had last surrendered myself to his care. My experience at the clinic had bitten into me and wouldn't let go. Doctors weren't perfect. They were only human. (Ah! If only *they* thought so!) And I had some rights, among them the right to challenge medical infallibility. So my communication, such as it presently was with Dr. G., was more strained than ever. I no longer trusted him or his judgment, in spite of reassurances that he was "a fine doctor." I suspected that even Len didn't like him or his attitude.

This time I had bothered to do some research, goaded by the specter of the snake man. I wanted to be prepared to argue the case for my body. I had learned of a new technique being used that seemed an improvement on outright ligation of the vena cava: fenestration—the insertion of a Teflon screen into the big vein itself. The screen would strain out any clot moving from the lower body toward the heart, and by the time the screen itself had become completely occluded—an occlusion that amounted to ligation—the body would have had time to adjust itself somewhat to the increased venous pressure by developing collateral circulation. It would mean less trauma and less chance of winding up looking like the snake man.

Dr. G. was having none of it, and quite plainly resented my having an opinion—any opinion; I knew that at this rate it was only a matter of time until he washed his hands of me entirely. He didn't like being challenged; he didn't like being questioned. He even offered to turn my case over to someone else if I was . . . dissatisfied . . . with my medical care, making me feel contrite and marginally guilty. In spite of my own growing sense of distrust, I didn't want him to feel *rejected*. I didn't want to hurt his *feelings*. I only wanted some information and a productive adult dialogue about the management of my case. He made me feel like a child who had to be talked through and talked over.

Len wanted me to bring in a consultant from another hospital. It was an option I had been afraid to raise with Dr. G.—who seemed exceedingly proprietary about his medical territory—although I had a growing suspicion that it was a course I should have followed some time before now. Len gave me the opening: a colleague of his at another teaching hospital—a brilliant young head of surgery—was well-known for his diagnostic acuity.

First Len spoke with Dr. E., and then I myself did. He was straightforward, informative, and quite definite. He agreed with me—preliminarily—on the fenestration issue. He additionally urged Len—and then urged me—to have another pulmonary angiogram done preoperatively. I felt pride in myself for finally having taken some hand in my own fate: it was strange and exhilarating. Seminal.

My platoon of specialists and quasi-specialists was visibly insulted. They thoroughly resented me for my meddling . . . especially Dr. G.; he disagreed with Dr. E. on both counts (according to Len), but felt obliged to capitulate in the interest of protecting his demonstrably vulnerable flank. While members of the medical profession dislike under any circumstances the ordeal of consultation and review (notwithstanding self-righteous protestations to the contrary), they *abhor* having to submit themselves to the scrutiny of anybody outside their own insular (read hospital-particular) network of professional loyalties who will poke through the refuse of their decisions . . . and the inevitable mistakes.

Surgery was scheduled for Wednesday morning; Monday and Tuesday were to be left for tests: X-rays, blood work-ups, another scan, venograms of both legs. "Now be sure to tell us right away if you feel faint or anything," said the technicians as they prepared to run needles into the tops of both big toes so they could record the progress of the dye as it sped toward my heart. I was standing on a ledge—my back against a kind of tilt-top table—restrained by straps. "Oh, I'll be *fine*," I stoutly assured them. "I'm hardly the type to succumb to the vapors." But I had never realized how sensitive the tops of the feet are, with their thin, tough layer of skin, resistant as plastic sheeting. The technicians had to push hard, as though they were punching leather, to get through the skin, and each try for the tiny toe vein made a creaking, then popping sound. I watched as if from a great height, strapped to my table, watched the blood trickling over my toes—which had turned white—and running down between them. "Uh-oh," I said, feeling my head sort of separate from the rest of my body and go floating toward the massive dark X-ray machine above me. "Uh-oh," I said weakly as the floor seemed to swing toward me, "I'm . . ." "Get her down," someone barked, and the tilt-top tipped me back as my stomach pressed up into my throat. It took four tilts—upright, horizontal, upright, horizontal—to get the needles in, where they sprouted from my toes like the tufts of hair on Hobbit feet.

*From a medical journal:* "Venograms of both legs failed to reveal a source of the emboli."

All of Wednesday was a blur of apprehension, confusion, grogginess. The angiogram had been scheduled to take place just prior to the surgery itself, for the reason that I simply and emphatically refused to have it done again without general anesthesia. My anesthesiologist—a kind, quiet Italian with an unexpected sympathetic streak—reluctantly acquiesced, being careful to point out the increased risk of doing the procedure under a general.

I was scared but fatalistic. My life was as much in order as it was ever likely to get. My in-laws had returned, my mother had arrived, Michael hovered reassuringly. I saw Michael in the morning before I was taken away; he kissed me tenderly and told me he intended to wait at the hospital until I was brought back to my room. I felt less shaky than I had before the hysterectomy, largely because I had refused to be "premedicated"—a doctors' convenience, at any rate, rather than a patient's. I wanted to be in full command of my faculties: if I sought a high, it would have to be a better one than Demerol could provide.

I expected to regain consciousness somewhere near evening, and dreaded the pain I guessed would accompany my new, wraparound wound. Instead, when I came to, although I was groggy, I felt pretty good; in fact, there was no pain whatsoever. Neither was I in the recovery room, but in a small holding area. The clock on the wall said 10:10: either I had been in the recovery room for many hours and had only now awakened on transfer (to say nothing of the splendid painkiller I must be full of), or something had gone wrong, somebody had changed his mind. I felt my body for bandages. The surgery had not been done. There was only a small gauze pad in the crook of my elbow where they had done the angiogram.

"What happened?" I asked a nurse who came by to take my blood pressure.

"How are you feeling? We'll take you back to your room soon."

"What happened?" I repeated, hating medical obtuseness. "Why didn't they do the vena cava thing?"

"I can't tell you anything about that," she said. "You'll have to ask your doctor."

"But did something go wrong? You must know something about what happened!"

"You'll have to ask your doctor," she said firmly.

Michael and his father were standing in the doorway of my room, conferring quietly, when I came back. (I had been moved, the day before, to a considerably more cheerful room on the sunny side of the hospital.) My father-in-law looked gray and strained; Michael looked swollen around the eyes and strained. I was still too dopey to concentrate on much beyond why I was back here in my room, and on the fact that I was ravenously hungry.

"They found something when they did the angiogram," Michael said, as I faded in and out.

"Can I please have some food?" I wanted to know.

Then Michael was gone, or maybe his father was gone and he was still there. I dozed, dreaming about magic cakes like the ones in children's stories, which invariably have many layers, icing oozing creamily down the sides, a cherry on top.

My room seemed suddenly full of people, floating like apparitions, all white. At least some of them were my doctors. They rotated in place like a troupe of skaters; someone was close by, perhaps sitting on the bed.

"Are you awake? Are you paying attention?"

Maybe. Yes, maybe. The anesthesia hangover made it so hard to focus.

Angiogram . . . shadow . . . good thing we did. . . . Shadow in the heart. Marked progression of the embolus . . . complete occlusion of the artery to the upper right lobe . . . middle and lower lobes are also occluded. . . .

"I don't understand. What is . . . a shadow?" The membrane of dulled drugginess stretches and thins so that I can almost see through.

(In the heart, a shadow. A clot . . . passing through. A tumor, growing and pushing open the little doorways, chamber into chamber, letting the draft in. . . . A clot, surprised. Perhaps a tumor.)

"Did you hear me? We can't know for sure from the angiogram. We can only see that there's something there, something that wasn't there before. We won't know until we do the open-heart surgery."

Wait. You left me behind. Open? Heart? It's all gone wrong, my blood and my breath.

"Open-heart surgery?"

"We can't schedule you yet, of course, you understand, but next week . . ."

I was to understand, which I was struggling to do.

The cardiac surgeons were all in Houston . . . a big meeting . . . no one was around. Schedules were so full already . . . because of the meeting . . . in Houston . . . DeBakey . . . there was no one now. So sorry. Such a long stay, we know, but we couldn't possibly schedule you before the end of next week. . . . Rest. You can rest in the meantime. . . . There's no point, of course, in doing the fenestration now, we'll do them both together . . . next week.

"Wait." I am meek. "Can I please have something to eat?"

Although my open-heart surgery is a week away, there is no time to be lost. There are so many tests to be done immediately—right this afternoon—in preparation for it. I may not eat, in spite of being able to think of nothing else. They never allow you to eat before tests.

Another cold, darkened room. My Princeton doctor, second in charge of my lungs after Dr. L., leans over me . . . looms. His preppie blond face comes into focus, his pale eyes shuttered by rimless glasses. A piece of straight, no-color hair separates from the rest—the rest combed back ever so neatly—and falls forward into his eyes, and he tosses it back without touching it, the way I did when I was eleven and experimenting with movie-starish styles. ("Where *is* your barrette," my mother would ask with ill-concealed distaste as I blew and flipped the hair off my face.) Then he has a green shower cap on. He is pushing my hospital gown up, above my waist. I have an insane impulse to put my arms around him and draw him to me: maybe he will make love to me, his soft cheeks blushing prettily, my young doctor with an initial for a first name, a name for a middle initial.

They are painting my hip, my stomach, my groin, painting me yellow-brown: shit and piss. "Hold still. A little prick." More pricks and my groin tingles. Something—they do something—and hot water runs over my hip, between my legs. I lift my head. It's not water, of course. Of course it's blood. Of course. I cannot keep my eyes open. Perhaps I have been drugged again.

Whatever they are doing to me, on this table, it is taking too long. My back hurts, the table is so hard and cold. My spine feels like a string of wooden spools. And my groin aches where they are pushing and pulling, where the little catheters, the tiny hoses, thread in and out. I cannot understand what they are saying to each other; maybe they are talking behind their hands. Machines move into place above me, move away: black clouds passing overhead studded with colored stars. The humming of the machinery lulls me back to sleep.

*From a medical journal:* "An inferior vena cavagram demonstrated total occlusion of the vena cava with collateralization around the vena cava suggesting a large amount of thrombus. The iliac veins were also diffusely involved. . . ."

It was dark when I returned to my room. Food smells awakened me. I was weak with hunger. Hungry. Weak. Eat and sleep. That's all I wanted to do.

Michael was there. Michael was waiting. Michael had been waiting all day. Dear Michael. Sweet husband: hands shaking, red eyes.

"How are the children?"

". . . Yes. . . ."

"May I have something to eat, please? You can't imagine how hungry . . ."

The doctors were all still there. A committee. A committee meeting in my room. They were talking to Michael, and then he began to pack up my things into the little folding suitcase I had brought.

"I'm going home?" I asked a nurse.

"Moving. You're being moved. Don't worry."

"But I like it here. I like this room. I just *moved* here."

The place was crawling with doctors—my medical past flashing before my eyes. My mother came, sat on

the edge of the bed as she used to do when I was little
and I was sick. Smoothed my hair. Held my hand.
Kissed me, the little hairs on her upper lip stained tan
with nicotine brushing my mouth; her blond hair—dark
roots showing—crinkly with setting, smelling of hair
spray. She looked drained and her face was paler, more
swollen than usual. She would drink too much tonight.

"I love you," she said, "my daughter, my child," and
put her beautiful hand with the pearly, oval nails under
my chin to raise my face.

Michael, hovering.

Len, Dr. G., somebody was explaining. ". . . Don't
know how this could have happened. We are moving
you to Intensive Care, the cardiac unit. . . . We can't
take a chance, the catheter may have dislodged. . . ."
I fought to make sense of what was being said. "If the
thrombus breaks loose . . . a massive insult to the
. . . You need monitoring, constant monitoring. . . .
At least you won't have to wait till next week now, you
are scheduled for first thing in the morning. . . ." I am
beginning to understand. "An emergency. Yes. An
emergency."

It's a nightmare; perhaps this isn't happening. I reach
my hand toward the doctor to see if he's really there.
My fingers make contact with the white coat.

"I thought there were no cardiac surgeons available?
I thought they were all in . . . where? . . . Houston?"

The doctor averts his face. "We'll get somebody.
We'll pull from another hospital if we have to. Let *us*
worry about that."

I don't think anybody will worry about that. They're
trying to kill me.

I think they're trying to kill me.

The room clears, the pretty sunny room I have occupied just one day, and I see they have scoured all signs
of me from it, as if there has been a storm that has
blown me and my belongings clean away. I am not to
move around, even to go to the bathroom. ("Don't

dislodge the . . .") How can I still be so groggy? Maybe it's shock.

Someone else. Len. Len for sure this time. He sits on the bed and holds my hand in his and shakes his head. My terror bubbles up, boiling to his touch. "I'm scared." I'm scared of dying. I'm scared of being dead. "Oh, God, I'm so scared!"

"I've arranged to be there," he is saying. "I will scrub in. They're not happy about it, and it will be hard to explain, but I will be there." Keep watch, Len, bar the way out. Keep my soul from tumbling from my body. Oh, God! Oh, help!

We look like a parade on the way to the Intensive Care Unit. Me, wrapped up like a bunch of wilted flowers fading on a steel tea cart, steered through a maze of corridors. Michael alongside, riding shotgun, carrying my little tapestry suitcase. ("I'll have to take it home," he says. "No personal belongings allowed." "But I need my hand cream, a book!" I protest. "No. Only your toothbrush, they said, your comb. There's no place to put anything else there.")

I know what that's really about: it's about making you a nonperson, extorting from you your few tokens of identity. (Put them in a plain brown paper wrapper, to spare the recipient embarrassment.) They want *you* to forget who you are. *They* want to forget who you are: it's not part of the deal. They would rather cut up bodies than people.

Through the air locks into the cardiac ICU: mission control—busy as the ocean, the dark shimmering with islands of fluorescence. Nurses scurry like ants over an anthill, dragging equipment. All the beds are in a circle, attending the supervisor where she stands in her ring of readouts. Above each bed a raft of monitoring devices, anxious blips dancing across the screens like a chorus line of electronic guardian angels.

There is a place ready for me, right in the middle, facing the command center: a good view of all the little dramas of life and death. Electrodes are attached, tubes inserted. I am affirmed in the flicks and streaks of light, in the beeps and whistles.

"Stay, Michael, don't leave me." I want him to insist on remaining with me through the night. I want him to defy all authority with his love. "I'm so afraid. They will stop my heart, won't they? They'll use the heart-lung machine. What if it doesn't start again?" (They used shocks; they shocked the heart again and again if they had to, to make it start.) "I'll be dead during the operation; what if they can't revive me?"

"I love you," says Michael. "Don't forget I love you. And the teenies need you." (At our most intimate, our most affectionate, we referred to the children as the teenies.) "Nothing can happen. You won't die. I know it. I promise you."

The children. If I died, they'd soon forget me—they are too young not to. Michael would remarry, give them a mother. In the meantime his parents would help.

"If anything happens to me, don't let them forget I was their mother. Don't let them forget how much I loved them." He could give them a picture. He could remind them. They would forget, of course: I would subside into a vague, primitive sensation they would experience only in the depths of sleep or in the inchoate splendor of lovemaking when something in them would resonate to other arms and a wet, cadenced comfort.

"Good night, I love you; good night, I love you; good night, I love you," he says, backing away from the bed. The whole big room seems to sigh, as he retreats and shrinks: it is such a long way to the door. He turns on the other side of the glass and blows a kiss.

Jell-O and ginger ale for dinner, now when I was too frightened to eat, now, when the anesthesia had finally worn off, leaving me unblinking, comprehending, defenseless.

A cheerful round nurse came, with merry blue eyes and chubby, capable arms, like Mina's. She made a sleeve-pushing-up motion, in spite of her sleeves being quite short, and plunked a basin of warm, soapy water down on the bedside table, singing to herself under her breath. She pulled the curtains around my bed and slid a waterproof sheet under me.

"Okay, off with the hospital gown," she said buoyantly, and proceeded to shave me from the tips of my ears to the tips of my fingers to the tips of my toes. I shivered and jumped as the razor tickled its way down my body.

"Why? Why shave everything?"

"You never know what part of the body they are going to need to be available." She rolled her eyes. "Hair is *loaded* with bacteria!"

"But I have no hair on my *chest*," I said indignantly as she made tracks through the lather in precise circles around my breasts, leaving a broad satiny ribbon of exposed flesh.

"Ah, yes, you do. You have hair everywhere . . . that is, you will until *I* get through with you." She helped me into a clean gown. I felt like an elaborate dish being painstakingly prepared for a banquet.

She left the curtain partially closed. Under the thin covers, I ran my hands over my very very naked body. I was smooth as a newborn, smooth as polished metal, warm and still tingling from the shaving. I thought about how life could leave a body: it would be only a piece of meat. Bones. Cartilage. Flesh.

That might be me tomorrow. Would I be back in this bed tomorrow, twenty-four hours from now? Or would I be cold as stone, cold as polished metal, lying on a slab in the basement, waiting for a doctor wearing a mask against the stench to rend my corpse, breaking open the breastbone like a bony egg, peeling back the silvery fascia, separating the lung tissue like segments of a peeled orange, poking into the pink, the gray, the dull red to find out what went wrong and why the patient died?

How could things have gotten so fouled up? How many miscalculations were there to make? And when did they stop? Tonight? Maybe tomorrow? with one final climactic extravagant miscalculation?

They said the surgery itself posed only a 10 to 15 percent threat of mortality. But what about *beyond* the surgery? What growth or polyp or lump was in there?

It didn't look good.

I wanted a priest. I *really* wanted my mother, or my husband, but there was no way to talk to them and I couldn't ask them to come back: this was possibly even harder on them than it was on me. I had no choice. I knew what I had to do. But I had to *talk* to somebody, and a priest seemed logical.

I didn't know any priests, hadn't been to church in years. (Michael could have found a rabbi, but I didn't want a rabbi. Back to basics. Forgive me, Father, for I have sinned.)

. . . Actually, I did know a priest—a Catholic priest. A Catholic *ex*-priest, whose little girl played with Alexandra. He lived in our building. He would do. He would have to do: I couldn't think of anyone else. Catholic, Episcopal, defrocked . . . it didn't matter. It was close enough. He would know what was necessary.

I begged the nurse on duty to call him, watching while she frowned and wrote the number on a scrap of paper. It was eight thirty.

"He said he will come," she reported. "He'll be here within the hour."

Nine thirty. Ten thirty. I gave a start every time the door to the waiting room opened to admit a doctor, or a nurse, or a visitor who would steal in—eyes wide, voice shaking—to lean over some half-dead loved one, murmuring words of comfort, crying, touching tentatively, or sometimes just standing as if lost in thought, watching the patient labor to breathe.

Ten forty-five. "Please call again. He has to come. Maybe he forgot." I had watched the clock jerk from minute to minute, all the way around, twice now.

"He says he's been held up. He's coming soon."

At twelve thirty the supervisor came over on her way

off duty. "Can't you sleep? Do you want something? Why don't you turn off the light?"

"Because I'm waiting. I'm still waiting," I said, tears welling up in my eyes. I wanted official absolution, somebody to tell me what to do, how to die.

"Oh, heavens. I *did* forget to tell you. Your friend, the priest . . . he called. He can't come. He said he was sorry, but he wouldn't be able to make it."

How could he not come? It was a sign, an omen, a final cruel irony in a series of cruel ironies. I was denied even this small, simple comfort.

If there was to be any absolution, I would have to grant it to myself.

All the rest of the night I watched the clock—tick, leap; tick, leap—the same kind of clock we had above the door in high school, that I had watched the same way, as the minute hand stammered out the hours. I dozed occasionally, but having slept all day I became more and more clearheaded and awake as the night bled out and the lingering effects of the anesthesia wore off. "Get some sleep," the nurses said as they came by to confer with my angels. But sleep seemed superfluous and profligate; whatever finally happened, I would have plenty of time to . . . catch up on my rest.

I used the time instead to work on myself, harden myself, weave myself a tough, sinuous fiber of resolve. The crying was over. There would be no sniveling or clinging or trembling. The only element in this drama over which I had any control was myself. And there was only my dignity to salvage, dignity I had always wanted but never knew I really had.

It was between me and God now. Even the doctors were out of the picture.

I was ready when they came to get me at seven.

Light. Brilliant, beautiful early-morning sunlight streaming through the high windows of this special operating theater (kept for the "big," the "interesting" procedures), scattering down the rows of seats piled to the faraway ceiling. Doctors and nurses—so many!—ricocheting around me like billiard balls, colliding in consultation, breaking, moving in and out of my range of vision. Len, drifting over me—protecting me, I think—touching me often with affection and concern.

"I'll be here, right here," he says, pulling my hair from under me and allowing it to cascade over the edge of the operating table so that its weight eases my head back. (They have spared me the final humiliation of having my head wrapped.) I fold my hands on my stomach, aware of their posture, of the articulation of the fingers, and then open and close them a few times in succession so that they look like the speeded-up films of flowers blooming and collapsing. Len is very quiet, standing there amidst all the bustle, stroking my hair.

I do not see our old friend Dr. H., who will perform the open-heart surgery although he has not done this operation—by his own admission—for a couple of years. It doesn't worry me. It doesn't matter.

They are making final preparations—everyone so kind, so gentle. I look at the blindingly white windows until my eyes water. I may rise through one of those windows, up near the white ceiling, drawn through it, melting through the glass into the sky where I could diffuse like a fragrance on the air. I can feel Len next to me, but I don't look at him; I am concentrating . . . arranging my mind and my soul like a still life that must look perfect at the moment the lens flashes open, so that that moment of perfection is captured forever.

I can feel the sting as they start the Pentothal. Len moves slightly next to me. In my mind—only in my mind—I throw my arms up toward the light, and as my last conscious act, take a deep breath.

# NOVEMBER 1971

◆

## PART TWO

THERE WAS A HUMMING, A SINGING, A STORM OF SOUND.
A rushing, a whooshing. A lapping.

Hot. It was hot and I burned. And cold, crystallizing
between my fingers, drenching me so I shivered and my
teeth chattered and I felt flayed, stately, rotating in an
icy wind.

I didn't move, but things moved. Things in me:
squirming, insistent, kicking up into my chest like a
changeling in the womb. Things outside of me: things
that banged and buffeted, things that pushed and pulled
at me, little sucking mouths kissing me and biting me.

And breathing sounds. Slowly in . . . click, click
. . . slowly out . . . click, click. Resonant and husky,
like the sound of a foghorn, deadened in the swelling
white fog.

Pain. But not mine. My body's, not mine. Little red
houses of pain awash at the far far end of the broken
stone piers, poking through a gelatinous wall of fog,
barely connected to the sighing beach, the singing
sands. (Like the eastern shore of Lake Michigan,
where I spent every childhood summer: the beaches a
white powder so fine, so minutely ground by the gla-
ciers, that no one stepped silently; the grains hummed
against each other as they gave way underfoot.)

Voices, faces, wove in and out: "I think we'd better
. . ." "She's not . . ." (Loudly, urgently.) "Can't I get
some help with this . . . ?" "Quick! We need a . . ."

Michael close. "I'm here. It's okay. It's okay." His
familiar, salty smell. The tiny pricks of light burning

backward in his green eyes, the spots of high color burning forward on his cheekbones.

My mother, her stale cigarette and perfume smell, her cool hands. I can't hear what she is saying as she bends over me.

Michael's mother: a flash of her gold jewelry, her beautiful, steel-gray coif, voice muffled.

(What? What? I can't hear you. . . .)

Something in my throat, terrible gurgling sounds, terrible pain. I would move my hands in front of my face, clear away the sticky webs of confusion and agony, but no parts will obey me. Maybe I am tied down. I am thinking very loud: please leave me alone. Let me sleep. Take away the hard things, the sticking things, the sucking things. Pain burns through the clouds, red and indelible.

I'm cold.

I'm hot.

I can't breathe.

Light. All the time. Even when my eyes are closed a glaucous thin glow filters through my eyelids. Someone reminds me to Wake up! Wake up!, but when I open my eyes, the light shatters my eyeballs and cauterizes my brain. I have single moments but I can't string them together, moments of startling lucidity when all my planets are in conjunction: "What day is it? What time is it?" It seems important. "How long did the surgery take? What did they find?" Somehow I am never conscious long enough to register the answer, but I am sated with the simple asking.

I begin to wake up regularly when they come to bother me—come to do things to my body—and look down at myself, naked and slack, when they turn back the sheet. (I wear no gown: there is only flesh; rough linen, plastic, and rubber; the funny, pinkish, old-lady antiembolism stockings on my legs; light.) A ridge of puckered skin runs toward my throat—higher than I can see—and down the other way over my pubic bone, where the gray skin is shaded with stubble. No dressing, no bandage, just this pale, bald range—its center split by a raw gash—laced ever so neatly with heavy black thread in rosebud knots and ladders.

I survey myself. I take note of the topography. There are delicate brown crusts like the deckled edge of fine stationery where I have bled and been cursorily cleaned. There is a tube sneaking out of a hole in my right side: it disappears over the edge of the bed. And there is one remarkable intact inch directly over the stomach.

"Why?" I mouth, indicating the stretch of the incision and the single inch of relief. A doctor laughs. "You figure it out." I look puzzled and he winks at an intern. "If we just cut you open from stem to stern we would have a hell of a mess. Everything would fall out. Besides, it helps us to get you back together again right."

I am confused.

"You know." He is being explicit. "Like trying to put on a dress with a lot of little buttons. You could get down to the end and find out that you have buttoned the whole thing up unevenly so that there are two extra inches on one side. This way we can get the edges back together again right. Nothing left over."

"Really?" I croak, working my tongue around the plastic breathing things in my mouth. I want to know. "Is that the true reason?"

"Doesn't it sound right?" he says, and the intern laughs.

Days and nights are the same in here, in Cardiac Intensive Care, twenty-four-hour eerie green day/nights that spill from one to the next and back again, slopping luminously around me. I am so thirsty.

"No fluids," they are saying. "Nothing by mouth."

I think: if I could just wet my whistle. (That *is* funny. My mouth slings into a lopsided smile; my lips split and bleed.) All I need to do is wet the whistle.

My tongue is dry and can't talk, a squashy, furry bird nested in my mouth. My breath honks in and out around the tubes in my throat.

A warm cuddly nurse lifts my head.

"Try this. It will help with the thirst." She puts more furriness in my mouth, tasting of lemon.

"Specialty of the house. Glycerine lollipops."

I make a chewing motion on the tongue depressor wrapped in batting.

"Don't eat that," she cautions. "Just suck. It's cotton."

I smack my lips contentedly.

My mother-in-law stands next to the bed. "The children are . . . Lamb chops . . . Your mother . . ." Her charm bracelet jingles and I am seized with an old familiar sense of mischief.

"Want to see my incision?" I chortle like a naughty child and whip off the sheet. She begins to look away but her gaze snaps back to the carnage. She gags. I feel wicked and satisfied.

They force me to sit up and then pound me on the back. "Cough. Breathe this. You must cough." Some kind of mask is pushed over my nose and mouth and I shake my head to escape it. It is like the ether they gave me when I was four and had my tonsils out: a heavy black mask that hissed at me with the florid smell of decay, a filthy big animal squatting on my face. Their voices pierced the suffocating stink, sonorous, echoing, wired into my head: "Do-o-on't be afraid. Take a de-e-e-ep breath." The running-down sound of an ancient phonograph.

You don't understand. I can't breathe. I can't *breathe*.

I'm drowning.

There is a new doctor. He is chatty while he checks around the stitches for infection, telling me about what they have done in the operating room. "We cleaned out all the clot. The vena cava, everything. What a *mess*." He sounds delighted. "An unprecedented amount of embolus."

He is holding his hands about a foot apart. "One of those basins . . . this size. We *filled* it with clot. *Filled* it." His eyes dance deliciously as he remembers—a clever child who managed to pick all the raisins out of the muffins.

The same doctor. (Is he still here or has he come again?)

"We're going to take this drain out of your side now. It won't hurt." A nurse hovers at his elbow.

But the rubber drain must have grown into me, burrowing deep, because when he pulls it out, I sense the unraveling of the small intestine: slurp, snap. The hole bleeds and oozes, pops and breathes. A pulsing vacuole. "Oh, God. Oh, God," I mumble with my thick tongue.

"Watch this. Magic." He is distracting me. "One two three." He takes hold of two black threads, does something to them, and then pulls. The hole closes like the diaphragm of a camera, whirling in on itself. "That's called a purse-string suture," he announces in a satisfied voice. I look blankly at the navel-like depression.

"Sit up! Cough!" I can't make them understand. I can't sit up. There are no muscles to hold me upright. After the first abdominal surgery it was a long time before I could sit unsupported, cough, or laugh without pain.

That's where the joke comes from: it only hurts when you laugh. From abdominal surgery. Sneezing was excruciating. And now they are insisting: have they no idea of how painful it is?

"Cough. You *must* cough. More. More."

"You'll get pneumonia. Pneumonia for those who can't clear their lungs. This is something you have to do for yourself."

*  *  *

I dream about water, fear drowning. The fluid in my lungs—the drainage from the wound, the wounds—flushes up into my throat without warning so that I am *forced* to cough. Often coughing doesn't clear the airway, instead floods the breath-places so that I choke and claw the air, turning purple.

If it weren't for the abdominal incision I could help myself more: roll over, sit up, cough with real strength instead of the genteel "heh heh" that makes the nursing staff raise eyebrows and shake heads. Finally I devise a system of turning on my side in self-rescue, throwing the far arm over my body and pulling myself toward the near bars. This eases me over. Sometimes, in this position, the ichor seeps out of my open mouth onto the woodeny pillow without impeding my breathing.

But when I gasp and blow like a surfacing whale—when the maneuver doesn't help and I panic—someone must help, running over to jackknife my heavy, resistant body into a sitting position and pound me on the back. I soon find that a pillow helps immeasurably if someone uses it to push hard into the curve of my body. It is something to cough against; my own arms are too weak to immobilize my gut and muffle the shrieking pain, so I enlist whoever happens to be near: "Push. Harder! *Harder!*"

"I'm afraid I'll hurt you" says my mother, says Michael. They look squeamish.

"No, no. If you *don't* push it hurts much more. Please. Help me. I won't let you damage anything. I'll let you know if it's too hard." But it is never too hard.

They push, I cough.

On the third day I am up for a few minutes at a time, seated in a chair dragged over to my bed: symmetrical, unresisting, like a condemned person about to be electrocuted. The curtains are pulled around my bed, either to spare me the sight of my roommates, sick unto death, or to spare *them* the sight of me, recovering.

When I am sitting up I am put on the breathing machine. I cough and sputter like a good girl. There is a new loose dressing over the incision, held on with translucent paper tape. They have removed some of the outer reinforcing row of stitches—the puckering as opposed to the closing row—so that I feel less tightly strung. And I am dressed: a breakaway hospital gown that comes in two vertical halves to accommodate tubes, IVs, drains, held together with cunning little ties at the shoulder and down the arm.

My lucid periods are longer but not yet long. I notice more consistently when someone is with me; I am able to manufacture my half of a short conversation. But with intravenous morphine on a four-hour schedule I sleep and sleep and sleep, surfacing to dream and then to wake when there is someone near my bed, or when the pain becomes intermittently unbearable. No one has to tell me when the four hours are up: I hurt so much I can only whisper, sneaking out my words.

When the pain comes on, the room spins above me as I descend into the maelstrom and I have to grab the steel rails on either side of the mattress to keep myself from flying apart. I pant and sweat with the effort, as if I were giving birth; my jaw is sore from gritting my teeth, my wrists and fingers ache. When the nurses mercifully deliver me, jamming the needle of the syringe of morphine directly into a rubber tributary of the IV tubing (How easy! How splendid!), the drug radiates into my arm and then into the rest of my body like a benediction. The spinning stops; I feel warm and glowing in my center. The drug lifts me and tips me into a vat of dark, sweet, melted chocolate, and I sink, sink, sink.

"We're so pleased with your progress," one of the doctors is saying. (They have all become Doctor, bowling words at me from far down an alley.) "As soon as Admitting gets us a room we'll have you transferred back to the floor."

I am elated. It is the beginning of the end of this long ordeal. I will be going home soon, good as new. Or maybe better than I ever was. There was nothing in the heart except a backup of those nasty clots; my lungs have been cleaned of their jellied, bloody sludge; I have a nice, neat, clipped vena cava and religated veins deep in the pelvis. Tuned up. Scoured of trouble. Ready for the open road.

Sometime on the fifth day after the surgery I awake to find myself miraculously back on my old floor, in a sunny, spacious corner room kept for the very sick or the very privileged.

# NOVEMBER 1971

## PART THREE

A SMALL CONTRETEMPS. I WAIL HOARSELY LIKE A voiceless baby having a tantrum and cling to Michael's arm, begging.

"Stay with me tonight. Just tonight. Oh, please stay with me. I'm afraid to be alone. I'll choke to death. The nurses won't come. Stay with me." What I don't say is that I'm also afraid of the dark, afraid of the pain, afraid (having relinquished the comforting presence of the beeping, bounding points of light, the solicitous surveillance of the nurses, in the ICU) of the absence of a watcher—a guardian while I sleep—to keep part of me from wandering off in search of easement, never to be found again.

Michael's parents argue for a private-duty nurse, for which they are willing to pay ("Spare him this! Look at the strain he's under! . . . And how can *he* help you? You need a trained professional!") but I am the sick one and totally selfish and I don't want someone who cares on an hourly rate: my limited experience with private-duty nurses suggests that they were usually asleep precisely when they are needed, snoring on the vinyl hospital chairs with their heads fallen back, mouths and knees fallen open. I want Michael. I want somebody as scared as I.

It is arranged. All the first night out of Intensive Care Michael stays with me, sleeping on the couch in the corner of my room, getting up again and again to lift me and tilt me forward, to burp me of the mucus and the watery drainage. He tenderly wipes my mouth after I cough and choke, then my eyes and my runny nose because the coughing makes me cry in pain. When I am tidied up and limp with the effort to breathe, he takes my weight full in his arms and lays me down again on the hastily fluffed pillows. I hold his hand, or his arm, or his sleeve, and will not let him go until I fade into sleep again. (What I really want is for him to climb into that narrow hard bed with me: to hold me, to keep back the dark. I am afraid to let go, to relax; *someone* must hold tight for me, crowd me back into my body: I fear leaking away.)

The next morning Michael goes home early, wan and unshaven, to see to the children, to get them to school. He is not working: his Wall Street firm, in a sweeping gesture of generosity, has urged him to take all the time off he needs.

A period of adjustment: the day here is very different from day in the ICU. For one thing, I know that it *is* day, though for the first week I am uncertain as to *which* day, which night. There is hustle and bustle, a constant blur of motion through my room—an incessant displacement of its spaces by bodies and equipment—and a cascade of people noise . . . more distracting, more fatiguing, than the machinery noise of the ICU. I dizzily feel that perhaps it is *I* who am moving, my bed chugging past these busy purposeful scenes full of busy purposeful people as if they were a series of dioramas on twentieth-century health care. The scurrying nurses, the interchangeable doctors, are there and then not there and then there again. Family and friends materialize and then evaporate. Everything is so confusing, such an effort, that I just want to sleep my morphine sleep and dream my morphine dreams, the dreams that have a way of curling into reality—past into present—the way a broken yolk curls into the fluid white of an egg, dream-stuff seeping through every waking minute so that I am myself now, myself long ago, sometimes even a self I never was.

Reality has become friable, breaking off in chunks just when I think I have gotten a really good grip on it.

Barbara appears the second night. She is my oldest and dearest friend, godmother to my children, who has long since forgiven me (though I suspect she still has a reflex of distrust) for having convinced her against her better judgment to pull down her pants on the playground when we were in first grade. I am grateful, relieved. (She and Michael are the only two people in the world to whom I feel I can expose my big-baby self—my mewling, puking, scared big-baby self that needs to be wiped, and straightened, and tolerated.)

As usual, her grace and beauty stun me. I feel shamed and sickening, unworthy of her ministrations. She has just gotten married; she belongs in the glass-and-chrome box poised high over the glittering black East River, arranging tall brilliant flowers into her characteristic spare, elegant compositions.

But I need her too much, and need has no pride. I am still frightened, unwilling to be left alone. All the long night she drifts in her lace robe from the couch where she huddles and pretends to sleep, to my bed, parting the thick quiet air with her radiance. She has in fact been caring for me since we both became approximate adults in high school: baking me dozens of cookies, embroidering an apron, writing cheery notes of encouragement when I was depressed: a depression that sometimes sprang—though I never told her this—from what she was so naturally that I could never be (not with all the prayers and determination in the world), from my envy of her sweetness, her popularity, her purity, her blond perfection. I was the difficult, the neurotic, the sensitive one. The intellectual one. She was stable and normal. Tactful and thoughtful. Perhaps I was her danger. She was certainly my safety.

Still, she and Michael are the only people who can really make me feel safe.

* * *

My mother does not make me feel safe, and when she comes to sit by my bed, reporting on the well-being of the children and my three younger (but grown-up) siblings, telling stories of her friends back home ("So I said to Betty—you remember Betty—anyway, I said to Betty . . ."), I feel a clutching inside my head that reminds me of how she used to grab my upper arm when I was little, digging in her long, red nails. There is everything and nothing between us: I must be visibly grateful, gracious—she has, after all, been willing to uproot herself and live in my (disheveled) home, take care of my (spoiled) children, and tolerate my husband's aggressive silences ("She disgusts me," Michael says churlishly, referring to her Scotch habit. "After five o'clock when she starts drinking, I can't trust her with the children.").

Somewhere I can feel my baby self—so irrepressible, so close to the surface now—plead, Mommy! Help me! Please don't talk at me . . . help me! as if mommies could really soothe away the pain and the fear and make everything better just the way they were once able to, when we believed in their omniscience, their omnipotence, their eternal and unconditional love. As if my mommy could, or would. But she won't. Or can't, can't cross the gulf that was either created or widened (I would never know) when she divorced my father and I refused to. Instead, when I breathe noisily and then cry, willing her to come to me and hold me, she holds herself away, pulling her pastel cable-knit cardigan around her shoulders, tightening her coral lips and shaking her head ever so slightly so that her dime-store dangle earrings bob.

As she drones on—a tickle of complaint in her voice—I turn slowly, self-protectively from her (from the guilt she makes me feel for my lack of love, my lack of understanding, all my betrayals) as if asleep, tumbling over and over into a soft stupor, lulled by the buzz of her voice and the rumble of hospital machinery, warmed by the drugs and yellow light by the bed and the sun bending around the curtains in the window, teasing up my mother fantasy, my dreams of comfort and reassurance.

I am four or five, in my red maple bed with the turned posts, in my red-and-white house on the prairie. My room has been darkened against the fiery flat light of the Midwestern midsummer midday sun because I am sick—measles, I think—and must rest. There is a droning I recognize with a soar of pleasure: insects' midget voices blending with the sound of far-off planes—the planes of my childhood with their clattering propellers, high in the burnt blue sky, masking for their few moments of passage over the vibrating prairie the furzy sound of cicadas.

Because I am sick, my mother has cleaned up my room, and the uncluttered, nubbly maroon rug seems to roll as far away from me as the fields outside the window. There is only a sheet over me—it is so hot! —and the radio plays softly. I stretch my feet out from me, reaching toward the bottom of the bed, feeling gratified at my straightness, my flatness, at the short distance from my shoulders to the two little hummocks of my upturned toes. I am also pleased by the breadth of the landscape of my maroon rug, my ordered shelves, my closet door neatly closed rather than hanging open disgorging mess. My mother will soon climb the stairs with a glass of ginger ale: I know that I will hear the ice knocking against the inside of the glass before I hear her nearly silent step.

I remember all this because I need it now, cherishing it because it speaks to me of my innocence. It is the last time my world seems totally ordered, totally safe, predictable and benign, full of prettiness and roundness, full of the love and the protection of my mommy, who is everything to me, everything I wish for myself. (Mother's baby / Father's mouse / Little fairy in the house.)

The prairie ticked like a bomb.

Mothers and daughters. What deep, profound ambivalence there is (I know!) in reproducing oneself, to see oneself as a child in a child, the confusion of otherness and identity. For my mother and me it has been a bloody battle, fraught with misunderstanding, resentment, even—I suspect—jealousy . . . for what I have had and done that she, with her superior gifts and beauty, had been forced to forgo. I love my mother at the same time I dislike her; respect her—her fiery pride, her undauntable determination—at the same time I think her foolish and weak with her drinking and her meddling. I fail to comprehend her self-destructive bent—the methodical effacing and defacing of her gifts: her beauty, her intelligence, her dramatic and musical talent—although clearly it has a great deal to do with her humiliation by my father, by his having run off with the next-door neighbor—our baby-sitter—leaving her flat with four young children. In the best of times she was an astonishment—the best mother of all—funny and fun, stunning in her glamour and her presence, generous, well-liked; in the worst—and it is more and more often now the worst—she is difficult, bitter, self-contradictory, stingy, rigid. A strong believer in God, she seems not to be able to believe in herself, filling her life with superfluities and injunctions to those around her to shape up while she herself crumbles with alcohol, self-pity, and a corrosive, distancing defensiveness.

More than ever now I feel this ambivalence—my dear memories of her that I need so much (because where else is there comfort?) and the mistrust that colors all our dealings, one with the other. I have tried and still do try to stop this leaking of ill will and suspicion into our relationship, but it seems that I cannot suppress it entirely: it seeps around the edges of my consciousness, saturating my fantasies and dreams.

Once—it was my freshman year in college—I had another kind of dream about my mother—vivid, terrifying, debilitating. When I idly recounted it at breakfast, one of our number (a psychology major) stood abruptly, wiping her hands on a napkin and picking up her tray, and said, ruminatively chewing her toast,

"You should be careful who you tell your dreams to."
Until that moment it had not occurred to me that such
a dream might be anything more than one of creativi-
ty's messy nocturnal emissions; until that moment I had
not thought about that dream as the powerful allegory it
certainly was. This was the dream:

It is morning, and I have come downstairs to have
breakfast; the house is the one in which we lived at
the time, the one in which we were living when my
father left us. My mother greets me, her back to me,
and I see that where the door leading to the basement
usually is there is now a white Dutch door closed on
the bottom and with the top half fully open so that
I can see the glazed white beach lying beyond, stretching to the thin mean line of horizon where it meets
a deep blue sky, all empty under a pitiless blast of
sun. Waiting for breakfast, I lean on the bottom half
of the Dutch door. Nothing is moving on the beach—
not even the water which rests against the bleached
sand like a vast sheet of mirror lowered there to
reflect the exact blue of the sky. Then my attention is
caught by something, a speck, a tiny black fly of a
winged creature circling in the cloudless vault of sky.
It gets larger, each descending circle bringing it closer,
until I can see what it is: a great black scaly bird,
shining like a snake, a cross between a buzzard and
something prehistoric, it is so big and leathery: a
predictable spore of the blank sky and sea and sand
and sun.

It has landed on the beach, and as it shambles
toward the house—peering around as if looking for
someone—I am grateful that the bottom half of this
door is closed and locked with its shiny brass bolt,
and that my mother stands behind me in the house
doing something so ordinary as fixing my breakfast.

As the bird approaches I see it is even more
grotesque, more malignantly ugly, than I had thought.
I call to my mother with a reedy, quavering voice: she
should come and see this phenomenal beast that has
landed in our very back yard, our . . . back beach.

Absentmindedly pulling at the towel that she has
tucked into her waistband, she joins me at the open
Dutch door. "Oh, that," she says offhandedly. "Don't
worry about that. It won't hurt you. You're always so
afraid of everything." She begins to return to the sink
but I hold her by the wrist. "Don't leave me with that
. . . thing . . . around." I realize I am pleading,
but her voice is sharp as she answers. "Stop complaining! You're being quite ridiculous. I don't have time
for this." She turns away.

The bird is now a few feet from me, startling in its
blackness against the bright background. It is looking
at me, its unblinking yellow eyes boring into my own,
its long neck—black and glistening, the scales on it
shifting like night water sparkling as the moon plays
on it—writhing like a hose when the water pressure
is too high. I try to determine where the scales fade
into feathers, but there is no place where I can actually
see the scales extending themselves into the glossy,
stubby black feathers that cover the bottom of the
bird and bunch around its black and knotty legs. The
bird is remarkable in its loathsomeness, its ugliness,
its total blackness, everything black except the stony
amber eyes, from the great hooked bill—as oddly
mobile as a pair of thin lips—to the black feet, splayed
against the hard-packed silver sand, dancing to some
frantic internal beat. I narrow myself to the door-
frame, hoping the bird will lose interest in me.

My mother sees me drawn back in terror, hiding
myself from this bird—so large, now that it is at the
back door, as to comfortably rest its head over the
white paneled bottom half. "Look," she says gently,
coaxing, "this bird won't harm you—you judge too
much by appearances. It's really rather a tame, sweet
thing, and you're going to hurt its feelings. Be nice
to it and you will have nothing to worry about."

"Do you *know* this thing?"

"Sure, I've seen it around before. It comes occasionally and I'm always nice to it." She pauses thoughtfully. "It's always safer to be nice to this sort of
animal. Pet it," she says encouragingly. "You'll see."

"It won't bite?"

"No. Of course not. Here. Give me your hand."

She takes my hand in her own and I touch—briefly
—the hot obsidian head, convincing myself even more
thoroughly that I want nothing whatsoever to do with
this bird thing.

"You shouldn't be so *afraid*. You have to deal
directly with whatever you fear if you want to conquer it." (This is the sort of thing my mother is fond
of saying.) "Here. I'll show you." And then my
mother throws the brass bolt and turns the door
handle.

"Don't let it *in* here! How do you know what it
might do?" I am so terrified, backed up against a wall,
that my voice is a squeak.

"Nonsense," says my mother, opening the door
wide. The bird seems to smile at me with its thin
black beaklips; perhaps that is even a wink of its
yellow eye I see. The bird saunters in, moving slowly
but deliberately, then once in the house it seems to
lose interest in me—thank God, thank God—instead
following my mother around as she finishes preparing
breakfast. I stay plastered to the wall, not moving,
hardly daring to breathe, watching the bird bob
around after her as attentively as a huge, incongruous
puppy. She pauses every now and then to feed it something and I see the throat bulge and surge as the bird
swallows.

"Well, come on now," my mother says, holding
a plate of breakfast, "you'll never get this eaten
standing there like a ninny, being afraid like that."
She motions for me to walk ahead of her, past her,
into the dining room. "Come on. Let's go."

I edge around the snake-buzzard—keeping as much
distance between it and myself as possible while it
gazes at me levelly—and go into the dining room. My
mother follows me, and right behind her trails the
bird's black presence.

"I don't want to look at that thing while I eat my
breakfast," I protest. "If *you* like it so much, keep
it in the kitchen with *you*." Mother puts the plate on

the table with more emphasis than necessary, which is exacerbated by the lack of place mats, so that the plate makes a loud cracking noise.

"I want to show you something," she says in a tone that suggests she does not welcome argument, and taking my arm firmly above the elbow, her fingers squeeze what I used to refer to as my "muscle." She steers me through the dining room and toward the living room, which has a closed, white door—unlike our real living room, which had an open archway. She and I pause in front of the door, and it is then that I realize that the bird is still with us; is, in fact, bumping against me, jostling me, like someone in a crowd who is being provocative, looking for a fight. My mother holds my arm, the bird rubs against me, its scales whispering against my white clothing. Then my mother reaches forward and opens the door, swinging it wide as I feel the bird's weight leaning into me—dry and heavy—so that I am edged into the room.

The room is no longer our living room, but an unfinished, just-plastered room, the windows recently fitted into their raw wood frames, rough subflooring under a blanket of wood shavings and sawdust. The windows are so filmed with dust it is quite impossible to see through them, but they are blindingly white with the same blistering sun that falls on the beach. It reminds me of unfinished houses I played in as a child, in our area of middle-class boom construction. My mother urges me into the room with gentle pressure—helped by the insistent lean of the bird—and when I resist she shoves me, so that I stumble forward and just manage to catch myself on the sill of a window through which I cannot see. When I turn back to look at her, she has suddenly become someone I do not know at all, her features contorted and set. The bird stands just behind her and to the side— easily visible through the open door—and it nuzzles her hip and arm. The two of them quite definitely block the door. I look around the room in a panic, but there is no other way out. The windows stand like silent sentinels, locked with their gleaming brass locks.

Mother looks grim; her lips are stretched in a grimace and some of her pink lipstick has run at the corners of her mouth. The snake-buzzard, with a nod to her that she acknowledges with a nod of her own, slides around her, past her, and sidles into the room.

"Mommy! Don't let it in here with me! Mommy! What are you doing? Help me, Mommy! Don't leave me!" My mother and the bird have planned this. They have been waiting for this moment.

"You must be punished," Mother says sternly, pitilessly, although she has that look on her face that I associate with "This is going to hurt me more than you." She is standing with her hands on her hips, filling the doorway.

Then I am thrown to the floor by some invisible force, lashed facedown to the raw pine with leather thongs, my cheek grinding into the sawdust. I twist my head up toward my mother.

"*Mommy!*" I am screaming in fear. "Help, Mommy, help me, do something!" But she purses her lips for a moment and shakes her head ever so slightly. Turning, she shuts the door quietly.

"Help HELP *HELP!*" I shriek as the bird approaches and I hear the clickety-click of its green-black talons against the wood, the dragging sound of its great wings. It straddles me, walking up from the bottom of one leg until it stands over me where I lie spread-eagled, one foot at my hip; one pressed up into my crotch. My fear is so great I think I will faint, and when the bird lifts its wings as if stretching, my shirt billows lightly off my back.

The bird leans over. As delicately as if it were filleting a fish it tears through the white blouse and pierces me with its beak, gobbling at the flesh of my back with its black tongue. At the last moment before I awaken, I am above the scene, drifting over it near the ceiling, and can see myself lying there on the floor, screaming in pain, the white shirt torn, the bird spiking and rooting, laying the throbbing red flesh back from the pink-and-white spine, eating its way into my heart.

"I really must go," I hear my mother saying. "The children will be wanting their dinner." (What she means to say is, "I've got to have a cigarette.") I turn toward her as she leans over the bed, pursing her lips for a kiss which she plants on my forehead as if she were pressing a seed into the earth. I look for a moment into her eyes, searching for my idea of my mommy—blond, beautiful, graceful, musical—with her limpid cat eyes like discs of deep seawater. She isn't there, though I want her there. Nothing is the same, though I want it the same. I wish that *her* pain and *her* trials, the crashing down and shattering of *her* life, had never happened, but it is true that I wish it selfishly, more for my sake than for hers.

Her eyes are still green, but the iris is golden and ragged at the center, as if the black hole of the pupil had burned its way through.

It must be on the second day that my father arrives from California where he has gone to live with his third wife (who has since left him). I haven't seen him in a few years; he barely knows the children. I feel even less safe with my father—for my own sake, of course, but also for my mother's. I am anxious for my mother, who has never recovered from her love for him, has never stopped being bitter for his rejection of her in his taking and flaunting of other women while she played her greatest dramatic role: ideal wife. I myself have tried to be angry with him for his weaknesses and his adolescent priapism, but I am not good at anger . . . and I don't like the taste of bitterness in my mouth.

Instead, he makes me sad.

All the same, it is my father I most resemble, feel most in tune with. We are strung to the same key, so alike—dark, long-limbed, curious, irreverent. Hungry. With his usual perspicacity, only he of all my visitors—

all my watchers—knows instinctively what I crave: not
cheery chatter or distraction; what I want is disengaged
presence. Protective silence. (I need to think.) When
my father comes to sit by my bed, he stays for hours,
saying little, saying nothing, except when he murmurs,
"Go to sleep. Don't worry. I'll be sitting right here."
And sure enough: every time my eyes flutter open,
there he is, looking at me with . . . yes . . . love. I
recognize it as great love.

He is, after all, Daddy. And I have not outgrown
being his little girl (his joy), his firstborn (his pride),
his wonder, his love. His Galatea.

"Go to sleep. Don't worry. I won't go away."

I know that. I am certain of that as I am certain of
little else: he won't go away. And when he is there, I
sleep less but dream more, in my restlessness endlessly
adjusting the small parts of my body that do not hurt.
("I won't go away. I won't go away.")

(Oh! Daddy! Go away!)

The very first time I got stoned (very stoned) I had
three hallucinations. The first was brought on by the
sudden conviction that I had been blinded. I remember
standing in the dining room (it was Christmas Eve of
the first year I was married) and I realized all at once
that I couldn't see. I pointed my face this way and that;
it was quite certain: I could see nothing.

I fought down my rising panic, calling to my friend
who had brought us the marijuana. By the time he
grabbed my arm, I was flailing at the abyss of empty
space in front of me and screaming, "I'm blind, I'm
blind, I'm blind." He shook me until my neck cracked,
saying, "Stop it! Listen to me!" and when he finally
had my attention said very quietly, "Open your eyes."

I did open them. He was right, I wasn't blind, and I
was so immensely thankful that he had such command
of the situation I hugged him. In return he kissed me
full on the mouth, gently. At that moment, as I watched
his face, I could see in my peripheral vision the wall
behind him open up like a pair of French doors. I saw

first—over his head—a brilliant blue sky—a Mediterranean sky—that mesmerized me. Beneath the sky was a vista of daffodils, thousands, millions of daffodils, swaying in the sun. Then my friend's features rearranged themselves,, metamorphosed into those of my father, who, created against this backdrop of flowers and sky, smiled slowly.

The second hallucination took place somewhat later in the living room as I sat at Michael's feet. I happened to look down at my clothes and realized with surprise that I was now dressed in the kind of outfit that the jack wears in a deck of cards. (The defining label "knave" flashed for a split second on the screen of my mind.) Astonished at my odd attire, I looked back to Michael as if he might offer a credible explanation and saw that he had also changed, had retreated from me, and was situated at some distance, high above me on a massive throne, wearing a crown on his head and a long purple velvet robe trimmed in ermine that swirled down the steps toward me. I knew somehow that I was his subject, his vassal, and that I had been brought before him tonight to be judged. I was expected to plead for mercy, for forgiveness. But I would not be forgiven, my crime was too grave; and though my ruler was a just man, he would regretfully sentence me to death. I cowered at Michael-the-king's feet, wanting to say Forgive, oh, please have mercy, I am a miserable sinner, but the words caught in my throat like burrs. I knelt and folded my hands in supplication; Michael nodded his head at me and his crown teetered back and forth, threatening to topple off. Knowing I was to die, knowing there was no hope for me, I began to sob, provoking King Michael to reach way, way down to touch me. Then the moment before I was granted forgiveness he became just Michael-my-husband—looking bewildered in his Levi's and plaid shirt—and I became his hysterical wife, kneeling between his legs and pawing at his thighs. I cried uncontrollably for fifteen minutes because now, surely, there was no absolution.

I think the third hallucination of that evening was

related to the second. Michael was lying next to the Christmas tree on his side; I was now sitting on the couch. He was engrossed with something shiny in his hand. I wanted to know what it was that he held that fascinated him so, but I seemed not to be able to move toward him so that I could get a better look. He turned the object in his hands, fingering it, and it glinted silver in the dim colored lights of the Christmas tree. Suddenly I saw quite clearly what he held: it was a gun. And I as clearly knew what he meant to do with the gun: shoot me. I wanted to leap forward off the sofa and wrestle the weapon from him, but I knew I was not allowed, not allowed to interfere in any way with my destiny. I was allowed only to wait. For my own death.

Shortly the shiny object fell from his hand onto our Moroccan rug. It was a Christmas ornament—a Santa or an angel. I was only a little relieved.

Of all the hallucinations, the one about my father seemed finally the most remarkable and the least benign. His face in the yellow lamplight as he sat in the hard chair next to my bed, leaning his head back against the hospital-blue wall, evoked the daffodils and the hard blue sky greased with sunlight. The morphine craziness settled like a stone on this slope of memory, so that every time I awoke and looked over at him, every time he gave me a reassuring nod and smile, I was whisked into my world of daffodils, throwing open the white doors cracked by horizontal shutters as my father receded through them, as he backed away, smiling and nodding. I couldn't tell whether I was letting him in— coaxing him in—or pushing him out. I couldn't tell whether I was following, but something ached, something splintered in me as I stood (in my hallucination), following him with my eyes into the daffodils.

I was eight, perhaps seven. It was late at night and the house was quiet. My father and I sat in the massive Danish-modern tweed chair that the Christmas before had been the frame of presentation for my "big" present, a real, true, baby-sized baby doll, dressed in real baby clothes. (Christina Elizabeth was so outsized I had trouble toting her around; neither would she fit in my doll carriage, which was intended for more reasonably proportioned rubber babies.)

Now I sat snuggling with my father in the dark, the baby myself, being held, caressed. There were soft sweet words: I was special, I was bright, I was pretty. I would make some man happy sometime far in the future. I made Daddy so happy now! Such a special girl! Able to understand things far beyond my age! (That was why I had special, unchildlike privileges; why I went to the opera, why I went to the museums; why I was read to with such dedication—wonderful books: *Hans Brinker, Smoky, Treasurer Island,* my father's own boyhood books with their crumbly-edged pages and muzzy, faded color plates.)

And then many such nights of hugs and whispers become like one freeze-frame, or many freeze-frames of the same scene, all taken from different angles: I sit astride my father, on his knees, facing him (horsie, horsie, carry me/over mountain over sea/and when you get too tired stop . . .); his head is back—his eyes closed so that I do not have to look into their milky blue—or maybe he is looking down, so that I can smell the pomade of the early fifties on his shiny black hair that he wears combed nearly straight back like a movie star ("Wow Your daddy's *so* handsome!" said my friends, say my friends), looking down so that he can watch what I am doing as he loosens the tie on his pajama bottoms, directing me how to touch and hold and stroke. ("A little biology lesson: this is this and that is that. And then this is what feels good, what a man likes, what your daddy likes."). This thing is so soft. Softer than the latex of my baby doll, even when it comes alive and the velvety top of it waves at me like a flannel-pink flower. ("Oh, you see what happens? That is what happens when a man is pleased, when he feels good. You make me feel so good. You are my special girl. I love you.") The thing doesn't frighten me because it seems so harmless, some capricious appendage that is amusing when it is teased, like a little dog that sits up when you hold out a treat, like a bird that jumps to its perch in front of the mirror when its tiny bell is rung. (Children like to see things happen; they like to be able to measure their effect on the world.) Here in Daddy's lap I have a certain power.

And I have a very big, a very grown-up secret of my own.

I awaken in the hospital room, sweating. My father leans forward anxiously to see if I am all right. I cough and subside.

It is later, same chair, different house. (We have come up in the world. We are quite nearly R-I-C-H.) I am . . . nine. I burrow into my father's arms in the eddying night, whispering and giggling, listening as always for some sound of my mother—sleeping (I hope) the heavy sleep of the evening drinker: it is *so* much past my bedtime. (My father creeps upstairs to my bedroom to fetch me when the coast is clear, to bring me back down to the big chair in his library.)

I am saying rapidly, stifling my giggles, "So they don't want to have to both pay for a ticket to the movie so the big fat lady says to the little thin man 'Climb into my girdle and I'll sneak you in' so he does and so she goes to the ticket seller to buy the ticket and the ticket seller says 'Nice evening, real fine weather,' and just as the fat lady is about to answer a voice comes from her girdle and the thin man says 'Maybe it's nice out there but it's raining in here'" (breaking off at this point in mirth). My father smiles and makes the fizzy, throat-clearing noise that means he is amused and says, "Do you have any more?" I continue with the story of the farmer's daughter and the man she is forced to share a bed with, who answers in reply to her questioning, "Oh, that. That is my obstacle." And her resultant confusion which leads her to say in the morning, "Oh, your *ob*stacle. I thought you said your *pop*sicle and I sucked on it all night." (This joke I don't really understand; the idea of sucking on that pink piggy thing seems to me irrelevant at best and repulsive at worst.)

\*   ❖   \*

Same house, a little later, one night when my parents are giving a party and my father comes upstairs to say good night (there is clearly no time to read to me this evening): I stand on my bed to receive his embrace, and as he puts his arms around me, I smell his breath and he smells funny with a smell I can't identify except that it is sweet and cloying and I am forced to turn away. He hugs me and hugs me and then his hand slips past the elastic of my pajama bottoms. His breath is coming fast. (I am a little frightened by this development, but not much. He is my daddy; he loves me.) He touches me someplace between my legs that gives me a zing of pleasure and makes the blood rise to my face and the room suddenly feel warm. He strokes me for a moment, asks, "Do you like that? Does that feel good?" I squirm with the deliciousness of the feeling, wanting to capture his hand between my small thin thighs, wanting to keep that hand with me while he goes back to the party. "This is a woman's special place," he is saying. "It is very small on you, but when you are grown up this place will grow too and make you feel very, very good." It is already making me feel very very good, but I have a spasm of distaste as I picture this part big—a gross protuberance of dark red tissue, poking through the undergrowth of pubic hair such as my mother has on what looks to be a messy mistake on the part of the Creator: dark, red, turgid flesh scruffy with matted black hair fortunately bears little relation to my neat, shell-like, pearly parts, which I have dared to look at once or twice.

Suddenly my father whips his head around as if he has heard a sound through my closed bedroom door and withdraws his hand, exhaling his fruity breath so that I must hold mine. I want to say, "Show me again, touch that thing again," but he is rolling his thumb over the fingers of the hand that has touched me, and puts his hand in his pocket. He runs out the door, tossing a "Good night, sleep tight, don't let the bedbugs bite" back at me. I fall asleep with my own hand in my pajamas, trying to locate and replicate the lovely sensation I have felt—with no success. (I will not know what it is that has been touched until after the couch episode when I am seventeen. There is no pleasure for me in touching myself—I never seem to be able to find the right spot, though I am shown by a couple of men—till I am twenty.)

In that same bedroom. Summertime and the windows are open to a cacophony of night noises. My father comes into my room, to read to me I think, and then lies down with me, on top of the sheet, to "say good night" in one of the infinite variations of our extended ritual. Somehow, in my dream editing— my imperfect memories illuminating single moments like a strobe light—I am now turned around, lying upside down on him on my back, the bottoms of my ruffled summer pajamas—decorated with big blue polka dots—crumpled on the bed beside me. My legs are spread.

He doesn't touch me . . . perhaps he is looking, but there is not much to see in the dark.

In another strobe moment, my pants are magically back on, and he is holding me tight—too tight. His pelvis is moving against me. This time I *am* frightened (the only time I can ever remember being really frightened) and I try to push him away, but his big hairy arms hold me even tighter, and he squeezes me and pants in my ear, making my cheek damp with the heat of his breath. "Daddy" I cry, as loud as I dare. "Don't! What are you doing?" "Wait, wait," he pants, squashing me with his arms until I am afraid I will suffocate, and rolling half over me so that I feel totally powerless, my arms pinned to my sides, my pelvis and thighs bouncing as he slaps at me with his body; I can feel his penis poking hard at my belly. "Ah ah ah," Daddy says and suddenly relaxes his grip. At the same moment there is something hot and sticky all over my naked stomach (my pajamas bare the midriff). His penis flops down as he pulls away and makes the same mess on my legs, dribbling on my favorite pajamas. I am still somewhat frightened, but more indignant. "You wee-weed on me," I whisper fiercely and roll out of bed. He follows me into the bathroom, and his hands shake as he takes a towel and tries to help me clean up. "Hey!" I say accusingly, sniffing, smelling an unfamiliar, crushed vegetable smell. "This isn't wee-wee. What *is* this stuff?"

It was over that night, when I got frightened; our "lovings" were put away with Christina Elizabeth and with my calculated innocence. He was dangerous now: he had grabbed me and squashed me and someday he might hurt me by putting his thing in me (how repulsive!) rather than on me. His panting and his shuddering and his strength just made clear to me what I had already suspected: that it was no longer I who had the divine power, but he.

There were no more nights in the chair; in fact, there wasn't long left to us in that house: money problems (and fights); the move to a smaller house in a different neighborhood (more fights); Daddy around less until he wasn't around at all; Mother angry, Mother crying, Mother drinking. I didn't have to worry anymore, because Daddy had moved out, gone away with his (very) young secretary, who was also our babysitter. "Pregnant . . . Slut" my mother spat in the darkened dining room of our lonely house as she sat nursing her Scotch. She would not eat, but would sit in the dining room for hours after she had fed us children, smoking and drinking. The others scattered—free—but I felt compelled to stay with her, to try to stand by her. I was her daughter. But somehow I was the least able: we argued a lot. It was our only real mode of communication; strangely enough, I cannot remember the subject of a single fight in all those years—from the time I was twelve to the time I left home for college.

The fights always ended the same way though, with her storming through the house to where she kept her private papers, and storming back to throw the divorce decree down in front of me on the dining-room table.

"He doesn't care about you kids. He doesn't care about anybody but himself, like his parents before him. How *can* you betray me by being willing to talk to him, to see him? How *can* you reward him that way for his neglect? You want to see him? Good. Get out. Get your stuff and go live with him. I need loyalty, loyalty," she would moan, "and *you* are a traitor."

Ah. If she only knew. If only she knew how I loved her and feared her. If she only knew how I loved *him* and feared *him*.

*Live* with him? I was terrified of him, of what I had been, had done with him. What that made me. While she pushed he pulled. "Come and visit me. Why are you always so busy? You can't be *that* busy. I need you. I love you."

His eyes would fill with tears. My poor daddy. Poor foolish, intemperate Daddy. But I was his girl. *His* girl. I was all he had. For him I was bright. Attractive (though not in a high-school cheerleadery way). Sophisticated. He made me what I was, the woman he wanted. His Galatea.

He said that to me, a variation of that. I was helping out at his office, doing some filing, typing. It was Saturday and there was no one there but us. I was in the back in a cul-de-sac of filing cabinets, old lawbooks, and he was suddenly behind me, nudging me with his body as he tried to get past. I squeezed myself against a filing cabinet to give him room, and then his arms were around me, his mouth moving near mine. I was used to tolerating his embraces—they seemed undivertible—and I didn't want to be rude, rejecting, hurt him—he *needed* me!—but this one went on too long. I turned one shoulder into him, which he seemed to interpret as an invitation. He replied by pressing me up against the filing cabinets.

"You have the body of a woman," he said in a voice I almost did not recognize, harsh and urgent. "You've developed." (It was true; I had recently bought my first real nontraining bra.) His own body began to tremble so slightly that it might have been a charge of low-voltage electricity vibrating through him. One of his legs pushed between mine.

I put my hands against his chest and pushed. He backed away, stood for a second, and then came at me with a renewed single-mindedness, like an animal on the attack. His fingers worked at the buttons of my shirt, but they were shaking so that he simply yanked at my neckline, tearing my shirt open. "Who has more right than I?" he was saying breathlessly. "You be*long* to me. You're my daughter. Who has more right?" He hooked a finger into the front of my bra and pulled. I pulled back.

"What **are** you *doing*?" I **w**as as breathless as he. I felt dilated with fear. "Let *go* of me. Now you *let go* of me." His eyes cleared and he opened his fingers, releasing me. I turned my back on him, leaning my forehead against the cool metal of the filing cabinet, buttoning my shirt. One button had been torn off.

"I'm sorry," he mumbled, "but why do you lead me on?"

Lead him on. Lead him on? It was truly the last thing I wanted to do. I truly did not want to hurt his feelings; I just as truly did not want him to misunderstand the nature of my filial affection.

And yet . . . there we were in his car together, a '52 MG. I was sixteen—wearing a suit, stockings, high heels—and in that bathtub of a vehicle sitting was less than a lady-like affair. We were discussing my boyfriend—my relationship with my boyfriend—and as much as I tried to deflect the course of the conversation, he was surely headed toward s-e-x. Did I sleep with him? Horrified, I shook my head: of course not! Then, my father, hastily: if I *wanted* to (and it was after all the predictable course of events) he would talk to him—my boyfriend—about proper contraception; I should know something about such things and he didn't trust my mother to tell me. As he talked he put his hand on my knee. And then in the silence caused by my embarrassment, anchored by the roar of the motor and the whine of air torn by speed, my stocking hissed as he slid his hand quickly up my leg to where the nylon ended, up to my naked thigh under the black wool of the skirt of my suit. I lurched away from him, warning him. Between his teeth he said (quite clearly angry this time), "What do you expect? Huh? The way you tease me? Tempt me? It is your fault."

My fault . . . my fault . . . my fault. It was like an echo in an endless series of empty rooms, ricocheting from one to the next. I had never realized it. I had never figured it out. It was *my* fault. Yes. Of course. Why would a perfectly reasonable man, a grown-up person, do something so . . . incomprehensible . . . as my father had done with me if it were not at least partly—and probably mostly—my fault? My father had not forced me to do what I did; I had done it because it guaranteed for me a special place in his affections, because then he would think me extraordinary, wondrous, worthy of his attention and his time. I had signed on; could he help it if I lost interest in the middle of the journey?

What did I expect?

(During graduate school a professor will say in a class: ". . . And we find that most 'incestuous experience' between father and daughter is projection on the part of the daughter, a product of the daughter's great desire to replace her mother as the object of her father's affections. The daughter self-servingly misinterprets natural paternal affection because of her need to see herself as important, central." I blush hotly as the professor goes on, pausing only to brush a speck of something or other off his impeccably tailored blue blazer. "Little girls can be extraordinarily seductive. It's a wonder that incest is as rare as it is.")

My reveries. My dreams. Memories. My father sits here next to the bed, watching me, loving me, holding back my secrets like the boy with his finger in the dike who kept the whole world from being swept away, kept the force of the furious sea out of the low, green land.

I cough and sputter, fighting my way upright before my father can be up off his seat and make it to my side. I refuse to drown, here, in front of him.

I wrote a story in college which I subsequently entered in a fiction contest. Michael read it shortly before we were engaged, sitting on the floor next to me in what were then called "beau parlors." It was the story of a young woman about my age and her father; I named the daughter Kathryn.

Michael read it, looking up from the last page with a penetratingly analytic look.

He married me anyway.

This is the last part of that story; Kathryn is spending the night at her father's apartment. He has followed her into the bedroom in which she is to sleep.

"I'd like to sit here with you for a while, Kit, if you don't mind. If you're too tired to talk, we won't. It's just so long since I've seen you." He glanced around the room distractedly, then, without waiting for any sign of interest from her, walked to the record file, producing a buff-colored boxed album.

"New *Rite of Spring*," he said, waving it across her line of vision. "Directed by Stravinsky himself. Not as spectacular as some, but one has to assume . . ." His voice trailed off as he sat down on the edge of the bed, motioning her to move over as he leaned his elbows on his knees and folded his hands. He did not look at her.

Kathryn's gaze flitted over him. His hair had begun to gray at the temples. He was getting old. Old and lonely. She thought maybe she should say something kind to him, but she didn't . . . only lay looking at him with heavy, tired eyes. Neither of them said anything through the "Dance of the Adolescents," and Kathryn felt herself doze, dreaming in time with the music.

Then he shifted his weight, waking her. She tensed against his silence.

"Kit . . ." He touched her cheek. "Are you awake Kit? Listen to me." He paused and she did not move, wondering how convincing her feint of sleep was. "Hey," he said. "Kit." She opened her eyes. He smiled, leaning close to her face. She watched the pulse beat in his temples, avoiding his eyes. He took her hand, turned it over and looked at the palm, and laid it again on the bed. He stroked her hair.

"You must realize how much, how much you mean to me—how much I care about you. It's hard, it really is, being away from my children. I love you all, but you've always been special, Kit, you know that. I enjoy these times we spend together so much, and when I look at you, I think, this beautiful, intelligent young woman is my daughter—mine—I created her. I made her with my body and her mother's." He drew her hair back from her forehead and arranged it around her face on the pillow. "I hope you don't mind my admiring my handiwork." He smiled once more, almost wistfully. Kathryn closed her eyes to hide her discomfort. "I love you so much," her father said, "and I do need you—I need you more than anything, more than anyone. You're all I really have. I love you, Kit. Can you understand how much I love you?" He paused and then said sharply, "Are you asleep?" She shook her head almost imperceptibly, as if for her benefit rather than his.

"Look at me," he commanded.

She opened her eyes, and knew what he wanted her to say. He leaned closer over her, putting both hands on her face. She felt ashamed somehow, seeing him this close up, and tried to look past his swimming blue eyes.

His breath, heavy with alcohol, settled on her face like petals from some fleshy decaying flower so she had to avert her face. Her father straightened up.

"No. I know I make you uncomfortable," he said. "Never mind. Just let me sit here with you a little while. I won't bother you. Go to sleep if you'd like." For a moment it was quiet. "I love you so much," he said as though there had been no pause. "You're so dear to me. I wish you could understand how much I love you, Kit."

The record reject made a dry, empty click, and her father rose to change the records. He turned off the overhead light. The bed creaked as he sat down again, drawing his robe more tightly around him.

Minutes may have passed or half an hour, and all at once Kathryn was aware that her father was stroking her hair again. She opened her eyes and looked at him apprehensively. "You don't mind my touching you, do you, Kit?" he said very quietly. "I just can't help admiring my handiwork." He smiled at her and touched her lips with his forefinger. She turned her head and said in a muffled voice, "You don't understand. Please don't touch me. I don't like to be touched by anyone, except by . . . you know. . . ."

"Ah, Kitty, I see," he said. "The line between father and lover is a thin one." He smiled at her again and nodded. "I do understand how you feel about it. Really. I don't want to upset you—I just want to be close to you. You are so precious to me, so dear to me. Don't ever forget how much I love you."

Kathryn felt a wave of relief when he stood up, but he sat down again almost immediately. "Just let me hold you for a moment, just a second, Kitty, as a favor." He slipped his arms under her and pulled her to a half-sitting position. He hugged her tightly, not saying anything, and rubbed her back and neck.

Kathryn tried to pretend she was somewhere else, thought, If I can just live through this moment and this moment and this moment . . . She tried to focus on the lights of the city outside the window opposite her and let her arms hang limply over his shoulders. He gave her a last little squeeze and let her fall back on the bed, then leaned over, kissing her on the mouth. His lips were large and wet, and lay on hers like hot pudding. He hesitated a moment too long there, then lifting his face, he took up her hand and laid it against his cheek, kissing the palm; her fingers curled like a moth in fire. Looking at her searchingly, her father dropped her hand to flick back the lapel of the robe she was wearing. Then putting his hand on her shoulder, he drew down the strap of her nightgown. She grabbed his wrist and tried to push him back with her other hand.

He began to talk breathlessly and softly. "Just let me look at you, Kitty, my own daughter, let me see you just once. You show yourself to other men—who has more right than your father? I love you so much. Take your hand away, Kitty." It was a command. He slipped the nightgown down. "I won't do anything to you, Kitty. Just let me look. Kitty . . . beautiful." His voice sounded far away. She stopped struggling and opened her eyes. His white face rose over her body like the moon—hung there over her shoulder, over her mouth. He picked up her hand and kissed it, rubbing it against his mouth and cheek, then laid it down carefully, as though there were an exact spot where it belonged. He put his hand on her breast, touching it lightly at first, then caressing her with a sudden viciousness. Kathryn moaned and bit her lip, writhing away from him. He released her immediately.

"Never mind, Kit," he said without much emotion. "I'm sorry, I really am." She turned on her side and cried into the blanket. He patted her arm and straightened her robe. C'mon, Kit, you're all right. Nobody hurt you. Forget it." He stood, tied the belt of his black silk dressing gown more tightly, and took his time pouring himself a small glass of Scotch. She stopped crying and lay with her eyes closed while her father padded around, turning out the rest of the lights.

"Kit." He stood over her, next to the bed. She did not look at him. "Good night," he said, and she heard him go into his room and close the door.

Kathryn opened her eyes and looked at the gray luminescent rectangle of window. She brushed her hair out of her eyes and away from her damp cheeks and turned onto her back. Tentatively she ran her hands over her breasts, down over her stomach and hips, and then slowly caressed her thighs, stealing her right hand up the tender inner surfaces until she touched herself, as if it were not her hand at all but someone else's. An exquisite pulsing flush crept up from between her legs to her throat, where it seemed to concentrate and expand. The small of her back ached and the gray window whirled like a dingy pinwheel.

My father leaves to go back to California before anybody finds out what is really the matter with me.

# NOVEMBER 1971

---

## PART FOUR

IT IS PROBABLY THE THIRD AFTERNOON THAT NELLIE
appears: I skim out of a nap and there she is in
the doorway, leaning on one jamb as if it is her weight
that holds it upright. Again I feel her strange monitory
presence before I actually see her, and somehow her
being here—so unexpectedly—shakes me . . . as
much as I am capable of being shaken in my present
drug-cushioned state.

"Where did *you* come from?" I ask stupidly, as if the
other wing of the hospital were a continent away. "How
did you know I was here?"

She steps toward me, carefully, as if there might be
footing to lose.

"I heard you were back. I'm sorry."

"I'm back." It is a safe thing to say.

"How are you feeling? Are you having much trouble
with the pain?"

"Yes. No. Not right after the morphine. Other times
I think I might lose my mind with it. The worst part is
the coughing; they keep making me breathe this irritating stuff and then I cough and that hurts terribly. The
throwing up too. I still can't stand the throwing up."
What a relief to be able to complain this openly, this
freely, to say how I really feel! Nellie, I know, will not
interpret my sharing of my pain as an assault, she will
not turn away or urge me to be strong or murmur some
expression of sympathy or swallow hard because there
is, finally, nothing to say to somebody who suffers and
is beyond comfort though not beyond caring. For Nellie

pain is just another fact in a professional life circum-
scribed and defined by brutal facts.

"Otherwise?"

"Otherwise I wish I could take a bath!" (Thinking
of letting myself slowly into steaming water in a deep
old tub—the kind I have at home—resting there with
my eyes closed while the water dissolves and floats
away the lacy crusts of blood, the scrubby imaginary
pelt of dried perspiration, bluish skin, and the smell of
rot I am sure stands out around me like a frizzle of
electricity.) "And wash my hair! It's greasy, it stinks, I
feel so filthy. . . ." Nellie does not need details; her
concern is not just for a patient, but for another woman
who feels herself discomfited by her own lack of deli-
cacy. Her face mirrors my distress.

"Now that is something I think I can help you with,"
she says. "The hair, anyway. We have someone who
can come in and wash it for you. The bath . . . well,
you know why it isn't possible at the moment . . .
infection and all. But I know you'll feel better when
your hair is washed. I would." Unselfconsciously she
reaches behind her own head and runs her hand down
the long tail of dark brown hair that falls to the middle
of her back. It is the color and length of mine, straight
and thick like mine.

We look at each other: she is thinking of my hair
and I am thinking of hers. Then she takes a breath as if
she might say something, subsides, and again stands
quite still with her hands folded in front of her so that
her motionlessness makes her seem sad, distracted.

"Oh well," I begin brightly in my tiny voice because
she seems to need cheering up, "it's all up from here.
Things can only get better now, thank God. The worst
is over." She smiles and again makes that slight movement that implies she is about to say something. I try to
identify the strange feeling I have about her being here,
try to separate the element of warmth and reassurance
from one that I can only describe to myself as oppressive: it is as if I had been cold and she has provided a
wonderful, downy quilt that I eagerly crawl under, only

to find it too heavy, too hot, stifling; or as if I have wandered into a garden of roses on one of those muggy summer days when the perfume of the blown blossoms is overpowering and sickening, invading the senses like thick mud. I rush to throw off the sensation, to cool it and slice through it with chatter, and she seems relieved as she joins me. The two of us rattle on about my family, her job, our lives.

We exhaust our brief topics and I exhaust myself: visitors take such a concerted effort, one must focus one's attention to damp the noise of self-absorption, fatigue, pain, and drug dementia. There seems to be nothing more to say and we both fall silent. Nellie looks toward the window where the drapes are drawn against the low orange scorch of the afternoon light.

"Well." Nellie backs away from the bed and turns toward the door. "If you need me for anything—for anything at all—have one of the floor nurses get in touch with me. We keep tabs on each other and our patients." (The truth is, I think, that the nurses know a good deal more about what goes on in this hospital—know more about the patients and the personnel—than do any three doctors put together.)

While her presence has been disquieting, still, I do not want Nellie to leave; I struggle toward an attempt to articulate something that nudges me, that is around a corner, that I can sense but not see that seems to have something to do with why Nellie is here. Buying time, I block her way out with a plug of words: "Wait. I have something to tell you. . . ." (I am about to try to get her to share my vexation of spirit.)

She turns back to me, ever patient, ever attentive.

"I just want to say that . . . well . . . seeing you like this, it means something to me . . . a lot to me," I amend. "Do you remember that day when I was in the hospital before and you came and stood by my bed?" She had become—I want to say, somehow—the magnet that drew to it and organized all the scrap of that experience. "When I thought you were some kind of an angel? Or a spirit, or a visitation? Something happened to me. It was quite strange. And now it is hard not to invest your presence with all kinds of . . . import . . . ." I think to myself: she must suspect the drugs have gotten to me, that I am totally mad, delirious. It seems I cannot do it—locate and capture the remarkable feeling, the powerful response I have to her, a response to shadings and layers that may be her and may be some dim perception of my own self.

She nods as if she understands. "It's so complicated," she offers. "We all identify with you, with what you're going through, your husband, your kids, your being so young. It could be any of us, nobody is immune. Any of us could have . . ." She breaks off and looks hard at me.

Another deep breath, except that this time it is not a preface to speech but to gesture: she reaches toward me and touches me on the shoulder, touches the wrinkled stiff surface of the hospital gown that is like dried, ancient skin. A little touch, the gentlest pressure, and she withdraws her hand as if I were hot, as if the gown between us were not enough to keep her from burning her fingertips. Her hand coils into a fist.

"Well," she says again.

"Thank you for coming," I say. "It's odd, but somehow I feel I ought to have expected you. You're my best visitor yet . . . the most important to me," I correct myself. "Like a gift."

She jams her hands into her pockets, the fists filling out the front of her white nylon dress like a pair of stolen apples, and with her head down, she squish-squishes out on her crepe soles.

The night is not a good one, nor is the next morning any better. I feel sicker when I ought to be feeling weller, and as I wait for Michael—who is uncharacteristically late—I ponder the possibility of a relapse. Perhaps I am not trying hard enough again, perhaps I am letting it get the better of me . . . as I am urged again and again not to. They must be cutting down on my medication because breathing is more difficult, I hurt from the front of me all around to the back; my stomach feels wobbly and loose, as if it might at any moment become unmoored.

I don't like it when Michael is late, although I know he has his obligations, his life, and needs to have *some* time when all of us are not wanting more and more from him. I am the worst offender, of course, clinging as I never have, but it is his presence alone—the strength and resiliency of *his* fiber—that knits together the moments of the day and the days of the week. When he isn't here—when I suspect he is making a life without me—I begin to ravel with all sorts of unreasonable, fatuous desertion fantasies: he is fed up, he can't stand the sight of me—my pain, my cavil, my bloody need and total dependence. I look wretched, I smell (I can smell myself: I smell embalmed). He wants an intact, functioning wife, or no wife at all.

It is not true, of course, it is silly. I know that, I really do, he has been wonderful, they have all been wonderful, but I have such a time keeping the whiny baby—the selfish changeling—in the high-sided cradle of my psyche where it belongs. It seems I must wrest control of my body from a whole series of monumentally capricious forces that press it into regression, into a flabby entropy rather than a muscular lunge toward vigor.

It is taking all my energy, all my resolution.

I am feeling sulky without Michael; usually he helps me with breakfast and my morning *toilette*, but even by the time they come to get my tray of unappetizing, stomach-sparing food he has not arrived, and I must negotiate a major change of position by myself—from sitting up to lying down: not as simple as it sounds. In fact I wrench something that wrenches back, and I find myself caught leaning on one elbow, balanced on my side, hacking horribly and once more unable to get my breath. With help I could sit up and cough effectively; with help I could lie down and roll onto my stomach, tucking a pillow into the curve of my body to ease the jolts. In the meantime, I am stuck half up and half down, clutching at the sheet and swaying precariously over the edge of the bed. I fling a pale "Nurse! Nurse! Help!" down the hall after the departing tray-bearer, but as she fails to reappear it is clear that I will have to help myself . . . slack, damaged muscles or not.

The room lurches as I get prone in the only practical way, by letting the supporting arm flop out as if it has been kicked away, and dropping hard onto the bed: nothing matters but to get control of the coughing or I am sure I will suffocate. My fall forward gives me immediate relief because of the weight of my own body against the mattress, but I have also spilled partly off the high bed: my head is over the side and it is my hands and arms which keep me from tumbling off altogether. The protective bars I have begged the nurse to fold down keep me in anyway because I have caught at them with my hands so that I hang there like some large scrawny primate at the zoo—upside down, gagging, and bug-eyed. I cough and I cough until the ragged sawing wanes into surges of nausea and I throw up on the floor.

I feel so helpless, so foolish, so degraded as I lie there, draped from the bed toward the floor, my hair sinking into the puddle of water and bile in which I can see my swirling reflection. I find then that I cannot haul myself back up so, baby again, I begin to sob from pain, frustration, shame . . . which makes everything hurt all the more, which makes me cry more insistently, the tears running down my forehead into my hair. It is one of those ineffable moments of total surrender, when the will drops from the self like a satin gown from a naked body.

Then a racket in the corridor: doctors. I will be caught like this, soppily weeping, in this undignified position. The doctors will see me like this. In a hurry, I push steadily to raise my head and right myself. My hair falls stickily around me; the tears, absurdly, slip back toward my eyes.

Before I can return myself to an appropriate patient-

posture, the door is pushed wide open and they are all
in the room, clogging the wide doorway, my whole team
of eager physicians, with Dr. G.—always the optimistic
coach—at the point of a flying wedge, pushed forward
by the group like a child shoved to the front to make a
reluctant presentation while the others lurk behind.
They look so awkward standing there, shuffling their
feet, jostling each other, combed heads bobbing like a
bunch of balloons in a stiff breeze, that if I weren't so
miserable, I would laugh out loud at their expressions
of dismay, distress, and disdain as they take in the patient peering up damply, the mess on the floor. The
doctors variously nod and mumble morning salutations.
Dr. G. appears to be about to say something but
doesn't, so that his mouth opens and closes and opens
again like a fish's. His colleagues, still nodding—now at
each other, as if their heads have been set in motion
and must run down—back away and disappear, perhaps on cue, leaving Dr. G. standing by himself.

"Uh, and how are you feeling this morning?" he inquires.

All my wetness is nothing compared to his stupidity,
and he no more deserves an answer than I can form
one, so I continue to cry—now out of embarrassment—
and shake my head. So that he can see I want nothing
of him, I muster one last push of exquisite focus, managing to regain bed level and retracting like a soft,
soggy slug into the impeccable white sheets. I don't
mind feeling rude this morning; I am tired of pretending and tired of the good-patient pose. They have
helped to make me feel this way and I don't see why I
should hide my pain and resentment from them. I want
to be left alone and I don't mind showing that either, so
I gaze wearily at the ceiling.

"Well, I'll be back this afternoon, hon," announces
Dr. G., as if I might be glad to hear it. I close my eyes
in acquiescence. Then he is gone.

Michael arrives not one minute after Dr. G. has left.
"Oh, Pea," I sigh, "where have you been? You missed

the doctors! They were all here together, can you imagine? A real rogues' gallery."

"I saw them," he says, coming toward me. "I've . . . talked to them already. . . ."

"Watch out," I interrupt, indicating the mess on the floor by dropping my hand over the side and pointing. "Don't step in that."

Michael investigates access to the bed, then makes a wide circle to the far side, where he leans down to kiss me on the forehead. "What's the matter?" he asks, studying my eyes, concern rising in him like a blush. "What did they say? Why are you crying?" His face is tight, as if somebody has put a sardine-can key into his nose and twisted.

More tears—in response to his love, to the look on his face.

"Oh, I don't know," I sob. "It's the coughing, the throwing up, everything hurts. And I feel so sick. I want to be getting better and sometimes I think I'm not recovering at all. It should be downhill by now and it feels like uphill, so that I've forgotten what it's like *not* to be sick and I wonder whether I'll always be this way—weak and sloppy and helpless."

Michael looks pained. He walks away from me to the corner of the room, then walks back, then begins to pace—a habit of his I dislike because I have always interpreted it as his way of avoiding confrontations with me, though he has assured me often that this is simply his way of clearing his head.

He makes two quick circuits of the room until I say sharply, petulantly, "For God's sake, Pea, sit down. You're making me dizzy." He perches on the arm of a chair for a moment, and then is up and pacing again.

"What's the matter?" I ask, now more concerned for him than for myself. The tears have already dried in filmy transparent bands down my cheeks. "What's the *matter* with you?"

"I have to leave," Michael says unexpectedly, stopping his pacing so abruptly he might have run into an invisible wall.

"You just got here!"

"I'm sorry, I've got to go."

"You promised to spend the morning with me!"

"Something's come up that I've got to take care of.
I'll call you later." This time he kisses me on my
mouth, hastily wiped on the bed sheet. I am too worn
out to argue: he will leave if he wants to leave, because
while he is (almost) always punctual, he isn't necessarily predictable. I hang onto his hand—my last bid—as
if he might have to drag me with him.

"C'mon, Stephani, please." He shakes free. "I love
you," he says (a peace offering), and then he is gone
too.

I couldn't take it: all the recent abrupt comings and
goings, the weird groupings, the tension that strung the
air like a child's rubber band game. So I slept. The
drugs that made me viscid and malleable, the stifling
radiator heat, the velvety depression, muffled the din of
anxiety. Whatever was going on, I wanted no part of it.
I slept all day, waking to smile crookedly and blink at
my few visitors, wishing them away so that I could
again enfold myself in an impenetrable layer of leth-
argy. I can get through almost anything by sleeping it
off.

But you can't sleep off death. I should have seen it, I
should have recognized it; even somebody as out of
touch as I should have known . . . should have
known in Nellie's hesitant touch, in the doctors' embarrassment and flight. And Michael: I had never understood him well (he assured me I didn't understand him
at all) and he is good at hiding (or not having any)
emotions . . . but there is no way to accuse him of
lack of devotion or a shirk of responsibility. There isn't
much he will run away from.

Maybe I did see it and thrust it away, because it was
a final blow—a terminal blow—after many blows, each
heavier and less comprehensible than the last. They
had done it at last; they had rid themselves of this

troublesome patient with the undiagnosable disease at last; they had killed me.

My mother-in-law was finally, thoroughly right; everyone else was sweepingly wrong: I had cancer. It was terminal.

I was going to die.

# NOVEMBER 1971

———————◆———————

## PART FIVE

"SIT DOWN," LEN HAD SAID TO MICHAEL THAT MORNING, "I'm afraid there is some bad news. The pathology report has come back."

"What do you mean? What's happened?" said Michael.

Those "clots" in the lungs were not—it seemed—clots at all, but "necrotic fragments" of a tumor . . . a malignant tumor. "Squamous carcinoma," read the report, advertising the virulency. Three months, perhaps, said Len, certainly no more than six, so sorry.

"But *how* could you not have *known*," said Michael, horrified. "After *all* this *time*! All the *surgery*! You're telling me she has cancer and she's going to die and you didn't know it until the *pathology* report came back?"

Michael thought I must be told—immediately. The doctors demurred: I should not be told—at all. Let her think she is getting better, they said: a wiser course, she's a very sick girl, who knows the effect of such a revelation? . . . (Only our opinion, of course, they added hastily, but think it over, don't do anything rash.) You'll see. Protect her. It's in everybody's best interest. She'll find out soon enough.

Michael (even more horrified): "But of *course* she must know! How can you suggest not telling her? She's sharp, even now. She'll suspect right away. It's *her* disease, *her* life. Of course she must know, and she must know as soon as possible, certainly before anyone else."

He wanted them to tell me; he wanted those great-and-wise doctors to have to bear the onus of their sophistry. He would wait outside in the corridor to be certain they did as they promised, would wait to be with me afterward.

They never told me, they escaped, barreling down the hall, saying to Michael, "We can't do it now, today. She's too sick. Tomorrow. We'll tell her tomorrow."

"So you see why I couldn't stay there with you," Michael said later; "I knew and you didn't, and I wanted to think everything over. I wanted them to tell you. I would have given it away if I had had to stay with you all day, the way we planned. It was a terrible blow, after all we had been through—you had been through—and I just couldn't face you."

So that afternoon I slept and then awoke to stare at the ceiling and wonder lumpishly, vaguely, what was going on, until the effort mired my brain and I fell asleep again. Michael had headed right home and after a desultory conversation with both our mothers—sitting together in my kitchen over coffee—locked himself in our bedroom to read poetry, stare at the ceiling, and pace. It was about four when the phone rang. It was Len.

"Now, I don't want you to get your hopes up too much yet, but there seems to be some question about the diagnosis made by pathology," he said. "It's cancer all right, but some things just don't fit and it may be another kind for which there seems to be a pretty consistently successful cure. We won't know for sure until tomorrow, but there's a good chance that her disease has been misdiagnosed; this may be a cancer we haven't seen here at Epiphany for twenty years. Let's pray for good news."

"Yes," said Michael, even angrier than he had been that morning, but also mightily relieved. He said later that at that moment he knew—he positively *knew*—that no matter what I had, or what the chances were, I would not die, that somehow we would get through whatever was necessary. Michael has always believed in miracles.

"Are you okay?" asked Len, and then added, "Thank God we didn't tell her this morning."

It is Len alone, sitting on my bed the next day, who tells me I have cancer, but that I am lucky, I will not die.

"Cancer? Cancer of what?" (Thinking of my mother-in-law's pessimistic prescience, I am somehow galled by the fact that she was right.)

"A very rare cancer—cancer of the placenta. Chorio-carcinoma. . . ."

"How do you get chorio . . . what? Where did it come from?"

"It grows with a pregnancy—with your last pregnancy—in the trophoblast. It's a trophoblastic tumor. . . ."

"What do you mean 'it grows with a pregnancy'? Does Zachary have it?" My heart gallops like a spooked horse. "Does Zachary have cancer too?"

"Oh, no, no, very unlikely, nothing for you to worry about, but we'll test him. No, it grows in the placenta, not in the baby . . . if there is a baby: usually they are aborted spontaneously. It affects the mother only."

"But I don't understand! I had Zachary a year and a half ago! Was a piece of the placenta left that got cancerous? Or if it was cancerous before, why didn't it *look* funny? Why wasn't there something for the doctor to see? Why couldn't he *tell* I had cancer? I don't understand!"

"Well, we certainly can't know *now* about the placenta itself—something had to be there, of course (what we call the primary lesion). . . ."

"Was that why it stuck? Why I couldn't expel it for so long after Zachary was born?"

"That's impossible to say." It occurs to me that Len is in an extremely awkward position and that he is unlikely to say anything interpretable as incriminating—to himself or anyone else. "Anyway, there's little question that the cancer *started* in the placenta—somewhere in the placenta—but this kind of malignancy grows very quickly and spreads very quickly . . . metastasizes."

Metastatic cancer. I know what that means. Inoperable, like leukemia or Hodgkin's, filthy little malignant cells crawling through your body, burrowing in, nesting, multiplying. "Spread? Where has it spread?"

"Well, the lung for sure—that's where we got the cancerous cells from. The tissue taken out of your lung—out of the pulmonary artery and the heart—and out of the vena cava were tumor fragments. . . ."

"The emboli . . . those weren't emboli?"

"No, not emboli. They were pieces of tumor thrown off from a mass in the vena cava."

"What was a . . . mass . . . doing in the vena cava? I thought the cancer was in the placenta. . . ."

"It was, it was, but once it metastasizes, it begins to grow at the sites of metastasis. Pieces break off and travel through the venous system until they lodge and begin to grow again."

I shudder, imagining I can feel the infinitesimal animacules sniffing and searching for colonization sites, then settling in and growing into the grotesque, misshapen, bloody gobs that stopped up all the silvery pipes and tubes in my body, strangling it.

"But if this is . . . growing . . . all over my body, it wouldn't have been necessary to do a hysterectomy, ever."

Len clears his throat and looks away. His hand, which has been resting on my knee, gives it a little convulsive squeeze. "You never know," he says cautiously, "where the cancer might be. We would have done the hysterectomy anyway. You can't be too careful in a case like this. It is wise to be conservative." He still is looking away, reciting at the floor.

"Where else does this thing spread? Do I have it all over me?"

"Metastases to the lung are most common, but it can also spread to the brain and liver. We must test for that. Wherever it has spread, though, the treatment is the same. The same treatment whether you have brain metastases and liver metastases, or just lung metastases. The same drugs—the same chemotherapy."

"What happens in chemotherapy?"

"Drugs are administered, much like medicine for any other disease. You have one of the few cancers against which drugs are pretty universally effective. You're lucky."

He has already said that. I want to feel lucky, but I'm having trouble mustering appreciation for my good fortune.

"Can I go home? How is this done?"

"It has to be done in the hospital. Chemotherapy is tricky. The idea, of course, is to kill the cancer cells without killing the patient. The drugs are administered in nearly lethal doses and so there must be constant monitoring. . . ."

"Who does this . . . chemotherapy?" It is a touchy issue, but I have a certain well-honed resistance to allowing these doctors to give me drugs that could kill me. Len does not miss the note of alarm in my voice.

"Oh, we don't do it *here*," he hastens to reassure me. "We are planning to transfer you to a hospital that specializes in cancer treatments. No, this is pretty sophisticated stuff for us to do here; we're not equipped. There is a man at Quimbly Hospital here in the city who is an expert in treating choriocarcinoma—one of two people in the country who is (the other is in Boston). We want to get you admitted to Quimby as soon as possible so the treatment can be started. This Dr. J. has already been contacted and will be coming to see you—to evaluate the case—in the next few days."

"And then how long will I be there? How long will it take to . . . cure . . . me?" I'm not sure how much more of all of this I can take, even if I have an absolutely absolute guarantee that my troubles are about to be over. It has been so long *already*, and I am beginning to have doubts about my stamina.

"Not more than six months, I should think. You can probably count on being out by June." He doesn't say, "If you're not dead."

Six months? *Six more months?* Even thinking about it exhausts me. But I should be glad. People die of cancer, lots of people, and Len has said I won't die, that my chances are good. ("How good is good?" I want to know. "Eighty percent chance of survival," Len says brightly, "a very good chance. Consider yourself lucky.") Fortunately, I don't know enough about choriocarcinoma—or about my particular high-risk case—to be too scared, so I decide to be gracious and optimistic.

We have finally, after all, found out what I have had all this time.

"Thank you," I say to Len, as if I am leaving a long and extravagant party he has given. He smiles and pats my leg. He too looks relieved as he gets off my bed.

Anybody can go to a medical journal and read about a disease, and—except for the technical jargon—anybody can follow what is being said. Metastatic gestational choriocarcinoma *is* an odd, rare malignancy, in something of a class by itself: arising with the trophoblast of pregnancy—the part of the fertilized ovum that attaches itself to the uterine wall and provides for nourishment to the developing embryo—it is a "fetal tumour which invades the maternal host . . . and is distinguished from its host by the genetic contribution of the male parent." In fact, it functions much like a tissue graft—a tissue graft that if it were not for a certain genetic "match" would not take, would be rejected as other tissue frequently is, for instance in an organ transplant or skin graft. Our bodies "recognize" certain tissues and substances (like blood) and reject others: this is what immunity is all about—the ability of the body to cast off an "invader." Technically, the mother's body will *support* the essentially alien life within her—the parasite of pregnancy—but will reject any *invasion* of the fetal tissues, malignant or not. While the course of a choriocarcinoma is still imperfectly understood, it is clear that there is some "failure of [the] surveillance mechanisms," either because the mother has developed an immunological tolerance to the "graft," or because there is a rare compatibility between the tissues of the mother and the fetus—and by association, between the mother and the father.

Choriocarcinoma occurs in something like one in sixteen thousand live births (among Caucasian women), though there is a higher incidence of occurrence if all pregnancy-related incidents are counted. (More than three quarters of the time the fetus is either aborted or the pregnancy develops as what is known as a mole: a grotesque growth—like a bunch of spongy humanoid grapes—that mimics pregnancy, a pregnancy gone wild, degenerate, horrible.) Until the last couple of decades, this cancer was "probably the most uniformly and rapidly fatal malignancy of women. . . . Death, usually by rapid and extensive hematogenous spread, frequently occurs in a few months." Ninety percent of its victims died "usually . . . within a year."

The same profuse proliferation, however, that makes this disease so swift and deadly also makes it susceptible to chemotherapeutic intervention; to put it too simply, anti-cancer drugs are the most effective against the fastest-dividing cells—as is radiation therapy. (For similar reasons, drugs taken during pregnancy can have profound effects on a developing fetus.) Since the early sixties, single- and then combination-drug therapy has been saving a large majority of patients with this disease. Chances for survival are calculated against the duration of the illness, the spread of the tumor, the ability to locate the primary lesion, and the general condition of the patient.

Len told me my chances for survival were good; the major argument, however, for my recovery was simply that I had lived so long with the disease already—nearly two years, or a year longer than nine out of ten women with undiagnosed choriocarcinoma. (As one source offhandedly contributes: "All too often, the diagnosis is made post mortem.")

What Len did not tell me was that I was considered to be in the "high-risk" category where my chances looked considerably less good: one study reported that even with the new combination-drug therapy, only eleven out of twenty-eight victims recovered where the interval between presentation—or first symptoms—and treatment was over six months. Furthermore, my blood group is AB and "AB patients tend to have rapidly progressive tumors which do not respond well to chemotherapy." (In another study of eight AB women with metastasis "none responded promptly to chemotherapy and sustained remissions [were reported] in [only] two.")

So my prospects for survival had been slightly beefed up: I guess they all thought that what I didn't know couldn't hurt me. They wanted me docile and tractable and Out Of The Way, the sooner the better. Let Quimby kill me.

It was not, it seemed to me, excessive to think they perhaps owed me something—some consideration, some generosity, even an apology. But they never stopped; they never stopped with their fudging, their excuses, their pass-the-buck mentality, their arrogance. Choriocarcinoma *is* rare, but it is also distinctive enough—in terms of its symptoms—to be an easy cancer to get. My complaints were not the product of instability or hysteria; they were classic . . . as was my concern about them: women who are later found to have choriocarcinoma "almost always seek gynecological advice in the early stages of their disease," and medical journals urge that it be considered whenever a young women presents with menstrual irregularity and/or hemorrhagic bleeding accompanied by chest pain and difficulty in breathing, especially if she has had a recent pregnancy. It is pointed out again and again the "danger of relying on technical procedure as opposed to a meticulous history": "It is clear that choriocarcinoma should be suspected in unexplained cases of progressive pulmonary hypertension in young women,"—"in particular, tests should be made in patients with . . . progressive dyspnea. . . ."

And what is the major test? An arcane, abstruse assay that takes sophisticated equipment, considerable time, trained technicians, and extraordinary diagnostic sensitivity? The preliminary test, as it hapens, is a simple pregnancy test—one I could even have done on myself at the clinic while I worked there.

During gestation, a pregnancy will throw off for excretion in the mother's urine approximately 1000 IUs of HCG (or human chorionic gonadotrophin) during a twenty-four-hour period. The most basic pregnancy tests simply respond to the high concentration of this hormone in the urine; a more sophisticated test will determine the exact amount of HCG. In cases of choriocarcinoma, the level of the HCG titer (or the proportion of HCG in a twenty-four-hour urine sample) is used to estimate the extent of the malignancy: researchers have found that there is a close correspondence between virulence and activity. My own titer hovered around 100,000 IUs, or a hundred times what one would expect during a normal pregnancy. (That probably explained my nightmarish fatigue, the nausea, and weight loss.)

In any case, hysterectomy is neither diagnostic nor necessary: women in remission from choriocarcinoma have not infrequently borne more children without mishap. And open-heart surgery—though in my case it paradoxically and quite fortuitously saved my life—is incontrovertibly the long way around.

"God damn, God damn," Michael exploded later. "At some point—it seems to me—even the fanciest physician ought to consider it an obligation to sit down with a yellow legal pad and say to himself, How many things could this reasonably be? and list them, and then test for each and every possibility! The nerve! The balls! The arrogance! After what they told you about yourself, how they made you feel, like a crazy person! Even *I* can walk into a library and read about this disease; even *I* have some understanding of it. And where were *these* clowns all that time, all the time you were exhibiting *classic*—absolutely *classic*—symptoms?"

I cowered in the face of one of Michael's infrequent eruptions of wrath and then found myself irresistibly defending the doctors: "Anybody can make a mistake. It was my fault, really. I should have insisted." Although they never apologized to *me*—not for my humiliation, not for the unnecessary mutilations (the cutting and robbing), not for all that time, all that money, all that pain—I had to fight down a reflexive, twisted impulse to apologize to *them*, for having been so much trouble, for having been the agent of their making such self-righteous fools of themselves.

But if they had made fools of themselves, I had made a fool of myself. If they had pushed, I had pulled: this chain of misfortunes had not been forged in a vacuum—the culpability had to be shared. Why had I been so willing to believe them, so willing to be crazy only because they needed to see me that way? Why had I let them do as they chose with my body and my life? Why had I never protested, never said, "Hold it! Just hold it! Back off, don't touch me, let me think." I *knew* I wasn't crazy. I *knew* I couldn't conjure such a real, crushing pain and the poisonous purr of a damaged lung. But why then did I acquiesce to the fiction?

People asked later: "Why did you put up with that? Why did you accept it? Couldn't you have gone to someone else? Didn't you have *any* faith in yourself?" And the most rending: "How could somebody with your brains have been so stupid?"

Ah, stupidity. Stupidity comes not of the plunge into a delirium of excess, but of the tendency to mince between monsters. Stupidity, finally, is the delusion that one can please everybody and still save oneself. Because I didn't want to look stupid, I behaved stupidly; I didn't understand that excessive exposure almost guarantees a fatal vulnerability and my many varieties of fear somehow never included the (quite appropriate) fear of self-annihilation. The key was this: in some strange and perverted way I had always been in control, had *chosen* to bend to the afflatus of my guilt and my need for affirmation and an inspired, visionary helplessness.

Cause of death: a surfeit of romance . . . a glut of credulity.

Now there is nothing to do but wait . . . and wait . . . until the Great Doctor descends on Epiphany to determine whether I am fit material for the World Famous Cancer Center of which he is the exclusive property. As I continue to wilt, the first week becomes the second, prompting Dr. G. to threaten to take over the chemotherapy himself. "Oh, please don't do that, don't trouble yourself," I say evasively, undiplomatically. "I'll wait." I'm not about to give them another chance at me, not as long as I am still *compos mentis*.

The singular Dr. J. turns up quite without warning on Sunday night. He looks altogether like an ordinary person—plaid flannel shirt and sport jacket, medium height, a square florid face, and a rumple of curly red hair—which is why I am surprised when he walks in with no other introduction than an announcement of my name . . . as if he has run to its den a rare animal he had been tracking by its scat. Without bothering to identify himself, he takes a chair next to the bed and sits there, contemplating me with his hands folded, chin on bent wrists, eyes half closed. I am too astonished to ask who he is as he bends forward now, looking at me even more penetratingly, although it occurs to me that anybody who would walk into my room with such self-possession and so little concern or apology would have to be a doctor.

Dr. J. makes me an offer: he will take my case—transfer me to his hospital and make every effort to cure me—*if*, and only *if*, I guarantee no interference . . . and by *that* he means (to be perfectly clear) I am not to ask questions—*any* questions—of either him *or* his residents. I am not to meddle, demand explanations, or get tangled in the issue of accountability. I would promise to be a good patient, and if I didn't know what that was, he would take personal pains to inform me. He ran the show *his* way. He meant it. He was too busy. He would brook no compromise, and he has spent this time coming to see me—his Sunday night— to be certain I understand and agree to my half of the deal . . . or we can say good-bye now and I'm on my own. He likes this understood. In advance. He will then do the saving and I will do the getting well.

My choice seems to be between the denial of basic rights—the willful assassination of the ego—and death. I actually hesitate before caving in and giving myself over to the ministrations of Dr. J. and Quimby Hospital.

# DECEMBER 1971

———◆———

QUIMBY HOSPITAL IS NOT AN EASY PLACE TO GET USED
to. There are no obstetric floors, no nose jobs (except
to repair what cancer has eaten away), no garden-
variety gallbladders and hernias; there are few single
admissions and fewer short-term stays. In 1971, you either came here to die or to miss doing so by only the
narrowest of margins, and no matter how bad you had
it, someone else always had it worse.

The place is home and we are all family, family because we are so familiar to each other—with each
other—shamed in our unwilling intimacies. The mark
cancer puts on you—the twist it gives to the tree (the
twist it gives to the mind)—the consciousness of mortality—its personal quality—is borne like a limp
through the rest of your life.

And the place is a penitentiary and we are penitents,
begging forgiveness, catharsis, lending our small weights
to some incomprehensibly indifferent—but accurate
—scale: you on this side . . . you on this, sheep
and goats. Many of us arrive never to be discharged;
others return again and again until the final admission
from which there is no discharge.

Some of us will escape with our lives. None of us will
escape intact.


My transfer to Quimby was looked forward to as a
great adventure: anything to escape the insalubrity of
Epiphany, its feel of ineluctable doom; my excitement

overlaid any nagging anxiety I might have had about the possibility that Quimby could be even worse. I focused, instead, on the prospect of a different place, a new four walls, a fresh start where the people seemed to know what they were doing, even if Dr. J. himself (my single example of a new contingent of personnel) had hardly been awash with the milk of human kindness.

I was transported by ambulance, still too sick to go anywhere anyway but flat on my back in the splendor of the shiny red vehicle (spangled—like a child's toy—with chrome) which passed for the private ambulance service that these hospitals used to trade patients. Relishing the ride as I had enjoyed little else since the day I had deposited a portion of my lungs in a crumpled tissue, I watched the real world flash by through the ambulance's fish-tank windows and allowed this minor pleasure to eclipse the excruciating discomfort of having been exposed to an unending stream of visitors—toting candy, fruit, and flowers and wearing the ambiguous expressions of well-intentioned people about to do something they would rather not have to do—in the lobby of Epiphany, who averted their eyes politely and stepped neatly around my squat little rolling bed while Michael checked me out of the hospital. (I had pretended not to see anybody—turned my face in the general direction of the nearest wall—but still I could feel them looking. I was wearing a new bathrobe somebody had bought me—red-and-purple flannel with a high, discreet military neck like a cadet's jacket—buttoned up with little ridged gold balls—that hid quite effectively the padding of bandage with which I was stuffed from chin to crotch. I had combed my hair carefully (although I had some difficulty in raising my arms) and daubed my gray cheeks with rouge in deference to some near-lost sense of occasion.

The elation wore off quickly; the bumpy ride soon had my weakened, loosened body quivering like aspic. I was glad that the ride was over only long enough to realize how uncomfortable I felt in Quimby, where I was unceremoniously deserted in the echoing lobby under a brass plaque while Michael wandered off to attend to the red tape of getting me admitted.

Quimby's lobby was totally unlike Epiphany's: where Epiphany's was a quiet, muffled area of rugs and polished wood—like a vicarage—Quimby's was circular, cavernous, and cold. There were so many people dashing through and so much noise that I might as well have been in Grand Central Station.

Again I felt the self-consciousness and shame—surely they were all looking at me, nudging their neighbors and saying, Tsk, look at that one. Pity. (I know that such a reaction was possible: a couple of months later a young radiologist who was a friend of a friend came by to say hello. He happened to have seen me that day and realized he recognized me—without knowing me—having been notified of my impending admission by our mutual friend. He remembered my red robe and the masses of long hair splashed over the pillow of the stubby ambulance stretcher, saw my face only obliquely because I had turned it toward the wall. He said it had made him sick to look at me; he took the rest of the day off.)

I was first assigned to a little cubicle on one of the private-patient floors of the sprawling hospital complex, but was easily talked into moving into one of the nicest rooms, in the corner, facing north and east so it caught the morning sun. ("We can't afford it!" I had said in distress to Michael, for it cost almost twice as much as the little room. "My parents have offered to pay for it," said Michael. "They think that a more cheerful room will help you get well faster. You should have it, it's important. What else is money for?") So I accepted the gift of this lovely room, and it was from here that I was snatched and then delivered many times over in the next few days as I underwent the usual round of admissions tests, plus some designed especially for me.

So many tests. Again. And the air of efficiency notwithstanding, what one did most was wait. And Wait. And wait. It was during all this waiting that I got a real sense of my situation, got a feel for the place and for the people in it. All around me were other patients who waited, patiently, as I did—in this corridor, in that sparsely furnished lounge. As crowded together as we were—packed in like miserably caged animals—there was no talking, no companionship. There was almost no reading, either; instead, everyone seemed to be deep in thought, sitting (or lying) quite still, looking in whatever direction we happened to have been left facing—the wall, the window, the ceiling. We avoided looking at each other . . . but we couldn't avoid seeing each other. We came to be recognizable to each other by our habits and our markings, like Goodall's chimpanzees. There was a tall, remarkably thin man—thoroughly bald—who could have been twenty-five or fifty: his head shone under the purplish light like the orb atop a royal staff; his features had the perfectly white, smooth quality of molded plastic. There were the old people—so sick, so frail and yellow, so unmoving, that it was not easy to tell whether they were quite alive, and one sometimes had the sense of waiting in a morgue with the bodies being prepared for dissection. There were the fat people, bloated like mortifying, beached whales, swollen with decay and sickness and drugs, shifting their bulks in the tight wheelchairs, faces red and licked with sweat, hair matted, hanging. (None of us managed to look as if we ever put comb to hair—even after some effort: perhaps it was a reflection of a basic psychological dishevelment.) There were the ones with braces, pins, casts, and bandages in odd places; there were the ones with pieces missing.

The worst were the children, small people essentially indistinguishable from the rest of us except for their size, with wizened, pained faces, arms and legs like sticks that invited careless breaking. Their heads looked huge and ungainly, pumped out of proportion to their fragile bodies; beautiful fevered eyes dented their faces; their hair was thin and limp and sometimes gone altogether except for a fine, babylike fuzz; there were livid scars on heads and necks and the backs of hands from numberless tests, cutdowns, IVs. One tried most of all

not to look at the children; one couldn't. We had at
least had some of our lives—maybe most of our lives—
we had children of our own perhaps, we had had our
chances . . . now we had our regrets. But these poor
little children, so accepting, so graceful, could comprehend only their own exquisite pain, their own explicit
fears. They were denied the luxury of regrets; divine
abandonment was beyond them.

The simplicity of their suffering shamed us.

You learn the ropes; you learn what must be put up
with and what can be complained into change. You
learn to trade obsequiousness for perks. You learn to
amuse yourself during the endless waits without actually *doing* anything. You learn to survive in an environment in which you frequently see yourself as They
see you: as so many papers to be shuffled, mouths to
be fed, veins to be found; as so many flaccid, fulsome
bags of flesh to be tended to and carted around and
treated. You learn to be good.

After the X-rays and the blood tests and the exami-
nations come the scans to find out whether my brain is
invaded, my liver compromised. I am folded into a
wheelchair in my room and then deposited in a busy
hallway outside an unmarked room with a massive, pale
wood door. Today, as I wait, my mother sits with me,
visibly uncomfortable on one of the two orange plastic
chairs, tolerantly arranging and rearranging the pillows
I have brought along for support: sitting is such a painful business. The incision aches and pulls with a dull
insistence; they have cut off my morphine and it is like
having a migraine-of-the-body. Three pillows piled precariously into my lap allow me to lean forward onto
them, to rest my heavy head and to lapse into a half-
doze that is almost as effective as a painkiller . . . a
dense daydream, an alpha state. I wish I had the energy
to talk to my mother; I hope she will understand.

A male attendant rouses me briefly, handing me a
glass of something vile-smelling and violently orange.

"Drink this," he says, in the gentlest West Indian lilt, and then adds as I taste it and make a face, "It has a kind of brackish taste, I know. I'm sorry." It makes me feel sick and I can feel myself go white, feel the beads of perspiration ooze onto my forehead. (Thank God for the pillows, in which I bury my face and drift off again.)

Then a tap on the shoulder, and a white-coated technician says, "We're ready for you." My mother pries the pillows from my arms. Maybe it is something in the concoction I drank, maybe it is the long sitting and the pain, maybe it is whatever they are "medicating" me with now, but I feel terribly groggy and have trouble concentrating on what they are telling me to do. "Up on this table, your head in here, this way. . . ." And then they turn my head on my neck like a steering wheel. "Hold real still, this takes awhile," and I give in entirely to the drowsiness, the murk, until I am surprised into a kind of semialertness when someone says briskly, "Okay, we're done, why don't you climb right back down here?"

I want to move, I really do, but I feel dissociated from my body, as if it no longer belongs to me, and my muscles refuse to gather themselves up and redispose themselves into the chair. An arm tugs me to a sitting position—to hurry me, I imagine—which disorients me further so that I slide toward the arm like a melting triple-scooper; my head falls forward onto the lifter's shoulder. "C'mon, c'mon," the arm says pushing me up and away and shaking me a little. "Someone give me a hand here!" I am falling this way and that, loose-limbed like a drunkard, trying to help. "They always do this!" says a voice behind me. "They send the basket cases in a chair and the ones who can sit up on a stretcher. I wish they'd get their signals straight!" (One other time, waiting interminably for a chest X-ray, I let my head drop forward into my crossed arms where they rest against my knees, trying to relieve some of the pressure on my chest and stomach, only to be rudely aroused by an attendant who yanks my head up by the hair. "Sit up!" she nearly shouts into my startled face as she still holds my hair. "What's the matter with you? Don't sit like that in here!") How I long—all those hours—for the privilege of the same stretcher I had scorned six months before! How the world narrows: a stretcher, a painkiller, a good IV nurse.

As soon as the tests are completed I am launched on my first course of chemotherapy. While I have been found to have no metastases either to the brain or the liver, there is "liver damage," the nature of which is never clarified. Because of the "damage," however, I am prohibited from the use of the first line of chemical defense—a drug called Methotrexate. I will be treated instead with two drugs thought to be nearly as effective: Actinomycin D and 6-Mercaptopurine. The Actinomycin D is run into a vein; the 6-Mercaptopurine is taken by mouth. All the drugs apparently share the same side effets, side effects about which Dr. J. is somewhat less than informative—presumably to keep me from manufacturing what may not happen at all. What happens, happens: he limits himself to the rare comment. One night he walks in as I am pushing the food around on my plate and says—in an attempt at levity that comes out sounding ominous—"You'd better cat now, because you're not going to get much eating done for the next few months."

That will be the nausea; I know to expect that. The other great worry is my hair.

"Will my hair fall out?"

"Sometimes it does and sometimes it doesn't."

"Well, what are the *chances* it will fall out?"

"Somewhere between zero and one hundred percent. . . ."

(Exasperated, but already well aware of the need to step lightly, I phrase the question as delicately as possible): "If it *were* going to fall out, then when might it begin? . . . In other words, at what point might I consider myself to be home free? When does the hair usually go?"

"Anytime from now till forever," he says, thwarting me.

Clearly, Dr. J. does not like to commit himself. I don't know why I am surprised.

The next night I am to start the first course of chemo-therapy; again I am eating as Dr. J. walks in. "I'd watch what I ate tonight," he contributes.

It will be my last meal for three weeks.

The pills—the 6-Mercaptopurine—arrive by nurse and go down easily enough; they are white and innocuous-looking, could easily be mistaken for aspirin. A syringe of Actinomycin D arrives shortly afterward by resident. The resident is wearing rubber gloves.

"I didn't think cancer was catching," I joke.

"I spilled some of this stuff on my hands out there," he says by way of explanation for the rubber gloves, gesturing with his head, "and it took my skin off. I want to be very careful and not get any more on me."

I try not to be alarmed. "If it hurt your hands, what is it going to do to my veins?"

"Burns 'em out pretty good," he confides as he in-jects the drug into a swift-running IV line.

It burns all right. It feels like the angiogram dye—like a rush—frying the vein in my arm, sizzling up into my chest, into my head (where I imagine I can feel the hair follicles ejecting hairs in protest), all the way down to the tips of my fingers on the other hand. It is like being purged with acid.

I get in only two hours of a sleep shallow with antici-pation, waking about midnight to the familiar tug of nausea. Intent on ignoring it I curl up tighter, self-protectively, squeeze my eyes shut, and will myself to go back to sleep, to sleep through it. Will, however, is nothing against nausea; leaning on my IV pole, I stag-ger to the bathroom and lose my dinner.

It is just the beginning: I throw up again and again, all night long, sleeping distractedly and badly between bouts. By morning there is nothing left but dry retching and an empty, inflamed feeling in the stomach. And this nausea has a viciously insidious quality: the throwing up, the empty stomach, bring no relief; there *is* no relief—just a steady sine wave of nausea, rising to retching, falling to simple motionless misery, then rising again and falling again, steady and rhythmical and predictable as a heartbeat. I lie rolled into a ball all day— often crouched on my knees with my head in my arms to relieve pressure on the healing incision, rocking with the primitive impulse to comfort myself, moving only to vomit or have my blood taken—which is done four times a day. (Only careful monitoring keeps the patient alive while the malignancy is being killed.) Talking makes my stomach shiver and shatter: my visitors leave hurriedly, glad to get away.

Anyway, I don't want anyone to see me this way.

For five nights I get the drugs; for five days I throw up, have violent diarrhea and lacerating stomach cramps. And then the second day after the drugs have been stopped, the nausea and vomiting cease quite abruptly, leaving me feeling like a used tube of toothpaste—all crumpled and empty. I have less than a day of relief when the next wave of injury takes over: my tongue begins to burn, then the roof of my mouth. In another day my mouth is a giant concave canker, one running, open sore. When I go to the mirror in the bathroom and open my mouth—as much as I am able—for a look, it is all red and raw—peeled-looking—except my tongue, which is bright red and furry white, in patches. My lips swell, my nose bleeds. The second phase of the reaction is the result of the breaking down of the fast-dividing cells: mucous membrane, skin, hair, nails. With the magnitude of the mucous membrane reaction, I am not feeling hopeful about the eventual fate of my hair.

\* \* \*

"How's the mouth?" asks Dr. J. cheerfully one night.

"Mmmmff," I reply, because even the slightest movement of lips or tongue is searing (plain water feels like napalm on the tongue; swallowing is a chore that takes all my concentration). I smile, to be neighborly.

"Ha! Still smiling," he pounces. "Not there yet! Wait till you can't even smile!"

I can't believe that this will get worse, but that turns out only to be a failure of imagination; in a couple of days even a twitch at the corner of the mouth makes me faint with pain.

I thought I would only worry about my hair, but now I become obsessed instead with my teeth, with elaborate fantasies of rot and decay and corruption and loss. My mouth is filled with a thick, yellowish scum that I cannot bear to rinse or brush away, a slippery, foul-smelling cheese caught around my teeth that squeezes out through my lips while I sleep, gluing them together. I stop praying that I will get through this with my hair and start praying for my teeth.

It is I who am sick; I must have *some* rights, so I start refusing to have testing done that seems to me to have no more value than to round out hospital records for some small mind obsessed with clinical closure. One afternoon as the vomiting is subsiding and before the chemical flaying of the mouth has begun, a chunky intern marches in, presenting his clipboard like a police badge: I am to have an arterial puncture and blood gas reading. "Why?" I ask sincerely, aware that I am setting my foot on the path of becoming officially difficult. He looks puzzled for a moment and then lights up with the answer. "Because they said so," he reports. "It's been ordered." Again he waves the clipboard, his evidence. "I'm not going," I say (it's that simple), crossing my arms sternly to give myself courage. (I am trying to look heavy and anchored, in case he should get it in his mind to remove me bodily.)

"You *have* to go," he counters.

"Why?" We are right back where we started. The intern's fat cheeks redden as he tucks the clipboard under his arm. "I don't feel well," I add. "I don't want to go anywhere right now, and I don't want another arterial puncture at *all,* not unless someone can explain to me why it's absolutely necessary." Between the four-times-a-day bloodlettings and the IV sticks once and sometimes twice a day as the veins collapse, I have had quite enough puncturing and poking.

He knows he is off the hook. *"That's* what I'll tell them," he says, relief softening his voice, ". . . that you're *sick!"* He takes the clipboard back out from under his arm and makes a note with the Mark Cross pen he has snatched from his breast pocket, mouthing words silently as he writes.

I feel in myself a building resistance to toeing the "good patient" line, even though my instructions on that score from Dr. J. could not have been clearer. When he sweeps into my room with his residents, interns, and students in tow, I cower diplomatically, try to keep my mouth shut, and learn through my mistakes: once I make the monumental error of asking a student if he would mind opening the window he is standing next to and am rewarded with a stale glare from Dr. J. (Once, much later, I happen to catch a glimpse—upside down—of a portion of his handwritten records, where I see this incident noted and his comment. "Depressed twenty-seven-year-old female," "neurotic," and "desire to control" seethe off the page at me like a swarm of ink-blue flies.)

I have been told by somebody that they are waiting for my platelet count to go up (both the platelets—which assist in clotting—and the white cell production—white cells fight infection—are depressed by the drugs used in chemotherapy: blood is also made up of fast-dividing cells) before they can consider discharging me for a few days before the next course of chemotherapy; somehow my enthusiasm gets the better of me and unwisely I dare to ask Dr. J. the state of my platelets one day as my mouth is beginning to heal. Dr. J. looks at me as if he has failed to comprehend the question—I am still, after all, gabbling confoundedly through my thick, sticky lips—so I stupidly repeat it. He has understood me all right; he simply is astounded at my shameless insistence on challenging his authority, compounded by the fact that I have had the gall to do so in front of a roomful of witnesses. In answer he turns—without a word, without an excuse, an acknowledgment, or a farewell—and stalks out of the room, his entourage tripping after him.

"Wait!" I call after him helplessly. "I'm sorry. . . ." He is certainly too far away already to hear me; he walks fast. Tears of rage well in my eyes and spill stubbornly and copiously; here I am, crying for the first time not as a child cries—from fear and pain—but from depression, anger, and impotence. I would get up and run after him, I am so angry, if only I could run, if only I weren't hooked up to the damn IV. Instead, I frantically ring the call bell for the nurse. She appears so promptly it is hard not to conclude she has been lurking in the hallway. She is looking over her shoulder, as if she might be followed.

"Uh-oh," she says as if she has expected this, "you tangled with Dr. J., didn't you?"

By now I am crying so hard, blubbering and drooling because my mouth has not yet healed, that I cannot answer her and I nod my head mutely. She hands me a tissue and watches sympathetically while I mop my face and get control of myself.

"Why is he like that?" I stammer. "I only asked him a simple direct question! How could he be offended by that? I wasn't prying, I wasn't trying to 'control' him. . . . Why isn't it all right for me to know my platelet count?"

"Don't take it too personally," the nurse says. "A lot of doctors here are like that, actually. Maybe it's because most of their patients . . ." (I can see her mind chew over what she was about to say, and then she plunges on) ". . . die. I mean, this can be a pretty depressing place to work. But Dr. J. is . . . well, he's more difficult than most of them, nobody crosses him." She leans over conspiratorially. "We're *all* afraid of him. We have a special signal for when he's on the floor. Everyone scatters."

She is smiling, checks the door once more just to be sure we are quite alone. "You know what the nursing staff calls him? We call him the Red Baron."

That is actually very funny, and I conjure an image of Dr. J. in a Fokker triplane, goggles in place and helmet flaps lowered, his white silk aviator scarf snapping rakishly behind him in the rush of air. It makes things easier, but not much, to imagine him swooping into my room, guns blazing, with his squadron behind him.

More and more I understand what this stay at Quimby will require of me. Even more than before, more than at Epiphany and with my other doctors, I find myself apologizing for being a person rather than a case, for having feelings and wanting—needing—to understand what they are doing to me . . . what is happening to me. Clearly any attempt to assert one's basic dignity and the right to have some small measure of control are met with exasperated tolerance, dismissal, resentment. Incidents like this one encourage me to maneuver into position the heavy artillery of my *own* resentment—much of it, admittedly, left over from the prior months and years . . . but still, the battle lines are drawn.

At least now I finally know who the real enemy is. At least now I am no longer fighting myself.

# CHRISTMAS 1971

CHRISTMAS LOOMS AND I FEEL THE SUCK OF DEPRES-
SION. I want to stay cheerful, I have tried to stay cheerful, to be helpful and optimistic, but the holidays reek
of loss. Like most people, I love the season—love it
and hate it for what it promises but doesn't deliver, for
what it should be and isn't, for its seductive nostalgia.
Like most people, I have probably always worked harder to sustain the illusion of Christmas more even than
the illusion of my own happiness.

Anyway, there's no avoiding it. It has infested the
bleak fluorescent hallways with its tacky cheer: the
light fixtures are done up like tarts with shiny colored
balls that spin and twinkle—with tinsel that dances—in
the air currents of the hospital traffic. Bright accordion
paper bells (imperfectly fastened open so that two or
three are always in a state of semicollapse) compete for
space with twisted crepe paper streamers; red mesh
stockings appear on a couple of doors, crammed with
sticky-looking candies—their colors run together—and
the kind of plastic novelty toy that elicits enthusiasm
from five-year-olds. Chattering, thoughtful volunteers
with hair done by stylists beguile with little felt and se-
quin handicrafts, urging them on one like a second
helping of dinner ("Just *try* it, dear, you'll see. It'll take
your mind off of . . . all this. Be a sport. Everybody's
doing one!"): occupational therapy for the maimed
and numb. Strategically placed radios squeeze out tinny
carols, ooze cheer.

One afternoon a week before Christmas anybody

who is remotely ambulatory is herded into the solarium by the clucking, cajoling staff. George Feyer has come from the Carlyle Hotel to play and sing Christmas songs and other old favorites ("Requests invited!"). We sit there in the fading light—a motley crew jammed in the small space cheek by jowl, IV pole by wheelchair arm, the latecomers consigned to the hall—all sad, sallow, watching, with expressionless faces, the kind Mr. Feyer effervesce. "You better watch out, you better not cry, you better not shout, I'm telling you why . . ." But it does make me cry, it makes my neighbors cry, we dare not exchange glances. He is a wonderful entertainer, he keeps on, soliciting requests, as merry as Christmas itself, while we sit or lean or lie like funerary figures in a dark, echoing tomb.

Christmas gets to me. It gets to all of us, and the tension pricks and burns like pine needles. Quimby has never been a friendly place, and the false note of jocularity makes us feel awkward, apologetic, and threatened.

I am determined to recover enough from this first course of chemotherapy (which I am distressed to find referred to as "mild") to get home in time for "Christmas with the family," God and Dr. J. willing; in fact my whole family, everyone—estranged, inimical, paranoid—is planning to come to New York. (My mother is already—still—here.) It is our first Christmas all together in fifteen years. Nobody of course mentions what I know they are all thinking, that perhaps it will be the last: the last together, the last for me.

In the interest of speeding my recovery I plan to walk up and down the hall once or twice a day. The project turns out to be overly ambitious: with the help of my IV pole—which I lean on like a supportive companion during a long forced march, I can just about manage half the length of the hall and back. The open-heart surgery, the abdominal surgery, the chemical assault, and six weeks in bed have made short shrift of me: I can barely stand, much less walk. And even when I am on my feet, balancing my ungainly bulk on unsteady legs, I find it impossible to pull myself upright: the wound has drawn together vertically as it has healed (the fetal posture of the last three weeks has not helped), and my chest seems to have imploded so that I stumble head down, hunched over, curled into myself like a tall, delicate fern closing for the night.

The unimpressive showing I make on my feet with my halting little excursions helps me to decide that—discretion being the better part of valor—I shall avoid letting Dr. J. see me standing up when I press my suit for release.

A few days before Christmas the place begins to clear out. It is just as well: the staff is shorthanded and harried. The hard-core sick are left now: a woman who has my disease who sits in a wheelchair in the lounge—large, staring, and impassive—a tracheotomy tube sprouting from the necklace of tape at her throat, to whom I proffer what companionship I have available, but who—because of the tube—cannot talk back at me; the boy (I think of him as a boy because he is in his early twenties) lying in the darkened room next to me, whose new wife, bowed into the sofa in his room—a round little rabbit protecting her burrow, who jumps every time I shuffle by with my pole (shuffle SQUEAK shuffle SQUEAK)—is still trying to understand how a routine appendectomy could have turned into a diagnosis of terminal cancer.

I want to get home, want to get out of here! See my children! (I haven't seen them since the beginning of November!) Sleep in my own bed! I'll promise anything, drink a gallon of water a day—to keep my fluids up—if I have to, even while my mouth is still sore; I won't expose myself to any germs that could make me sick—a real danger with my depressed white count. I'm feeling better: my stomach is calm, the thick immobility is leaving my mouth.

But Dr. J. guards his noncommittalness like a

Scrooge; I revert from tact to pressure (a mistake) in desperation for a clue as to whether . . . or even when. Shamelessly, I beg.

" . . . You see, I have to know, as soon as possible. . . . Everyone will be here—my brother is just home from Vietnam, my father is flying in from the Coast, one sister is coming from Boston, the other from southern Illinois. Maybe they shouldn't all come if I can't go home. Please. Please."

Dr. J. looks down at me as if he is measuring a distance by eye. I feel encouraged.

"Well, let me see. I'd say that's a CCL question."

I brighten. A game? "CCL? What's that?"

And then the slightest twitch, the look before the blow that I will come to recognize.

"It means I couldn't care less," he says as he turns to leave.

They don't call him the Red Baron for nothing.

But he does let me go home at the last minute, condemning me to my own inflated expectations.

Everyone is certainly here—everyone ARRIVES— coexisting in uneasy truce, circling and silent or rigid and voluble. The children race around like cheap mechanical toys that have been too tightly wound; the adults have confabs and secrets and hurt feelings and a dear determination to "make this really *nice* . . . for Stephani." My siblings slip in and out of the back bedroom where the air is thick with the sweet-oregano smoke of marijuana: they need it to dull the tension. My mother dulls the tension with Scotch and stays in the kitchen cooking steadily, resolutely, turning her head as if she has been struck whenever my father (who is trying to make himself scarce) is in her vicinity. We decorate the tree, we plan Christmas dinner: two geese (my young tradition), and I insist on making the dressing myself, enjoying my own defiance, wanting to reclaim some portion of my usefulness and identity, obstinately sitting for hours at my cutting board, pitting prunes with trembling fingers—and then sucking on the warm slimy stones draggled with golden-brown flesh, the kitchen lights dimmed around me. "Let her be," they whisper. "Let her do it if she wants. She knows what she can manage and what she can't."

The truth is that there is not much I can manage, obstinacy aside. In my enthusiasm to prepare myself for a few days at home, I had walked the length of the hall at Quimby not once but twice the day before I left for home—the day before Christmas Eve—and done something quite terrible to my lower back, where pain rests and grips my waist—just above the hipbone— like a brutal iron girdle. The young resident to whom I sheepishly report this development—the only doctor I can trust not to tattle—pokes me gently and pronounces some internal hemorrhaging around the kidneys brought on by my overexertion. Quite painful but probably not dangerous: hot wet heat should help.

I take his advice when I get home and lock myself into the bathroom for hours at a time, lying in my old tub filled to the brim with steaming water. It is only here in my own house, in my own bathroom, in my own tub, that I begin to do something I have not yet been able to do: vocalize my suffering. The sounds come of their own accord—as natural as breathing and somehow easier, soft moans bank and glide, bouncing off the white tile of the bathroom walls. It seems the only way to cope.

Because of this injury, and because of the nasty pull in the chest, I cannot sit for long. Pictures from that time show me balanced in a sofa corner, propped on all sides by pillows, the gay red robe buttoned discreetly to the neck, the family ranged around me. My hair, just beginning to fall out from the first course of chemotherapy (in the morning it is on my pillow like fine long grass; each pass of the brush through it brings out nightmarish handfuls), is pulled back and caught with a clip, emphasizing the fact that my part is strangely broad. I have lost more weight than I had realized: my face looks like a grinning death's-head perched precariously on a thin, reedy neck-stalk. My cheeks are hollow, and while the mouth smiles—with thin lips drawn back in a grimace from teeth now definitely too large (almost predatory)—the eyes look wounded, hungry, desperate.

I hold court on that sofa. I hold court in our bedroom—forced to retreat there when sitting becomes too much of an effort—where every available surface is occupied by my family and Michael's. We talk, we babble, we thrust and parry; fast emotional footwork is everything. My brother announces that cancer is nothing compared to what he has gone through in Vietnam: my two sisters reassure me that he is just looking for attention. We three sisters—in shifting dyads—talk about our differences with the third, then talk all together about the strangeness of seeing our parents together. My father is articulate, spoiled, exotic. My mother is shadowy and stolid. My family pulls together against Michael's: his brother can be difficult, his parents judgmental. Michael's family—in turn—thinks mine bizarre. His mother clucks over evidence of lack of organization, lack of precision and etiquette and cleanliness, lack of character and good citizenship. Michael's father and Michael's brother and Michael watch sports on TV.

Christmas Day is lovely and wretched. I feel comforted by the presence of these people who love me and have extended themselves; I feel defensive about not being stronger, less disturbing to them ("Would you get me some milk?" I ask Michael one morning as we sit at the kitchen table. "Oh, no," says my mother, intervening. "Don't you move, Michael. She doesn't need to be waited on all the time, let her get it herself. It's good for her."), defensive about my love for each member of my family in the face of acrimony from some other member, defensive about the disorder of my house (I can find nothing—everything has been rearranged) and the disorder of my mind. I feel really at home in two ways only: lying in bed with Michael (but oh! how I want him to gather me to him, to make obliterative love to me and blot out my pain and fear and loneliness) or sitting with the children, the poor puzzled children who have had so many mothers that I am just one more in-distinguishable substitute for someone they have lost long ago.

My one moment of total abandonment to a present uncouched in reserve and ambiguity is lunatic, when I ride the motorized race car the children have been given by my three siblings, careering maniacally around the corners of our large apartment, revving up on the straightaways, hooting warnings as I plow undignifiedly into and through knots of surprised people.

My family gives me a joint present. I have been sit-ting quietly on the sidelines Christmas morning, watch-ing the mad exchange and feeling slighted—it seems they have forgotten me—until there is only one large box left, plastered with a crazy quilt of wrapping paper. (I have thought it was some special gift for the chil-dren; everybody knows that good *grown-up* presents come in the *little* boxes.) They tease me: "Who do you think that's for?" but it doesn't work because I am too dense this morning and I just look blank.

"You!" shout my sisters. "Open it! It's for *you*, from all of us!"

It is a color TV, something I have wanted for a long time but we couldn't afford. It is a perfect present which presumes nothing. I also register that it is some-thing that can be enjoyed without me as well as with me.

The tension-shot, delirious Christmas fades like spec-tacular fireworks in the night sky; I dread and crave the return to Quimby two days after. Back there, I feel sur-prisingly, thoroughly relieved that I have checked out of real life and back into the truncated simplistic world of the sick and dying.

# JANUARY 1972

———◆———

Submitted once more to Quimby, I work on my New Year's resolutions, goaded to exceed even my usual enthusiasm for such fresh starts by the cancer patient's litany, the lilting incantation: Dear, *dear* God, if I ever get out of here . . . dear God, if I live to get out of here . . . I will be good, I will be better, I will be what I was meant to be and failed at: wife, mother, human being. Save me God. Forgive me.

Not that I am praying. This is purely a business deal with the Hard-liner, negotiated over a bargaining table of white sheets, the blue-and-white-striped hospital-issue seersucker robe, the sheepskin slid under my body to help prevent bedsores. I no longer know how to pray, having lost the ability somewhere along the line as I have lost the ability to believe in Santa Claus and the Tooth Fairy—all such fantasies and hopes of supernatural beings having been unceremoniously swept away in a storm of pretentious sophistication and too much analytical education. I wish I had my innocence back, my simple refulgent beliefs, my faith that Someone cares, that Someone watches and listens, that I am special and worth . . . saving. I wish to be more than a sick person who might die and then be put in the ground and left to decay and oblivion.

I want faith; I crave faith. (It is what patients here and their families retreat into, pulling the luxury of skepticism in after them.) I burn with envy for the Catholics fumbling with their rosaries; the twice-born; the Jews swaying and chanting, beating their heads

263

against their holy books and holy walls—everybody who knows and feels and *believes* in the presence and mercy of a God.

I myself do not believe in mercy, only in justice.

A tall, cadaverous minister wanders into my bright room, plucking at his black coat and tight collar in some fervid religious tic, pushing gloom and doom like a vendor.

"Episcopalian, aren't you?" The inquiry sounds like the pronouncement of a sentence.

Now how did they find that out? Perhaps a kindness pressed on me through Michael by an administrator, wanting to know whether I should have holy water thrown on me, a cloth tied around my head, or coins put on my eyes and in my mouth if I should die.

"Lapsed," I say shortly. I can tell by the expression on his face what he is thinking: that in this hospital nobody is lapsed, that we all become believers. How I wish. If I could buy faith I would take the jumbo size.

He wants to counsel me, to save me, to gather me to the bosom of Abraham and Jesus and the rest of that opal-winged cohort. We have a short and desultory theological debate.

"Try to pray," he hopefully intones. "We'll pray together."

"I don't pray," I say boldly, coldly. It would be hypocritical—especially now—to ball up my fears and regrets and hurl them in supplication at the Divine Vacuum. Negotiation was what was required at any rate: even when I was little, I made a point of avoiding the initiation of an outright request of God for some favor or special consideration, without making a mutually subscribed deal of it. All prayer, all communication, was in the service of penance, in service of mitigating my shortcomings and failures of character. (Me, kneeling very straight in the pew—not leaning back to show my resolution and earnestness—making offers: Dear God [a simple habit af address], if you let me find that watch I carelessly lost, I will keep my room clean

for a month; Dear God, don't let Mommy see the lipstick I got on her hat when I was playing dress-up, and
I will be *very* nice to my brother and sisters and give
them one soft drink each from *my* case.) I had always
seen the magnificence of the Deity in this way, in
vaguely economic, cost-accounting terms. Praying, asking for something, was—disconnected from the exi-
gency of complementary promises—like accepting a gift
from a relative you hated and feared.

This reflexive perception of a wrathful and judgmental God who has nothing better to do than track down
and punish the sins of naughty little girls (and naughty
big girls) unquestionably contributed to the freighted
and magical interpretations I could not avoid making of
what was happening to me. (It was too bad, for my
sake, that the impoverished "sophistication" of my intellectual approach to religion left untouched its roots
of aboriginal superstition and atavistic fear.) People don't
get cancer by accident; my torments were not arbitrary.
God does not play dice, and the implicit ordering of the
universe implied my sins and their price.

It was why I could not fight although I could endure.
I could not "fight" cancer any more than I could
"fight" God: one doesn't fight what must be borne in
dignity and suffered in silence. One endures the pain
and the punishment and perhaps in the end one survives. The reward—aside from one's life—would be an
earned dignity one had never before deserved, a dignity
won from the exercise of bowing the head—exposing
the tender neck to destiny and redress—and still being
able to raise it high when the torments had finally
ceased. Endurance, dignity, humility.

Survival.

The chaplain takes my two hands and patty-cakes
them in a simulacrum of a prayerful posture, bowing
his head and closing his eyes in preparation for the delivery of a message to the Deity on my behalf. I shake
him off.

"I have my own way of praying," I say, and then to

stem his wounded look I snatch at some platitude I had
had shoveled at *me* and, hoping I am speaking his language, offer as a close to our debate: "There are many
paths up the mountain."

"So they say," he rejoins sadly as he turns from me.
"But there is only one that is direct. It is easy to perish by
the long route."


That is specifically what I fear, the perishing. It is
this simple: I am afraid to die (though I'm not nearly
so afraid of death itself, believing, as I do, that it is
nothing but an inchoate straining of fate toward balance). Somehow I have found out that the first course
of chemotherapy has had little effect on the cancer, that
it was done mostly as a trial to gauge my tolerance and
response; I am consequently less optimistic in general
than I was before Christmas. Nobody will discuss results with me, talk to me about my chances—whether
the numbers have gotten better or worse. ("Numbers
mean nothing," they all say. "You just work at getting
well.") I realize now that the pre-Christmas depression
was more complicated than I had thought: it was at
least in part due to my rearranged perceptions of what
this cure might mean. After all this time—after more
than a year of this sickness—I am terribly weary.

It is something else to be afraid of—my own weariness, and the accompanying temptation to give in to the
disease . . . to refuse to endure.


The first day back here I struggled over to the window of my lovely room—kept empty for my readmission during the five days I was home—and, leaning on
the radiator, I contemplated the ten-story drop. How
many patients simply opened the window and let themselves out? Let themselves float down to the busy Man-
hattan cross street like a dried and empty husk that is
taken by the wind, falling not in a straight line but riding the air in dips and darts, all the way to the pavement below? How many of us wore thin, wore out,

couldn't see beyond the next course of chemotherapy, and grew to be as frightened of the cure as of the cancer? You could go through this and die anyway. You could endure the pain and the nausea and the crumbling of the self and still wind up on a slab in the basement.

There were so many deaths, big ones and little ones, long ones and slow ones. There was death by the steady munching of the voracious cancer cells as they gobbled healthy cells, finally consuming the body itself; death by drugs, death by vitriol and corrosion, the hunks of meat melting to flakes left clinging to the bone like leaves to an autumn tree; death by defeat and death by exhaustion. Death scrabbled at the windows and gnawed at the gut; it snuffled and lurched in the halls, lurking in the corners with the last bits of grimy night each morning.

I knew how cancer patients died—how languorously, how vividly, how agonizingly—aware all the time they were going, powerless to stop their loosening from life—tortured by regrets, wracked by fear, raging at God—and clinging to the people who loved them, wanting not to be surrendered to the enveloping dark, wanting to be nailed to their lives until at last the disease tore them away.

It is easy to forget that cancer is not so much death as life gone monstrous and out of control.

So it is at least partly a matter of will. I can feel the potential of death on me the way I can smell my own breath, like smothering thick fingers probing for ingress. One has to stay alert to it, to its danger and seduction. Fading into inattentiveness augurs a forfeit.

I have had the feeling before, when a kind of whiff of the magnificent and final wound by me at unexpected moments . . . standing in the subway station waiting for a train, for instance. My muscles would tense as the train roared into the station, and it was for a split second so thrilling, so compelling, to entertain the possibility of standing on the edge of the platform as if poised at the end of a diving board, and simply tip over into the train's path, trip onto the tracks: an ordinary movement, nothing that required special strength or ingenuity or equipment. The humblest shuffle, the babiest step, a moment's loss of precious balance, could accomplish the same astonishing end: all one had to do was to will it, to take that little bit of control (or choose to lose it). To shift, to lean, to relax into oblivion.

And it is back, the feeling. Only now it is more like hanging over the edge of a cliff (having already slipped and caught oneself), clinging by just the fingertips to a brittle ledge and having people yell, "Hang on, we're coming, don't give up, just hang on," and not knowing whether I can or not, whether I am strong enough or not, whether it is even worth it or not, and knowing how it would be the simplest of things, the smallest of gestures, the most impulsive of surrenders, merely to open the hand, uncurl the straining fingers, and let one's body sail into the void, tumbling over and over through the clouds.

My dreams are filled these nights and days with falling, with jumping from gigantic swings, with the crashing of planes which nose up into the azure air and then arc back to earth in a flaming parabola of death.

"Die? Of *course* you won't die," objects anybody I venture to express my fears to. "Don't talk about it, for heaven's sake. You're really being too silly. You have to keep the right *attitude*."

But of course I *might* die. I could die. I shape the shapeless words in my head and my mouth over and over, molding and remolding them the way a child worries clay. I have to think about this. I might be entering the most significant phase of my life and I have to be prepared. I have to die again and again in my imagination to prepare myself for such a possibility in reality.

I don't like to be taken by surprise, with my dignity down.

\* \* \*

"I need some help," I say to Dr. J. "Can you send someone for me to talk to? Are there people like that here, to talk to the patients?"

"There are the private psychiatrists," he says.

"Are they free? Or is there some special rate for patients?"

"They charge their usual fee," he says. "Fifty or sixty dollars an hour. . . ."

"But we can't afford that! Isn't there any provision for helping patients to cope with their illnesses?" I've *got* to talk to *someone*.

He looks at me as if nobody has ever asked for help before; maybe it is just that nobody has ever dared ask *him*. "If you feel you can't pay for a psychiatrist, I don't know what to suggest. . . ."

But one of the nurses knows. "Social Services," she says. "They will send you a social worker."

And they do: my own social worker for half an hour every other day or so. She is a young woman close to me in age and experience who is willing to listen actively and sympathetically to my fears and complaints as well as to encourage me to do some exploration of issues that reach far beyond the confines of the hospital walls and these last months.

It is in talking to Marilyn that I begin to figure out I am at least as afraid of life as death.

It is evening. Len comes in. He has appeared periodically since I have been in Quimby—ostensibly to check up on "his" patient—usually timing his visits to hours when visitors are forbidden. (After all, he is a doctor, with privileged run even of a hospital not his own.) This used to seem fun and daring, smacking of special dispensations. Lately it has seemed faintly invasive.

He is always solicitous: "How's it going tonight? Feeling any better?" I have not yet started the second course of chemotherapy so I feel better now than I suspect I will be feeling in a couple of days. He stands next to the bed, his black raincoat with the pile lining turned over his arm like a waiter's towel.

Ordinarily I welcome seeing him. He is diverting, a consistently interesting person to talk to, but tonight there is something in his manner that makes me feel uncomfortable and makes me wish I could stand up straight and face him. He is altogether too close to the bed, and the bedside lamp makes the front of his wool pants—at my eye level—shine faintly, as if there were iridescent fibers woven through the fabric. His presence is insistent and vaguely oppressive.

He touches my throat with his forefinger while he talks to me, running it up and down, occasionally tipping my chin up toward him. His hand drifts down my arm to my wrist, which he picks up—the hand depending like a wilted flower—and lays my limp palm against the warm serge at his groin. His belt buckle glints meanly like a steel eye.

"I've missed you," he says, covering my hand with his and pressing it. (Me? What could he possibly have missed that he can't get more efficiently from another woman?) I pull my hand away. He seems to interpret this as some kind of invitation—a tease perhaps—and immediately unzips his fly, digging into the front of his pants for his cock. I am not afraid of him but I *am* terrified that someone will come into the room—come onto this ludicrous scene. (They won't, of course: the nurses and aides know he is a doctor and they won't come unbidden into a room when a doctor is around.)

"I've missed you a lot," he says again, leaning slightly toward me. His black raincoat blocks my view of the door. I can feel the heat of the lamp on my thinning hair.

"Hey. How about it?" He strokes himself. I am incredulous; how could this be happening right here in Quimby Hospital? His cock is two inches from my face, one inch, trembling like the ruddy bald head of an old man.

Probably before then, but certainly ever since then, I have loathed the gesture common to some men: the presentation and flourishing of the penis—the waving of this flag of manhood—and the assumption that a woman seeks this mode of intimacy for its own sake, that she will *be* satisfied because she *has* satisfied.

Women do not feel about men's cocks as men seem to feel about women's cunts.

It strikes me soon after: I will not die because I am too angry—too angry at my own persistent acquiescence, at my fears of rejection and exposure, at my welcoming of the role of victim. Victims invite oppression; they create it. And then they embrace it because without it they lose their definition and cannot recognize themselves.

Choose: the lady or the tiger. Which do you want to be? I say to myself.

I will hang on.

The chemotherapy is begun again: five days—a week—of nausea, which takes me like a flash flood, strewing me around with its force. It is, as they have warned, worse. My stomach is always empty; I don't eat so there is nothing to throw up, but I squeeze thimblefuls of bile into a little tin pan, retching horribly. My nose bleeds, my lips tear, I get a painful vaginal infection. (The drugs attack all mucous membrane.) There is nothing to be done except to wait out the reactions, but some small relief is offered in the substance of Gentian Violet—an inky, indelible tincture that a nurse paints on the inside of my mouth, around my teeth, on my gums and lips, and a resident paints on all my private parts. It stains, it smears, I look as if I have eaten my way through an acre of blueberries and then sat in it for good measure.

Now every morning when I awaken my pillow is covered with hair fall; the long fine brown strands tangle around me like the silk of a spider web . . . in everything, stuck to everything, inhaled, itchy. (Much later I notice what is not so noticeable as it happens: the thinning of the eyebrows, the lashless lids, the shedding of the pubic hair.)

I have my hair cut, thinking that if it is short it will look less sparse, and a hairdresser that my best friend Barbara has commandeered comes to the hospital and gives me what I can only think of as a militant shag cut—a style I would have never chosen for myself, but one that disguises fairly effectively my present amount of hair loss. When he is ready to leave, the hairdresser refuses his fee, waving away the bills Michael has provided me with. "My mother died here," he says by way of explanation. "I didn't think I would ever have a reason to come back. I hate this place."

A Sunday afternoon, after the worst of the reaction is over. Michael brings the children, sneaking them in with the complicity of the nurses when the disapproving doctors are least likely to be around—strictly against the very strict rules. I have tried not to think of the children—it is too painful—and I must actively guard myself against visual memory of their little faces, shining against the walls and on the ceiling and even on the inside of my eyelids like the afterimage of flashbulbs.

I don't like it when people ask me how they are, I don't like being reminded and then having to talk about them as if they were still my children. Each reminder is a needle under the fingernail, a dance on the nettles.

I arrange myself carefully in an armchair, my thin tufts of hair fringing my thin rouged face, and hold out my arms in welcome as Alexandra toddles in and Zachary, now nineteen months old and recently walking, hides behind Michael. I finally coax Alexandra to sit on my lap, which she does stiffly, unyieldingly, watching for her opportunity to escape. Maybe I am not her mother. I can see it in her eyes.

There is no maybe for Zachary: at Christmas I was just one more vaguely familiar face and now he will not come near me. One of the nurses—on lookout in the hall—brings ice cream, but he will not take it from me, though I coax and gesture, twisting my burning mouth into a smile. "Num, num," I manage to say. But he is suspicious, looking from me to the proffered treat to Michael's face. Someone is playing a trick on him. Finally Michael takes the cup and spoon from me and Zachary's face lights up as if the sun has hit it. Michael feeds him steadily as he giggles and bubbles and coos. Alexandra, who has slipped from my lap, sits on my bed, seemingly absorbed with its magical features—its bending and extending, its humming and kneeling—which she is able to control with the handset she holds.

When Michael leaves to take the children home, I feel lonelier than ever. Maybe something irreparable has been shattered in my relationship with the children. Perhaps they will never forgive me for leaving them to a series of surrogate mothers.

Every term by which I define myself is garbled.

Thank heavens for Michael. What ever would I do without him? He is here always—every day, twice a day sometimes—sitting quietly, waiting and watching. I feel as if he is keeping me alive, as if he is that person reaching down from the precipice to rescue me. He is so kind, so good, so attentive; I cannot remember why it was that I was so unhappy before I got sick. Maybe our differences were just some kind of elaborate misunderstanding; maybe he was right about me. If I were out of here, out of this, I would surely be so happy, so grateful to be home with my husband and children.

My marriage has never been better; my life has never been worse.


One afternoon I meet Jack Gates, who pokes his head into my room just as I am feeling particularly sorry for myself.

"Do you draw?" he inquires briskly. "You look like the kind of girl who can draw." Jack Gates is about seventy—maybe over—tall and distinguished-looking, well-dressed, with the birdy look of someone who observes carefully and misses nothing. I wonder what he is doing in here with the brigade of blue-haired volunteer ladies. (The answer, I find out later, is that he is a retired architect who gives drawing classes to those he can convince to come and attempt to reproduce a still life he has arranged at one end of a long cafeteria-type table. The presumptive artists draw maddeningly slowly and obsessively, wanting each detail to be exactly right, guarding their work like children taking exams that they are afraid will be copied. Even this small effort takes on undue significance here.)

Jack takes a few steps into my room but stops as I roll on my side so that I can sit up. (I still do not like to meet anybody lying down.) Then something shadows his eyes; he has seen that I am in pain.

"You're not feeling very well today, are you?" My mouth moves to answer him, but it is still sore and stiff, which he also sees. He flaps his hand at me. "Never mind, don't talk. You'll come and draw with us when it's easier for you. In the meantime I'll stop in every day or so just to see if you want to join us, or maybe just to say hello. You're too pretty not to have company."

I'm not pretty at all anymore, I know that, but his is the first silly flattery I've had in a long time. (Mostly I am self-conscious and ashamed around men, turning my head away in the dim light, wanting to hide what I can of myself.) Jack doesn't make me feel that way; he is clearly not embarrassed or put off by disease and mortality. He becomes one of the rare people in front of whom I can really be myself, in front of whom I need no mask.

Jack, like a few other close friends, is an immense comfort. It is important—essential—to know that you are visible, that you matter—it is one of the things that keeps you going. Many illness fears are related to the sick person's human milieu; friends and acquaintances do strange things, show exotic aspects of themselves around illness that betray complicated feelings about themselves even more than they betray feelings about you.

It is embarrassing to show disease and infirmity—embarrassing maybe to be dying—in front of a mere friend. I find I don't trust some people now—don't trust their motives for visiting as I don't trust others' excuses for *not* visiting. In the first group are the ambulance followers, the voyeurs, the casual acquaintances who begin to hang around, turning up again and again like the Old Maid. They don't even know themselves who they are, but I know. I can see it, after they have been to visit a few times. They look at me too carefully, their eyes flickering, their tongues in motion; there is a slowness, a caressing viscidity to their words of concern; they roost on the plastic chairs like vultures, watching. They make me shudder and flinch.

In the second group are friends one might reasonably expect to see. They call periodically, promising to visit. But they never do. It is just as well. I try not to feel already buried.

It is not easy for me to be good visitee; it takes a great deal of effort to concentrate on a conversation, and the relentless, implacable cheer visitors bring in with them, as they bring in the brisk winter smell of New York, is a kind of reproach for my self-absorption, for my anxiety about being so offensively sick. I feel not very interesting, not very worthwhile, and it is daunting to seem to be expected to make the visit an event, so that the visitor feels suitably rewarded for having made it. There is the constant tension between my impulse to self-effacement and my need to *connect* and feel alive and reassured and protected and important, to have *mattered* in some small way, to know that if the waters close over me I will have left a ripple on the surface of their lives. And at the same time that I want sympathy and support, I am aware of the threat of its deterioration; I do not want to embarass those who are already embarrassed into saying things they don't mean.

Friends whom I trust are another matter. Without

them and without my family and Michael's it would be
so easy to slip away, to leave it solely to the doctors and
their battery of miracles to keep me alive. My friends
sustain me, each in a singular and loving way; my sister
comes down from Boston almost every weekend to be
near. There are times when I can't be amusing or even
amused, times when I am too sick to do anything but lie
here with my eyes closed, and still they come to sit
wordlessly by the bed and hold my hand, keeping me
company through the long hours.

Because we go through this together, I learn as much
about myself as I do about them. I learn something
about the more positive aspects of dependence, learn
that allowing somebody else to assume the major responsibility of caring and loving is not the same as taking without giving anything back. My friends need to be
supportive as I need to be sick, and when I stop inter-
preting our intercourse in a manner consistent with an
ordinary-use model, I have stunningly powerful experi-
ences of intimacy and sharing. My real friends ask
nothing but that they be allowed to care for me, and I
am astonished at how simple and unriven feelings can
be when they are not obscured by conflict and power
and envy and jealousy and unreasonable expectations.

It makes me long for a life of emotions I can understand, the simplicity of linear love.


The third week of January they send me home. I
dress slowly (but all by myself) in a pair of pink pants
and a sweater—navy, with a wide pink band that encir-
cles the chest on which little red hearts are scattered
(an irony that escapes me until later)—bought in the
fall. That fit in the fall. Now the pants bag and gape at
the waist so that I must pin them and then pull the
sweater low to hide the improvisation and remaining
slack.

It is this coy sweater that my favorite resident—a
cardiologist—raises to give me a final going-over before discharge. I lie on the bed, feeling odd and light-

headed as he bends over me and lifts the heart-shot sweater to expose my white chest—neatly bisected by the horrible purple ribbon of the surgical scar—where the breasts hang flatly sideways like fleshy gills, to listen to the heart beating.

"Breathe," he says, and then, "Cough." It is somehow an intimate moment fraught with a chaos of need and desire. I want him to rub his beard into the hollow of my shoulder, the curve of my neck. I want him to see me not as I am, but as I might be.

"I don't want to come back," I say, apropos of nothing—and a necessary sidestepping of what I am really thinking—"but I sure would miss seeing you." He takes his stethoscope out of his ears and very very gently pulls down my sweater. He looks at me levelly for so long it is finally I who am forced to break eye contact, reaching out my hand to him for a boost up from the bed.

"My rotation here is almost over," he says noncommitally, still touching me, "but I will miss you too."

# JANUARY–FEBRUARY 1972

SOMEHOW, IRRATIONALLY, ONE EXPECTS THAT THE world stops when one is not a participant in its events, a player of its games. One assumes—on some visceral level—that nothing changes even though one knows perfectly well that everything changes. In truth, it may be more accurate to say that one changes oneself in surprising and subtle ways simply because one is no longer anchored by familiarity and it is this, then, that makes the world—on reentry—seem so strange and alien.

I am home and I want to be home and I like being home. But I feel like an interloper, a visitor, in need of special favors and special consideration. My mother has retreated to the Midwest for a well-deserved rest—having been here since November—and I feel both abandoned and unburdened of a nagging debt of gratitude I shall never be able to repay. I am not alone in the house, however. Before Christmas the committee of family that ran my home in my absence hired an expensive—but competent and personable—young Brazilian woman who has been mother to the children and maid to Michael and the house; now that I am back she is deferential and solicitous, tiptoeing around me as if I might disintegrate at any sudden noise or movement. Between us we manage the cooking and shopping and the laundry. I leave the rest of the household duties to her so I can concentrate on the children, reinserting myself back into their lives as I might cautiously introduce a baby-sitter whom I must leave them with and

want them to like. We seem to—for this reason—watch
an inordinate amount of television together, which al-
lows us close contact without forcing us at each other.
Many hours I sit in the middle of the big blue sofa
watching Oscar the Grouch slam the top of his garbage
can, watching Mr. Rogers conduct daily tours of the
Land of Make-Believe. I am so happy just feeling the
squirmy warmth of the little bodies that lean into mine.

At night Michael too leans into me, but cautiously,
fearful of pressing or poking or jarring some injured
part. He rubs my back endlessly, tirelessly; it seems to
ache all the time now, since the kidney episode at
Christmas. Lying there in the dark with my back to
him, his hands moving over me, I tremble ("Did I hurt
you?" he asks anxiously) and sometimes cry (which he
does not notice, which I do not let him notice). The
fact is that I like to have my back rubbed, but what I
really wish is that he would make love to me—parting my
legs with fingers as tender as those that knead my back,
making the sad flaps of my breasts swell with my response to his desire for me and my body heave with
shared pleasure. (So long! It's been so long! Thinking
once crazily, inconsistently, that Michael would want it
too, I went so far as to ask Dr. J. whether the exercise
of conjugal rights was permitted—behind closed doors,
of course—in the hospital. I was so desperate for Michael to shed his diffidence and cool propriety, to shed
his clothes and push aside the metal and plastic that
surrounded the bed and to climb in with me, *Love
Story* style, pulling the covers over both our heads so
that only a shimmer of watery light could penetrate the
tent of sheets under which we hid and rolled and made
love. It was the only time I ever heard Dr. J. laugh out
loud.)

But I understand. I know Michael is afraid of my
frailness: he can't lie on me and all those fragile
cracked bones in my chest, all those knobs and points
the skin is stretched over like a fine drumhead. As for
me, I haven't the strength to straddle him. And then of
course there is the way I look. I have eyes.

I am some sight. My hair has been cut again, to a practical, heartbreakingly uniform two inches all over my head—it was going so fast it seemed useless to be anything but practical—and it is scraggly, spiky, with gleaming patches of white scalp as if the moths have been at me. Moth-eaten, that's how I look. Or maybe just plain *eaten:* I am gray, emaciated, hairless; I have livid ridges of scars, boils from the chemicals—ugly pus-y clods that spatter my body—black discs of necrotic skin that betray pressure points—elbows, knees, knuckles, each sharp flange of my backbone. I swathe my body in flannel to pretect both of us from the sight of it, but I understand Michael's position. It's not as if it were just as simple as closing your eyes and trying not to think about it.

Michael has been through almost as much as I have, and there is a limit to what one can expect.

I keep busy, what with the usual housewifely duties and the strain of my limitations. My very first project is to get myself a wig and get used to wearing it. I settle on a cheap, demented-looking Dynel business—an explosion of short brown filaments with deep bangs to hide behind (I have never worn bangs)—and feel quite comfortable . . . mostly because it is *so* unlike me that there can be no pretensions to camouflage: it is an outright disguise that announces its fakeness with its plastic sheen and its improbable bounciness. (It also complements thoroughly my current sense of myself as imposter.) I am careful to wear the wig in front of the children; I don't want to frighten them. Things like this are very hard; I want to be direct with the children, I don't believe in lies, they know I am very sick, but what is fair, what is right? Should I even be here, sitting with them while they screech with laughter at the antics of Big Bird? They were accustomed to being without me. What will happen when I go back to Quimby, as indeed I am sure I must? . . . and then what if I never come back again?

Is it the ultimate act of selfishness to love them and

need to be close to them as I do? To impose on them my mother love when they have learned to do without it?

It's not as if one can really get away from Quimby; one graduates from inpatient to outpatient. Once or twice a week I make my way over there either to see Dr. J. or to drop off twenty-four-hour samples of urine—which will be analyzed to determine the extent of the diminution of the activity of the malignancy. As the days go by, then a few weeks, I allow myself specks of optimism—maybe, maybe, there has been some extraordinary progress, maybe I *have* been cured with just two courses; I am strong, resilient, it is possible—although they tell me nothing. (The only information I manage to get from anywhere is embezzled from Dr. A., a tall, black, courtly staff physician on the gynecological service who covers for Dr. J. Dr. A. is at least accessible, and while he doesn't exactly encourage questions, he fields them graciously and thoughtfully, answering them as completely as he can. But I see him only when I am an inpatient.)

As time passes I allow myself to pretend that what has happened is all in the past, that there will be no more pain and humiliation and sickness, that the cosmos has reestablished its homeostasis in my immediate vicinity. But the impulse to pretend conflicts with the subliminal attention to reality—reality is an old habit—with the result that I have a bad case of nerves. I feel attenuated, jumpy, fatalistic. Every time the phone rings, my heart stops, I hold my breath, until I can be sure that it is not Dr. J.'s nurse saying "We have scheduled you for readmission. Please be here tomorrow at one."

So when the phone call comes—after I have been home three weeks—there is a palpable sense of release, an existential clatter made by the other shoe.

Someone else is now in my corner room; I am assigned this time to a small cell where the walls press in on me and the ceiling is flaking. This time chemo-therapy is begun right away: they have given me enough time at home to recover so that they can make me sick again.

This third course is exponentially worse than the last, as the last was worse than the first. It is so bad I can't sleep, I can't read. I can't watch TV. I can't even think. Horrid nausea simmers in my gut and the slightest mo-tion—the slightest failure of vigilance—brings on un-controllable retching. In one twenty-four-hour period I throw up twenty-three times, keeping count out of per-versity and boredom. I bar all visitors; I don't want any-body to see me like this, and until the worst of it is past, nobody may come but Michael and Barbara. I will not even answer the phone: listening gives me vertigo; talk-ing feels like a stick down the throat. All anyone can do for me right now is to steady me while I sputter and gag—or hold me from behind, as Michael does, drag-ging me upright and pressing his fists into my dia-phragm—and then empty the little basin. ("I'm sorry, I'm sorry," I say over and over again to Michael, not even sure just what it is that I am apologizing for, but all the same feeling waves of remorse and shame.) So much puking for a spoonful of thin yellowish bile!

Severe nausea is overwhelming and ghastly, a totally engaging experience . . . in a way like the cancer it-self—invading, expanding. Nausea is of a different or-der than pain because pain can be located, pain has a *place*. Desperate nausea has no place; it has every place. It is in you, through you, soaking consciousness right to the brain stem, right back to the reptilian re-flexes; it makes you feel as if you have dissolved, en-tropy has taken over, you have no boundaries. The room swims, the bed rocks, there is an endless whirl-pool of convulsive discomposure. It sucks out your brains and your eyes and your organs, leaving a hollow, resounding shell in which a hot wind bangs and blows. At least with pain there is an "it-ness," an otherness: "it" hurts—a part signaling the whole of its injury—and one can say, "There. There is where 'it' hurts."

But nausea is different. It becomes a travesty of the self because it invades so totally, and part of its special terror is this possession of the body and fogging of the mind, as in a severe psychosis. Wresting one's body from the grip of this singular insanity and one's focus from the panic-stricken fascination with the vortex, with the hypnotic heaving and yawing, is a formidable enterprise: it snatches back.

I pray for wholeness. I pray for the distance of pain.

The fourth night I feel so filthy sick I give up on stoicism and call for the resident to give me something, anything. My abdominal muscles are unbearably tight from vomiting and will not uncramp enough even to allow me to lie flat on my back or stomach. I don't think I can take this any longer.

The resident is unlocatable for what seems like hours; I sit in an armchair, folded in half over a pillow, my head between my knees (for some reason this alleviates the dizziness and spinning), waiting because there is nothing else to be done. He finally appears, sullen and contentious. It is nearly midnight.

"Couldn't you give me something?" I plead. "Something to help with the nausea?"

"Nope," he says. "Nothing I can do for you." Over his shoulder he says to the floor nurse, "Is *this* what you called me for? *This* is no emergency." His eyes narrow as he looks at me appraisingly. "You'll live," he says.

I can't be sure of that, or I wouldn't have called him. I suspect he has never been desperately seasick, or he wouldn't be so flip. It makes me think of the old joke about seasickness: first you're afraid you'll die, then you're afraid you won't. I look up at him in anguish, my vision jumping like a film with torn sprockets.

"Look," I say, hoping to appeal to his compassion—a commodity I have learned is in short supply in the medical profession. "I have been vomiting for four straight days. I can't sleep. I can't think. I feel very . . . *sick*. And I can't believe that in this whole big famous hospital you have *nothing* to relieve nausea. I just can't believe it."

He slumps into the other chair and shakes his head. "Really. I'm telling you. You've been getting the Compazine. If it doesn't help you're just out of luck. There's nothing else to give you, no way to treat this kind of drug reaction. You just have to ride it out. Anyway, we have to be very *careful* what we give you. You're very . . . vulnerable . . . right now. You'll be over this in a few more days."

"Please." I start to cry, though I intended not to, I would not stoop to it, but sickness keeps crying very close to the surface. The crying stirs my stomach once more and I grab for the little steel basin. He waits until I am through, then silently takes the pan from me and empties it into the toilet. Flopping into the chair again, he shakes his head. "I don't know. I don't know what to tell you."

I still don't believe him. If they think they can cure cancer, they *must* have developed something to cure the cure. I cry noisily because I am trying to stop (stifling sobs seems to make them louder) and it's very late and I am thinking he has no pity or no imagination or both. He sits unmoving, adamantine, watching me for what must be a long time. I rock; he sits. It must be a good sign that he hasn't walked out. Doctors are quite capable of simply walking out.

"Maybe," I venture, "if there is nothing for the nausea, at least you could give me something to make me *sleep,* so I could sleep through it, get some rest, some relief. I really *can't* take it anymore," I add quietly, lamely.

The resident seems to be thinking. His face is dark and he has made a tent of his fingers, which he beats against his pursed lips. "If I give you anything like that," he says, "I have to get permission. We can't just go giving that stuff out indiscriminately."

We are getting somewhere. "You could ask," I prompt. "You could ask whoever it is. . . . If I could just sleep . . ."

It is another half hour before the order comes through. As the grandmotherly head nurse stabs me with the needle she says in a thick brogue, "Now, thank the Lord, you will get some sleep, poor thing."

And I do.

The next day I tell Michael what has happened, galvanizing him into action: anger arouses him. He marches off to Dr. J.'s office to challenge him, sure now—as I have been—that drugs are being pointedly, calculatedly, withheld.

Dr. J. admits it to Michael: we are right. He also does not intend, he says in defense of his judgment, to *start* administering nausea-reducing or sleep-inducing substances (read "narcotics") citing the "regrettable tendency of women to become addicted." He will not be told his business, he knows how women are, and he is unwilling to take any chances with me. No drugs. I will survive.

In defense against what I cannot control I begin to cultivate an interesting state of semiconsciousness: it is almost as good as drugs. From what I read later, I decide it is a conditioned retreat into alpha, a state of "waking sleep" in which one is minimally attentive to environmental distraction and which shares many features with deep meditation. I am there and yet not there, available at the same time I have checked out. Time stands still in this fog, and yet the stretch from moment of arousal to moment of arousal is unpredictably elastic.

My mind is like Yeats's long-legged fly on the stream, moving on silence. Prancing in the void.

* * *

Blood transfusions. They are giving me blood transfusions. Perhaps they have miscalculated and killed me more than they intended; it feels that way.

I try not to take it as a bad omen.

When you are sick, everything becomes an omen—sometimes good but mostly bad. One looks for clues to one's fate in the simplest things; every happening, usual and unusual, is freighted with enchantment, portent. One keeps score involuntarily: I will live, I will die, I will live, I will die. . . .

My friend Joan—the friend with the snake-man book, who lives in my apartment building—comes to visit. I am in the mouth-burn phase and conduct my end of conversations with a pad of paper and a pencil. (I have tried a Magic Slate, but the first words seem to dissolve before I get to the last ones.) We have a short visit—even writing is an effort—and then she asks suddenly, just before she leaves, "Did you hear about Sharon Carroll?"

No, I shake my head, and then write, in big letters, turning the pad to Joan who is standing at the foot of my bed, "What?" Sharon Carroll lives on the other side of our building—on Joan's side. She is a few years older than we are and has two attractive, quiet children. I last saw Sharon in the lobby when I was home, and she seemed oddly shrunken and bloated. Her face was swollen, with the skin stretched so tight it was shiny, and her eyes glistened as if she had a fever. After all this time at Quimby I should have recognized the signs.

"She died," says Joan shortly.

I am horrified. My hands shakes as I scrawl an "Of" over the "What?" and aim the pad back at Joan.

She shifts her weight from one foot to the other, crosses her arms over her own generous bosom, looks down at the chrome footboard. "Breast cancer. She didn't tell anyone. There was apparently nothing they could do. Somebody told me that near the end she just lay in her bedroom with the door locked and cried and cried." She pauses, looking uncomfortable. "Everybody said not to tell you, but I thought you would want to know."

Of course I wanted to know; I wish I had known before so I could have said something when we met in the lobby, not that it mattered now—or even then. But she must have known about me!—everybody knew; I could see them stop and look after me when I passed, whisper behind their hands. Why hadn't *she* said something to *me*? Was it so important to her to face her death alone like that?

I feel inexplicably ashamed, as if I should apologize for still being alive, for being so obvious.

It comes at you from all sides, from everywhere at once, like a bad smell. Death.

I can't help thinking about it, in spite of the reassurances, and feeling so sick does not help scrub it out of your thoughts as if you were going after germs. In Quimby morbidity runs like sludge in the corridors, but finally its proximity is less the issue than its ubiquity. We see each other with our wounds and our death masks, our shiny heads and invalided bodies; we see the tubes and the metal and the "empty" stretchers whisked down the hall heralded by a drum roll of closing doors (they know that we know that the stretchers aren't *really* empty but just made to seem so, with their sheets—brushing the floor on both sides—draped casually over them, so that the billowing linen hides from view the body secreted on the shelf underneath); we see the Maltese crosses—slashes of red on white, the blood of the Paschal lamb—on some doors, underscored with the warning: CAUTION: RADIATION. We hear—we cannot shut out—the sounds of machinery, a symphony of modern medical technology: breathing machines, blood-pumping machines, monitoring machines, a throbbing, steady cadence broken periodically by a doctor's scolding or inflated joviality, a singing, tremulous cry of pain or despair, the whisper of wheels, the slamming of doors.

The boy with the bunny-rabbit wife is dead. The woman who also has choriocarcinoma, the one with the tracheotomy who made addled chewing motions and stared at me as if I were as strange to her as she was to me, is also no longer in evidence.

I am feeling so sick, so beaten, it makes me afraid. I bargain with God: how different I will be if I get out of here, through this! (I cannot and will not beg, but bargaining is not so unpalatable.) And then I must inevitably think of the possibility of *not* getting out, *not* getting through this. All the things I will miss—aside, of course, from my sweet children: what if this is it? Right here? What if my last view of the world is the cracked ceiling, the peeling green paint, instead of the sky and the trees and the Hudson in the late-afternoon sun? What if I have long since eaten my last carrot (I love carrots, I love their . . . integrity)? my last heavy, dark, moist chocolate cake? with a glass of sweet cold milk to go with it? What if the last sensations I have from my body are its surrender to disease—the fatigue of decay—rather than the heavenly relief of resting a body tired from honest exertion—from running like the wind, from physical labor, from making love?

And then there is what I haven't even known to miss. Twenty-seven years, and what do I have? What have I done? There are the children: I can grasp that, press it to myself and feel *something*. I have done *something*. But the rest? What—as my mother would say—have I to show for the row I have plowed and sown? A harvest of illusions, a reap of irony. What if I die?

What if I die?

I ask Marilyn, my social worker, what would happen if I got sicker and sicker, so that it was clear I would not get well. I want to be very careful how I phrase my concern.

"In case," I begin delicately, "I were to take a turn

for the worse, in case," I say, "I find out I'm not going to make it, is it possible to . . . get hold of . . . to make arrangements for . . . some . . . something—some pills, perhaps . . . enough pills?" I don't want to disintegrate into a foul, mucilaginous puddle of dying cancer patient; having the disease is bad enough; I choose not to die of it.

Marilyn has been doodling on the edge of a manila folder while I have struggled to be euphemistic. Now she looks up. It is a long moment before she speaks. "Arrangements can be made in . . . such a situation—in special circumstances—if that is what the patient really wants. If *we* can be sure that's what the patient really wants. . . ."

"Can *you* help me make that kind of . . . arrangement? Could you help me that way if I wanted help?" I am *so* relieved.

"There is always somebody to help," she says. "Always somebody."

I don't know whether she was telling me the truth or not, whether such an option was in fact available. But she made me *believe* there was one, and that was all I needed.

Maybe Dr. J. is right. Maybe I do want control. But that feels like a step forward, not a step back.

My hands swell from the IVs, sometimes the whole arm, so that the appendages extending from my own bony shoulders seem no longer to be mine, but grotesque balloon arms—balloon fingers—copped from one of the huge inflated characters that float over the Macy's Thanksgiving Day Parade. It becomes harder and harder for the IV nurses to find a good vein—they collapse, protesting their excessive and unnatural use—so that the lines have to be started again and again: my hands and arms have needle tracks like a junkie's. The IV team is creative, every possible place is used, from the knuckle of the thumb to the inside of the wrist to the elbow; this or that part is taped to a board to immobilize it and keep the little butterfly needle from working its way out—or into the surrounding tissue.

"I *promise* to drink enough," I say to Dr. J. (The intravenous protects me from dehydration, shock. It guarantees a line in case something suddenly and unaccountably goes wrong. And presumably it has something to do with washing the toxins from my body; I feel like a piece of plumbing with the constant flushing.) I will drink a gallon a day if I must, sipping steadily through a straw arranged for minimum contact of the fiery water with my raw, flayed mouth. "Besides," I say, naïvely proffering what seems to me the clincher, "there are no places *left* for any more IVs."

Dr. J. must see an opening for his idea of drollery. "You mean there are no places left that are acceptable to *you*."

My hair is finally gone, leaving only a few senile strands plastered across the crown. ("Skull and bones," Michael says in jest one day.) I feel bereft, mourn it, almost more than I have mourned my lost childbearing capacity. It is a final blow that makes mock of all the blows to my femininity: the void in my belly; the flabby, deflated breasts; the menopausal changes in my body; . . . the loss of all that long, silky, shiny hair. I am vaguely surprised at the impact it makes on me now that I am bald; I expected it and it is, after all, just hair. And it may grow back. It is *likely* to grow back, although Dr. J. is not committing himself to any prediction on this score.

Nobody has much sympathy for my feelings about my hair, which makes me feel misunderstood. "What's more important?" the purveyors of optimism try to convince me, "your hair or your life?"

I don't need convincing: of *course* my life, of course. But they have missed the point.

In a hospital of rare diseases I am still rare enough to be the subject of a number of presentations by aspiring doctors on rotation through Quimby (this is one of the major drawbacks—to be weighed against the undeniable benefits—of being treated at a teaching hospital). Each presentation requires that the resident or intern who is doing it examine me from top to bottom, inside and out. This procedure is unpleasant, but not just because it is annoying, repetitive, and (often) uncomfortable. It is most unpleasant because it is humiliating.

I don't need a witness to be humiliated by the way I look, although knowing that Michael watches me when I am home, that his mother sees me when she helps me bathe in the hospital—undressing and dressing me, handing me in and out of the tub (when I stand to have her help me dry off, I am painfully aware of the flabbiness, the whiteness so much whiter in contrast to the discolorations, my genitals mercilessly exposed in their hairlessness, their slack gaping from childbirth)— leaves me with an aching, sinking feeling. But I am a woman! And sometimes, somehow, these nervous, bright-eyed medical boys inspire in me lubricious fantasies (perhaps erotic fantasies function as an escape, a compensation for the rigors of reality, a primary life-force that refuses to be curbed, even here—or perhaps it is *because* it is here: Eros in a futile contest with Thanatos). I climb up onto their tables and lie down, buckling my dumb wig as my head falls back on the fresh, waxy paper, and surrender myself to their probing and poking . . . to their shadowed eyes as they bow their heads intently over my thinness and desiccation. My wreckage.

Lying there on their tables, knees up, body exposed, eyes closed in an eruption of modesty, I feel degraded, unidentifiable, a biological specimen of passing medical interest. I am only to be handled with tongs, tweezers, rubber gloves, an absentminded kindness.

I can hardly remember what it was like to be made love to.

I am sitting on the edge of the bed, swinging my knobby twig legs and staring at the floor when there is a knock. (I keep the door closed now; I do not wear my wig unless I am expecting visitors, and I do not like people glancing in as they walk by to see me naked, without my hair.) It is Jack, who sits and tells me stories of architectural projects he has worked on, knowing I have been in architecture school myself (my undergraduate major was art history), knowing that it interests me without requiring anything of me.

"Dear Stephani," he says after a while, patting my cheek as he stands to leave, "I fear I am tiring you. Why don't you lie down?" Months later he remarks to me, "It broke my heart, the way you were just sitting there, staring. You looked so lost and forlorn, like a waif, an orphan."

It was just that there was so little left of me.

# FEBRUARY–MARCH 1972

I HAVE NEVER FELT SICKER . . . ALTHOUGH I HAVE been sicker. Perhaps it is because I am more alert, more attentive—more resonant—to my body's travails than I was after the open-heart surgery when I was so heavily drugged. Coming out of this is like coming up for air, moving so slowly against the resistance of the drugs and the disease—pulling my way forward—that progress is hard to assess and the distance to recovery deceptive. As when one is underwater, the objective shimmers and plunges: it is hard to know where I am in this sickness, where it is in me.

And yet . . . there is a *feeling:* light filtering down from somewhere I mean to be. I have the unassailable conviction that I am flooding back toward life rather than leaking toward death. The drugs are working, I am sure of it.

My mother-in-law picks me up from the hospital—one more chore in the many chores she has taken over for us: how would we ever manage without her? I am settling myself in the car as she pulls away from the patient-loading ramp, about to breathe my habitual sigh of relief, when quite suddenly I am overtaken by uncontrollable weeping, surprising myself and startling her.

"What is it?" she says with concern, slowing the car. "Are you all right?"

In truth I do not know what it is, and although I am sure I *will* be all right, at the moment I feel as if all the tears of grief for what has happened to me are spurting from the lump in my throat and the ache at the base of my skull as if an artery of misery has been punctured.

"What is it?" she says again, now alarmed, as I sob and gulp.

"I . . ." It will sound stupid. But she is looking at me, waiting, with her foot on the brake pedal and her fingers tightening white on the steering wheel. Impatient drivers honk because she is half into the traffic and half out of it. "Go on. It's . . . nothing," I murmur. She continues to cast sidelong glances at me.

Then I blurt, "It's just that . . . I'm so glad to be out. And . . . I can't go back there. It was awful, the worst, this has to be the last time. I'm never going back. Never." I don't care how hysterical I sound. I am aware of drivers in other cars, watching me in the crawl of traffic, tears streaming down my face, my wig knocked askew. I want to roll down the car window and shout at them, "I'm out and I'm never going back."

The farther away we get from Quimby the calmer I become, as if I have gotten out of range of a deadly ray. Ten blocks north the tears have ceased; I stare straight ahead, unmoving, all the way home.

When I get home I know it for sure: I am stronger—in spite of the devastation of the last hospitalization. The future is no longer a brief stretch of road, melting into a scrim of haze, but a highway unrolling into the virescent distance as far as the mind can see. I allow myself to think of next year. I allow myself to think of the children growing up, getting married, having children themselves. I allow myself to think of dying quietly in my own bed when I am very old. My body feels to me like an exhausted, infuriating child, spent from months and months of tantrum and now in need of comfort, support, and forgiveness.

I must work at being normal, at being well, at being indistinguishably whole. They have gotten along without me—all of them—and I must elbow my way back in, make them need me. I finally have the desire for that and the beginnings of the strength I will need to accomplish it. I am remembering where I belong, where I have always belonged. I will not be displaced.

Here I am, the wife and mother. Here I am, the able student. It's me, the keeper of the house—Hera, the goddess of the hearth. The one luxury in all this pain has been the time to think—an activity for which I had little inclination in the past simply because it complicated more than it simplified. But I have thought and thought; I have felt . . . change. Surely I am a different woman than I ever was! Perhaps finally the woman I should be—the woman I have been brought to this point to be—and I must become her as certainly as a rose must open to its deep blood red. Something immense has changed, I'm not sure what, but I can feel it. Perhaps the earth has moved.

I want to put this poisonous experience behind me ("It never happened, it never happened . . ."). What needed to be learned has been learned: I just want to scrape the plates this hash has been served on, wash them and put them away. I want to forget. I will work at it. Because I have never believed that pain and suffering are character-building. Pain and suffering are pain and suffering, to be gotten through and dispensed with and forgotten as soon as is humanly possible. And when all this is over and in the past, when my life is once more sunny and balanced and predictable and I am new and chaste and purified, I will still work on consigning what lingers in the consciousness of this stint in hell to oblivion, where it belongs.

Memory torments, it does not refine.

It is three weeks before the hospital calls and shatters my grim optimism. The road to the future snaps back on me like a bullwhip.

"One more time," they have said. "It should be the

last." "Don't worry," they have said. "This is just the extra margin of safety." I believe them. I am getting better. I can feel it.

For my fourth course of chemotherapy I am put on a semiprivate floor, into a room with three other women. Until now I have been more or less isolated in the privilege of a private room, obsessed with my own pain and my own sickness and my own fears and losses. Sharing a room—which means sharing in the most intimate possible way three other lives—brings me up short in my tendencies to self-pity and gives me a good deal to be grateful for.

We are arranged in the four corners of the room like distant game partners. We have little to do but watch each other, talk to each other, sympathize with each other, facing as we do. We are audience and chorus, each for the three others, which means that nothing happens to one only, but to all four.

The youngest (myself) and the oldest (Annie) are opposite each other, as through a time warp, next to the windows. Annie is withered and dried, with a puff of yellowed no-color hair. Her nose and chin quite nearly meet: Annie only bothers with her dentures when she has to eat.

Underneath Annie's nightgown is her colostomy, which is acting up: it is why she is here. (She thinks. The rest of us think she is here to die.) Annie fusses endlessly over her colostomy as if it were an infant that has to be soothed and fed and changed and looked after—which in a way it is. She is sweet but tiresome, complaining monotonously in an old lady's querulous way, so that the rest of us are periodically forced into a sham of sleep in the hope of stemming her incessant nattering. A calm little husband comes occasionally and bends himself stiffly into a chair in the corner next to her bed where he patiently nods his way through what must be a familiar monologue of cavil and gossip while he surreptitiously reads the Yiddish newspaper in his lap, still nodding punctiliously, until she slips into sleep—her head dropping forward, gentle snores burbling from between her pink gums—when he escapes, tipping his hat apologetically to each of us as he scurries out.

Mary is kitty-corner to me—the farthest away and the one who interests me most. Mary lives upstate with her five children and her husband . . . when she is home: she has spent the better part of her recent past in Quimby. She is here this time recovering from the last in what must seem like an endless series of cancer operations: she has just had her adrenal glands removed; this is supposed to help arrest the spread of what she calls "inflammatory cancer," my understanding of which is that when cancer has eaten up the rest of you—has no organ to lodge in, no place to seize and occupy—it begins to sort of break out all over, like a brush fire. Mary has already lost her breasts, her uterus and ovaries, her colon, and one lung to cancer; now she has an angry rash that starts on one side of her neck and cascades down her body, which apparently has something to do with this latest manifestation of malignancy. I wonder about her children (not much older than mine), what she tells them, if they know she is going to die (unquestionably she is going to die, surely no one survives such virulence). And I am fascinated also with her relationship with her husband, who rushes in looking terribly distracted, to have tense, whispered conversations with her, and then rushes out again. It almost seems as if he is never here long enough to take off his coat—though of course he must be . . . but whenever I see him his coat is on.

Mary is stoic, philosophical, self-possessed, with a massive, quiet courage that prods me, shames me, for my now relatively small concerns and relatively unwarranted plaints. She is alone most of the time—her husband must stay with the children, *somebody* must stay with the children, and they are not rich—and she is obviously in great pain, but she smiles and embroiders and only rarely do I catch her with the vacant astonished look of an animal frozen in the headlights of a speeding car.

My third roommate—next to me—is a coarse, friendly woman with spatulate hands and a slab of a face. "Sumpin' in my mouth," she says good-naturedly. "They're gonna take out my teeth and give me new ones." She has never been sick, clearly, and is one of those hardy, innocent souls who does not yet have the proper awe for current venue. She wanders from bed to bed, slapping us on the back, wanting to talk, wanting to smoke—which she goes out in the hall to do. They take her away after a couple of days for her "new teeth." She doesn't come back, which we all notice, but pretend not to, averting our eyes from her neatly made-up bed as if it were the scene of an accident. We ask the nurses how she is, what has happened (after all, she is *one* of us), but all they will say is that she is "in recovery" ("In recovery?" we echo cynically), and then they will not even say that, shrugging their shoulders and shaking their heads: it has nothing to do with them. Four days later orderlies bring back unrecognizable carrion and roll it into the bed. Our garrulous friend has been relieved of half her lower jaw, all her teeth, and her tongue. In the moments when she is conscious her eyes are wild, panicked, and when they start feeding her Sustagen, pressing and pouring it through a primitive-looking contraption constructed of a funnel and a length of rubber hose (the rubber hose goes through the torn hole that used to be her mouth and down the throat)—her gullet rising and falling like a baby bird's—I must draw the curtains around my bed.

What are my mouth burns to her no-mouth? I lever my concern about not being able to eat, drink, talk, or swallow, against her.

All the same, with all the horrors, it is astonishing what is accomplished in here: we are all still alive . . . and we should be dead. To think that somewhere, in some lab, a man or a woman sits hunched over papers, reports, statistical studies, that will bring the same extension of life—that will maybe bring a cure—to a cancer patient! To think that some years ago tumors were induced in mice, or in rats, or in rabbits, and then they were injected with a chemical that could burn the skin of the experimenter, and then that researcher wrote a paper, and then those drugs were used in special studies with human beings—because there was nothing else to be done for the poor wretches—until the dosages and drugs were got right. And then they were used on me, and have kept me alive when I should have been dead. Five years ago—even two years ago—I would have died of my disease as so many others will die of theirs.

I used to think, Why me?—at least in those moments in which I wasn't convinced I *knew* why I had been singled out—but now I find myself thinking, Why not me? Or rather, why am *I* getting stronger, getting better, when Mary with her pale-moon face and sensible-lady brown hair—Mary with her five children—lies dying? Why can't they come up with something to help Mary?

It cannot be that everyone who has pain deserves it.

The nurses on this floor, while more harassed and overworked even than on my previous floor, are at the same time more gracious, more patient, more generous. I am fascinated by their dedicated enthusiasm and their competent benevolence. I am right when I guess that they are just out of nursing school.

"Why do you do it?" I ask, wound up with curiosity. "Why would you take an assignment like this? Such hard work, and it's got to be terribly depressing. . . ."

"There *is* an awfully high rate of turnover," Bonnie the nurse says reflectively as she tucks in the hospital corner she is making on my bed. (I know she is Bonnie because that is what her plastic ID pin says, like a waitress.)

"But why do you do it? Why should someone take

this on in the first place? Idealism? Experience? There must be *much* nicer places to work!"

"Some of the girls have a sense of . . . mission . . . or something," she says, "and it is an . . . extraordinary . . . experience . . . but . . ." She stops fixing the bed and looks at me, her hands on her hips. "Do you have any idea what they *pay* here? For a first appointment? I can make twice as much here as anywhere else."

This last course of chemotherapy has been mild—not at all what I feared; just, as they promised, a "cleanup." I even eat real food one night before leaving the hospital, which Michael brings in an aluminum cake pan from the local Greeks: steak and French fries which I eat in teeny-tiny pieces, chewing cautiously and swallowing whole whatever is resistant to mastication. The last few days in the hospital I do things I haven't been able to concentrate on for months—watch movies on TV, embroider, read.

Dr. J. asks me to step out in the hall one day shortly before I am released.

"I just wanted to tell you," he says, squinting against the bright light in the sun-streaked hallway as I lean against the wall. He rubs his nose and puts his freckled hands into the pockets of his coat. "I want to tell you what I have not been able to tell you up until now with any certainty: that you will live, that you can expect to lead a normal life. It looks like we have a cure here."

I had *known*, but it's different being told: I nod mutely because I'm not sure what to say. Dr. J. and I have shared such antipathy (this is the first time he has ever spoken to me like an adult, treated me like an adult) that it is difficult for me to regard him generously, even if he *has* saved my life—one of the few men in the world who could have: being free of cancer also means being free of him. But whether I like it or not, he is a momentous link in my chain.

"Then it's over? For sure? I will never have to come back again?"

"Recurrences are fairly rare. And as far as *I'm* concerned, you're cured. But we will monitor you very closely for the first year."

I search his face, looking for some kind of clue as to how he feels about me; my feelings about him have always been pretty clear. What goes on behind his doctor mask? Does he congratulate himself for a job well done? But what must it be like for him, women dying away under his hands, one after another, wasting, disintegrating, stinking? When he goes home and lays loving hands on his wife does he ever see her as he must see us? And because he is a powerful man who must contend with his powerlessness more rather than less of the time, does he come to loathe all of us for our mortality, the chiding and jeering of the corruptible flesh? I'll bet he is very lonely, I say to myself. I'll bet he makes himself lonely.

I pull myself together. "Thank you," I say as clearly as I can with my slow, sore mouth, "thank you," and shuffle back to my room.

It is a real leave-taking this time: I have been cured in nearly record time, I won't be coming back, I am through. As I pack I look around the room. One, possibly two, and maybe all three of my roommates will never leave Quimby. I alone have been spared. I alone. . . .

It is almost Easter, and the clammy, gusty breath of spring is unmistakable, ballooning in the dead spaces left by winter.

When I walk out of the hospital I am bald, ninety-two emaciated pounds, and hunched over like a baboon, skipping on unsteady legs. But I am out. I am free.

I have won.

# PART
# TWO

---

*Remission, n. 1) forgiveness, pardon, as of
sins or crimes.
Remission. From the Latin remittere . . .
to send back.*

# SPRING 1972–SEPTEMBER 1974

AT FIRST, OF COURSE, THAT IS WHAT I DID FEEL . . .
what I thought. That I had won. That I was therefore a
winner. I considered myself a victor and expected to
march in triumph through the rest of my retrieved life.
I had been forgiven and I was very very grateful.

What I should have known and somehow missed
were the subtle and deadly correspondences between
mind and body, reflecting distorted images of the self
like a pair of warped mirrors. What I should have
known was that to be cured is not necessarily to be
healed; that surviving death does not necessarily equip
one to survive life: to survive as a wife, as a sister, a
mother, a friend. To survive as a good girl.

I had always wanted to escape life and its responsibilities, but I couldn't. I thought I had escaped death,
but I hadn't. And of all my oversights—of all the failures of vision of my newly opened third eye—the grav-
est was not recognizing that one escapes nothing:
these things cannot be run from but can only be run
toward; they must be faced and embraced.

One learns to lie down with darkness.

Thinking back to those first few weeks I was out of
the hospital, I do remember the initial serenity of surrender, of being swallowed whole by my old life which
had been lying in wait. I didn't think much in the beginning; I didn't have to and I didn't want to: if something
wasn't perfectly obvious I wasn't interested. My tasks

were clearly defined—perfection of the work was for the first time imaginable—and I did all the simple, orderly, stable things that keep the earth on its axis, dropping into my accustomed slots with a reassuring click: into my side of the bed, into my post in front of the sink, into the straitened niche between the children on the sofa. I cooked and washed clothes and shuffled to the park. I cleaned closets and rearranged furniture and located long-lost items so that I could deposit them in their original spots. I took great pleasure in this reordering—building myself a fortress of resolve—and took strength from feeling necessary in my familiar roles, throwing myself into every endeavor of narrow ambition.

I worked at everything. (Everybody said you could do anything you really wanted to.) I worked at my marriage, I worked at my home, and I worked at being good. Because I had promised. I worked at getting better with the same determination I had once worked at getting happy, happiness being at this point a redundancy for someone who could fervidly kiss the icy panes of glass in the morning simply because the sun floated there on the other side. I rested just enough to be thought temperate but not a self-coddler. I ate well. I exercised moderately, walking each day until I was barely short of the moment when I would have to lean gasping against a building, and tried to remind myself to "Stand up straight!" as my grandmother had always chided me, although it was no longer a matter of a lazy adolescent slouch but rather a fight to the finish with the strap of scar tissue that cinched me from neck to crotch.

I began to gain weight almost immediately, looking quite soon less like a concentration camp victim on whom dastardly experiments had been performed and more like a distressingly wan version of my old self. In those first months at home the drama played in the mirror was like watching a movie run in reverse and at triple speed: the space between my legs—they touched only at knees and ankles, with great gaps of white air

separating them—got narrower; I filled out and looked
less like a deflated rubber doll whose latex breasts and
belly and buttocks hung in soft empty folds; the black
spots wore away, sloughing onto the sheets and towels,
and although the boils still came on for months, my
skin gradually took on a creamy translucent quality that
was disquieting in its intimations of injury but nevertheless not unattractive. The predatory look around my
mouth softened as my cheeks rounded; the hunted look
in the eyes was less piercing. It was as if I was cushion-
ing all my damage with this extra flesh. "And to
think!" people said, clasping their hands in front of
their faces. "To think what you looked like . . . well
. . . just six *months* ago!"

Eating comes naturally to me; getting fat has always
been a barely suppressed ambition. Gaining weight,
resting, renewing myself was the pleasurable challenge.
What was less easy was the consecration of myself to
the rest of my life.

My marriage was my center—I insisted on its being
my center—and more than ever I suspected that if the
marriage did not hold, I could not. Michael had always
defined me for myself; it was a responsibility I had
been glad to give over. And as he had once given me a
meaningful life because he shared it with me, so now he
had given it to me once more; I didn't think I could
have survived without him, couldn't have endured without his unflagging support. I owed him a great deal; I
owed him everything. "He *saved* me. I would have *died*
had he abandoned me." I said this at night as if I were
saying the rosary, listening to his regular breathing in
sleep, moving close to him and hoping for some answering tremor. The rhythm never changed. "I love
you," I would whisper fiercely at his cool dark back,
riffling the hairs on his shoulders into a riot of commas,
leaning into my conviction of love like a hiker into the
wind. When he was awake I tossed him the bouquets of
my gratitude at unexpected moments, hoping to seduce
a smile from him, a hug, perhaps even a kiss on the

neck: "Thank you for everything you did. I would have died. . . . I couldn't have gotten through it." Me, smiling to encourage him. Me, hopeful and eager. He had promised too, after all. He had promised me a new life as surely as he had given me a new life.

But he also needed to recover. We would grow into our promises, into our rededication of ourselves to each other and our family.

The children were harder. Although I had always been insecure as "wife," as "mother" I did more than recognize myself: as "mother" I *knew* myself. Motherhood was an island of calm and surety in all the stormy seas. But as distant, as unpredictable as Michael was even in his solicitude and kindness after I arrived home, the children were more so: I had to remind myself that children do not forgive easily nor forget quickly, that children have no more conscience than cats. I had left them, deserted them, so it followed that they did not trust me, avoided me, found reasons not to go with me or be with me—choosing anyone else more familiar. They gave me a wide berth, sidling away from me to Michael, to Michael's mother, to the Brazilian housekeeper. Warily, they watched my movements like little lab animals alert for the next experiment, letting me close to them only when they were confused or distracted—at night for instance, when they sometimes had nightmares (a new development) and awoke shrieking in terror. Then I sat in a rocking chair late into the night with a baby in my arms, crooning nonsense and old show tunes while they clutched and whimpered like newborns.

Part of it was my fault: there just seemed to be so many ways in which I couldn't think straight, stumbling again and again into childish behavior when what they needed from me was to be their invincible mommy. I kept getting confused about what they should and shouldn't know, and how things ought to be presented to them.

For the first weeks I was home I was careful to wear

my wig around the children, keeping my head covered as I kept my body covered. But clothes are easier to wear than a wig, and it wasn't too long before I decided that I just could not leave it on all the time, day and night. They would have to get used to seeing me without it.

I wasn't sure how to introduce this current anomaly to them: Zachary, I thought, would accept it better than Alexandra: at twenty-one months his presumptions still seemed elastic enough to accommodate a bald mother. Alexandra was another matter. She was three and a half and she knew what her mother was supposed to look like: she had clearly already stretched her imagination thin to tolerate the short fluffy wig.

I was not very creative and uncomprehendingly insensitive, retreating into clowning. "Look, sweetheart," I said quite without warning one day, "look what I can do with my hair!" and I whipped off the wig, making a face, making a joke of it.

Alexandra's mouth dropped open and a look of horrified disbelief masked her eyes. I had blundered again, done entirely the wrong thing when with all my heart I desired to do the right one. "Look how funny Mommy looks," I said weakly. "Just like a new baby." She had crossed her arms and shrunk back into the corner of the bench on which we were sitting. I put my wig back on and took her hand, which she let lie in mine like a dead minnow.

Years later she said to me in a whisper as if it were a secret she herself did not want to know, "But you looked so much like a witch, Mommy. Your head was all . . . hard, and your nose was so . . . pointy . . ."

Now why did I do that? It remains one of the unsolved mysteries of that period and its strange accommodations to stress. I was someone the children didn't know. Worse, I was someone *I* didn't know, behaving in bizarre ways, feeling provoked, oversensitive, jumpy. We were all jumpy, trying to rewire the essential circuits of life as an intact family, used—as we were—to the tyranny of arbitrariness. Cancer's capriciousness, its invidiousness, becomes a caricature of all life's uncertainties: when I wasn't assuming a psychological posture of conditioned woodenness that was easy to mistake for stoicism—a reflexive bracing for blows that became habitual—I was angry with no cause and reckless in a way that was not brave.

I couldn't relax. It was as if I were waiting for something, suspended in a state that can only be described as a slow-motion frenzy.

I wanted never again to have to think about or see Quimby Hospital, but being "closely monitored" required continual contact. It was bad enough to get the periodic phone calls that made me recoil because I never knew whether the familiarly anonymous voice would say "Please bring in another specimen," or whether it might just as easily say "Please plan to be readmitted." It was the not knowing what they thought, what they were planning or doing, that was so corrosive. One day I could be living, the next day dying. It was all the same to them.

Every couple of weeks I took the bus over to Quimby for blood tests and to hand in my titer—the twenty-four-hour collection of urine by which tumor activity is monitored—delivering it in a flimsy hospital-issue box done up to look like a milk carton that hid the thick plastic specimen bag.

I transported my half-gallon of urine in alternating Tiffany and Gucci shopping bags, praying that the ominous sloshing sounds it made as the bus lurched forward and jerked to a stop didn't forebode a leak. (More than once I picked up the bag from the floor and left a little—but nevertheless olfactorily identifiable—puddle, which I pointedly ignored, stepping away from it with the self-righteousness of one who has learned to live with the New York City dog problem.) Frequently I saw Dr. J. on these trips; we maintained a professional distance and a kind of gelid cordiality.

It was on one of these visits that I found out that Dr. J. was to speak on choriocarcinoma at a national conference on cancer chemotherapy to be held in New York. At once I wanted to attend; perhaps some objectivity would offset the disconcerting singularity of subjectivity that had taken possession of me. It felt like one more step toward becoming responsible for myself.

The warmth with which Dr. J. received my request to go to the conference so that I might hear him give his paper—the ease with which the arrangements were accomplished—floored me; for a doctor who seemed to guard jealously the inner chambers of medical arcana—to say nothing of the anterooms of simple basic information—he was unexpectedly gracious about accommodating me in my desire to learn more about my disease and the current state of research on its treatment.

The conference was in early June at a large downtown hotel. I dressed modestly and colorlessly, hoping to blend in with all the medical honchos, trying not to look like an ex-cancer patient. ("There's one of them!" I imagined them saying as I bent over a table to register, conscious of the Dynel hairs pricking my forehead. "Who let *her* in here?") I lurked near the back of the hall and couldn't see, not really—Dr. J. was a tiny, red-haired figure beneath the great blank eye of the screen on which would be projected legions of figures demonstrating the efficacy of various interventions—but I could hear, and his familiar intonations—amplified, disembodied—came at me from the back and the sides and overhead. Yes, Great Oz, I said to myself, it's me, Dorothy, the meek and mild.

And then he was talking about me, or rather, talking about a recent case, that of a "twenty-seven-year-old woman" (S.C.) who had been "because of the long duration of the disease prior to onset of the chemotherapy, . . . considered to be in a 'high-risk' category and was initially given combination chemotherapy." I listened, rapt, as he described my symptoms and the initial course of nondiagnosis. "The patient is presently in remission," he finished. I felt hot, embarrassed, but of course no one knew he was talking about me. Nobody in my row turned to look; there were no significant throat clearings or elbow jabs. Did he remember that I had intended to come? Did he think about me—for one scant moment perhaps—sitting in his audience? Or did each of us—even those of us immortalized in the sheaves of conference proceedings—fade from his mind's eye, become interchangeable, as soon as we were discharged and our thick files closed and buried in the Records Room?

On the way home I thought about it, and decided I had been wrong and unfair. "Have you written Dr. J. yet? Have you thanked him properly?" my mother-in-law would prompt periodically, appalled at my bad manners. "I don't owe him anything," I would snap. "He was just doing his job. He got paid for it. He doesn't want or need any thanks from me. Anyway, I thanked him in the hospital." Months had passed, but now, finally, I *was* ready to thank him. I hoped he was still ready to accept my sincere—my heartfelt—gratitude, as well as my compliments on his presentation.

A week later the phone rang and I flinched my usual flinch. And then there he was.

"Hello. This is Hugh."

"Hugh?" I echoed. Did I know a Hugh? But I knew the voice.

"Hugh J.," he supplied helpfully. I took a deep breath. At the same time that he was consummately recognizable there was also a quality to the voice I had never heard and it threw me off guard. What could he want? Did I have to go back to Quimby?

"Uh," I said, paralyzed.

"I got your note," he continued conversationally. "It was very nice. I wanted to call and tell you how much I appreciated it." There was an awkward pause.

"I'm sorry it took me so long," I said. Another awkward pause. "I liked your speech," I ventured. "I felt very proud that you are my doctor."

"I'm glad you liked it," he said.

"Listen," I blurted, "I hope you weren't offended by what I said" (which had been something like "I was difficult, but then, at times, so were you"), "because I didn't mean to offend you, but I know we never got along too well, and that certainly had something to do with my reticence when it came to thanking you properly."

"Let's just say it's a rather deep-seated emotional problem," he said gently, "and leave it at that."

I bristled. This had started out so congenially, such a . . . surprise! And now he was after me again. He couldn't resist. My palms were sweating and my cheeks burned.

"I think anger was not an inappropriate response," I said, choosing my words carefully, "everything considered. Nor was my . . . neurotic . . . self-absorption. Nor my depression. I was under a lot of stress."

He laughed, the second time I had ever heard him laugh. "Oh, I didn't mean *you*," he said. "I meant *me*."

For some strange reason I had nurtured the illusion that everything would be fine and back to normal once my hair had come in again. By that time, I promised myself, I will have gotten used to being out of the hospital, I will be settled into my routine, I will have shed the last veils that hide me from my own sight.

But even as my hair came in during the summer—looking like a cap of velvet flocking—even as I became firmer and livelier and fatter, there was some persistent vacuum at my center; in a mocking reversal of what had happened when I had got sicker and sicker, now I got weller and weller without, somehow, *feeling* better. The harder I tried to get happy and to fit into the place I had vacated, the more restless I was and the more convinced that either the place itself had been a conceit or that if it had really existed, I no longer fit into it.

I had expected to come out of this experience purged and made new; I had expected the sickness to be flushed from the body and the soul hosed down and cleansed of every bloody particle of mortal illness. I thought I had won. But now it was almost as if the shrinking of the cancer had left a void into which ballooned some new malignancy: disease replaced by dis-ease. Dis. Ease.

Of course there were adjustments to be made; one would be foolish and naive (and I had been worse) not to expect to have to make some adjustments. But I was powerless to stem the perturbation, the unhappiness, that should have been cured with the cancer, the poisonous impatience with normality. It was just that everything was so . . . *bland*.

In the last year I had been reduced to some highly concentrated essence of myself. I was beginning to suspect that nothing ever again would be as real to me as the cancer had been.

Certainly something was happening to me. Or maybe something was not happening that I expected and needed to happen.

"What do you *want*?" Michael would ask, exasperated and bored with me—as much with my inability to answer his question as my instability. "What's the problem *now*?"

What *did* I want? To matter, I guess. To make a difference to *some*one. To have been worth saving because I was essential to *some*body. When I was sick at least I was sick; now I was merely unhappy. I cluttered Michael's life—was a distraction and an inconvenience—keeping him from himself and his habits of quiet concentration. For me, in turn, Michael was a thin, tough membrane through which I thought I could just glimpse what my life ought to have been; he stretched like a barrier between me and it. I was not indispensable even to the children, and that was a presumption that was particularly painful to surrender. They had managed—they had all managed—without me; they had managed quite well.

In a way I was a hindrance, an impediment to the regular rhythm of lives that no longer depended so

thoroughly on me. Worse, I'd become a trouble-maker—
suspicious, distant, difficult. In spite of myself.

Somehow I had looked forward to the swelling
strains of Wagner; instead it looked as if the musicians
had simply packed up and gone home.

During the summer and fall of 1972 I filled my life
with things that were manageable because they were so
reasonable, things I understood. I finished my master's
degree in family and community relations. (Ha, I
thought. Some joke.) I entered a Ph.D. program in
counseling psychology (a not unpredictable move: it
has always been my impression that people frequently
go into psychology as a profession because they themselves are troubled). I read books that might help me to
comprehend what I was going through, educating myself more thoroughly both in issues of life—like sexuality—and aspects of death and mortal illness. I wanted
labels for my crises: clarity and control achieved
through the rituals of naming, a very primitive imposi-
tion of the self on the world. I began therapy so that my
understanding of this odyssey might be more complete,
so I could learn to accept reality. I could handle this.

After all, I had survived cancer. And if you can survive cancer, you can survive anything.

"We're *fine*," I told the psychologist. "It's just that
we are so *different*. We want different things, we have
different ways of expressing love for each other. But
that doesn't mean we can't make it work. People live
together like that and have strong marriages. It happens
all the time."

"Are you happy?" asked my therapist, going for the
jugular.

I looked away, twisting my hands in my lap. "We're
working on it," I said finally. Happiness was something
you had to beat into submission to reality.

"Do you love him?"

"I've always loved him. Always. If only . . ."

"If only what?"

"Nothing."

A long pause. Then Dr. P. said, "Does he love you?"

"Of course he does."

"How do you know?"

How did I know? "He says he does." It sounded good. "He's always been very supportive of things I have wanted to do: work, school. And he was wonderful to me when I was sick. He took such good care of me. He took such good care of everything. The children. The house. . . ."

"Does he tell you he loves you often?"

"When I ask," I said in the tiniest voice, thinking of my begging, Do you love me?

"How else does he show you he loves you?"

All I could think of was that he always let me out of the car right in front of the building, so I wouldn't have to walk in the cold, and parked it himself.

"Do you *feel* loved?" pressed Dr. P.

I almost never felt loved. But it could very well have been, as Michael often said, that I had deep misconceptions about what it was to love and be loved, that my view of love was a dismal mix of Walt Disney and True Romance, a comic-book view of what two people were supposed to feel for each other that you grow out of. Because certainly I had felt something different with my high-school love, certainly I felt different with my Yale swimmer. I had even felt different with Michael . . . until we were married. But it was hard to remember what it had been *like* then, so long ago, when we were so young, when we were the golden couple.

"Don't you think you deserve to be loved?" asked Dr. P. gently.

Now I had never thought of that, that someone might *deserve* something as impalpable as love. And I wanted to say yes, because I knew that was the right answer, that I should say everyone deserved to be loved, but I didn't say it. It would somehow have been like lying under oath.

"Don't you think you deserve to be loved in a way you understand?" Dr P. persisted.

Maybe I should be trying to understand the way in which I *am* loved, rather than trying to be loved in a way I *understand*, I thought to myself, but I said, "We'll make it work. We *have* to make it work. I owe him too much, I owe his family too much—everyone has been so kind, so generous. . . . And then the children, of course." My vehemence built with my determination. "I'll make it work."

"Beware of your illusions," said Dr. P. when the hour was up. "Don't think you don't have them."

And I *did* try to make it work—as I had promised: I don't know that one really has a choice about one's illusions.

But then Michael found out about Len. (He asked one day, out of the blue, playing on my addiction to honesty. He asked. I told. He found out.) He shouted at me from the bed where he was lying, his face knotted in fury. "The two of you—you knew all the time and I didn't know. I treated him as your doctor when he had been your lover. You have humiliated me. You made a fool of me."

"Try to understand," I pleaded. "It happened at a time when I was terribly needy, when I wasn't sick yet—when I didn't know I *was* sick. And then once I knew—once I had the hysterectomy and everything else came apart so fast—then I *couldn't* tell you. Don't you see? I couldn't tell you then. I was so scared. Anyway, it was over."

But he would not forgive me, not because I had fucked Len but because I had fucked *Len*. And he would not forgive me because, unlike the case of my prior transgression, in this instance he had not been informed; I did something that he didn't know about or even suspect until long after and that he had had no control over . . . that he had not given me permission for. I would always think therefore that it was my defiance he hated—my willful and bold secret—more even than he hated Len.

"Now things will never be the same again," he said. "Never ever. I will never love you as I once loved you. There is no going back, no mending."

This cut me to the core, right through the anger and defensiveness and the sense of having been misunderstood in my wickedness. How was it if he had once loved me that he would never love me again? What was I going to have to forfeit that I as yet had failed to apprehend?

One day I was lying in the bathtub, thinking. Michael was rummaging around the bathroom, scowling. ("My mouth just naturally turns down," he would say. "Don't take it personally.") I was seized with an impulse, and before I knew what it was I meant to say I had said it and heard it with the same surprise that Michael did: "Do you want a divorce?"

His head turned, slowly. "No. That's not it," he said flatly.

"I can see you're not happy," I hurtled along, "and I can never be happy with you when you are so visibly unhappy with me. You don't want me, you've never wanted me, you never wanted a wife."

"I don't need anybody," he said thoughtfully, as if this were an answer.

In spite of my daring offer of liberation to Michael, I would not give up. (Where would I *go*? What would I *do*? How would I *manage*? I thought I would probably rather be dead than alone.)

If I could not build my life around Michael I would build it around the children. If Michael could not need me or even want me, I would make the children need me as they had once needed me. I didn't exist if I were not needed.

\* \* \*

Feeling isolated as I did, I sought the children's closeness, holding them when they would let me before squirming out of my arms, taking naps with them so I could watch them sleep. Alexandra more often had to be caught on the run: she was all mercurial flash. But Zachary at two and a half was placid and soft and sleepy as I often was. He would snuggle facing into the curve of my body in the afternoons and fall instantly into a heavy torpor while I watched him succumb, thumb stuffed in his mouth, swollen fetal eyelids closed over dreaming eyes that traveled back and forth under the lids. He was very responsive to me, even in his sleep; perhaps it was some early memory of the comfort we had given each other as he nursed during his whole first year. If I moved away from him—getting up to see what Alexandra was doing, or to answer the phone—he would lapse into a fit of loose grasping and thrashing, searching for me in his sleep as little tremors flung his small hands in my direction. Sometimes, needing to get up and not wanting to wake him, I would shove a soft pillow at him, which he would accept, sighing, mistaking its warm resilience for my body and subsiding once more into deeper sleep, pulling at his thumb with an almost inaudible tik tik tik sound.

After their baths—which the children took together—I would pull them out of the tub, one at a time, lingering over the small slippery bodies as I dried them, smelling their sweet smell, touching them, wanting to rain a shower of kisses over the unresisting flesh, holding them, tickling them, raising the hair off the backs of their necks to see the velvety white napes which spawned their masses of dark gold hair.

If only one could be loved again as one's mother once loved one! If only loving a child and being loved by a child were enough! But even with the children and their sunniness I longed for something darker, a loamy, fecund love that they could not give me and I could not want less.

\* \* \*

The marriage slipped by notches: my reprehensible involvement with Len—and Michael's resultant sarcasm and punitiveness; my brisk, naggy orderliness, Michael's turned back; my loneliness and fears of further evidence of my emotional corruption, Michael's scorn for my frailties and the excesses the frailties bred. He was right. It would never be the same again and my stubborn desire to make it so—no, to make it in fact what it had never been—only belied what I had known but failed to understand about the nature of the bonds between us. We were quickly getting to the point where it would be impossible to forgive each other for anything, where everything felt like betrayal.

We never fought (so useless, so noisy) but rather nursed our respective injuries and the illusions that engendered them with the care and denial lavished on the terminally ill. In trying to be "ourselves," we struck at each other and then withdrew into our respective and separate understandings of this process of disintegration. Always more prone to "acting out," I gave Michael reasons to withdraw; in turn he frustrated me by rarely giving me a direct, concrete reason to hate him, to loathe him, to want to be free of him. My damage to him was all sound and fury, his to me like a contusion that swelled and bled under the surface, subtle and devastating, devastating for being so subtle. He scowled, disapproved, turned away; I slashed back: pay *attention* to me when I am talking to you, pay attention to me even when I'm not. Love me. Want me.

Then Michael slipped and did something atypical and overt, something I could blame him for and hate him for (although it was not something I would leave him for; there was perhaps nothing I would leave him for). Something that justified my anger and revved me like a motor, pitching me out of the virulent nest of my immobile and convoluted rage. Until then it was always easier to be a martyr than to feel guilty.

In the early spring of 1973 I had plastic surgery on my chest: wires were pulled out of the breastbone where it had been closed after the open-heart surgery—

the breastbone in healing had crested upward so that I looked like a pigeon—and the bone itself was shaved down, the rosy lumps of scar tissue peeled away. If it had been a purely cosmetic procedure I would probably not have had it done. I was so afraid of going back into the hospital—hysterical, almost, at the very thought— but this knuckle of growth—like a fist pushing up above and between my breasts—was as tender as a row of carbuncles: a child's head slipping back to rest in my arms made me yelp in pain; anybody hovering over me or near me who might press me or bump me or put weight on me made me hunch my shoulders and turn my side to the threat.

I don't remember how, but Len knew I was going to be in Epiphany for a few days for the operation; perhaps Dr. G., who had referred me to my plastic surgeon, had told him. At any rate, Len called soon after I was admitted to say that he would try to stop in later to say hello. He knew how much I hated hospitals.

My relationship with Len had been cordial and detached since my release from Quimby; we talked on the phone occasionally but did not see each other as he was no longer either my doctor or my lover. I suppose I should have felt badly treated, taken advantage of, after the incident in Quimby, but I had always suspected that even the kindest men were capable of the most abject cruelties where women were concerned—especially where women intersected with the immediacy of their sexual needs. Anyway, I still felt grateful (no matter what Michael thought) for our electric interlude almost two years before, when I had first begun to grapple with my succubus. Len had been a flying leap, a midair stunt between trapezes where I was still floating, waiting, it seemed, for someone who wanted to catch me.

It would be nice if he stopped by, I said.

When Michael called from the office to see if I was settled and to tell me what time he would come to the hospital to see me, I thought it only fair to mention that Len might look in.

"Call him back and tell him not to come," said Michael, "or *I* will not come."

"I don't know where to reach him. I think he's on rounds or something. What if I can't find him?"

"You'd better find him. I'm not coming unless you guarantee me that he won't be there."

I understood his feelings, his mashed pride. I had been wrong in telling Len he could come, failing once again to consider someone else's most obvious sensitivities.

"What if I can't find him?" My voice cracked and rose. Doctors are not always easy to locate in the late afternoon.

"You'd better find him. I'm not discussing it anymore."

I couldn't find him. Or rather, his answering service said they would have him call me when he checked in with them, was it an emergency, should they page him and if so, what was the message?

Perhaps I should have worried less about my pride and more about Michael's, but somehow I just couldn't bring myself to tell them to pass along the information that a certain irate husband insisted that Len not show his loathsome face. The whole thing was stupid, I hadn't thought, it was my fault, I had underestimated Michael's anger, but I just couldn't do it. It was humiliating. It offended me.

"Then I'm not coming," said Michael mildly when he called back, as if he were commenting on the weather.

I had thought he would yield, forgive me. He didn't have to *talk* to Len. This could be handled with dignity.

"*Please* come," I begged. "I'm frightened." Which I was. How could he not soften? "I need you."

"No. I warned you." There was silence while the phone crackled.

"But he may not even *come*. He only said maybe. And he's likely to stop by after visiting hours if he stops by at all."

"I'm not coming," said Michael again. More crackling. My face felt hot and crazed, like an old plate that has had one too many rounds in the dishwasher. I could feel myself breaking. How could he be so hard?

"Well. Good night. Good luck tomorrow. I'll see you when the surgery is over." And then there was the click of disconnect.

For some reason I couldn't get it out of my head that I might die, that my heart might burst along its barely healed seams it ached so, that my lungs would collapse, there, on the operating table, during this simple procedure. Not having Michael with me the night before was tantamount to having been denied Last Rites—I would die with my sin on me, smeared like egg yolk. In fear and despair I cried myself to sleep, cried to myself under sedation the next morning, and then found myself still crying when I came out of the anesthesia in the recovery room, where my chest hurt so much I promptly vomited from the pain.

I had survived, it was true, but the idea of survival was coming to mean less and less because so much of what I hoped for seemed to be dying, or dead. Michael had had his reasons for abandoning me, to be sure—and they were undoubtedly good ones, a solid defense for his actions that would stand up in any court. But at the time I didn't understand them completely. I understood only that he seemed *un*reasonably angry, unrealistically harsh, and unfairly punitive when I was vulnerable and terrified.

Long after, he made explicit his feelings about Len:

"Len, who promised to deliver Zachary and didn't; Len, who breached the code of professional ethics by sleeping with a patient, my wife, who was half-crazy at the time by her own admission; Len, who arrogantly criticized the performance of the other doctors; Len, who delivered to me the mistaken news about your terminal cancer; Len who admitted to me that he should have caught the cancer.

"Your illness was an extreme experience for me as

well. It tested me to the fullest in many ways. You know I was the one who held it all together. To think that the experience should never have happened, that Len was too arrogant to think that the great him was at fault, that he did not have the requisite detachment and objectivity because of his relationship with you—these things not only depreciated the experience for me but made it seem like an elaborate joke. Yes, my pride was hurt but this was the least of it. So something snapped.

"I did not come to the hospital because I did not trust myself in the same room with him—and still don't."

For my part, I thought that pride was *not* "the least of it," and I couldn't help thinking how jealousy distorts and self-righteousness blinds . . . everybody.

Yes, Len had missed a gynecological cancer, but it was a gynecological cancer that metastasized while it was still asymptomatic in the pelvis, and it had not been to Len that I had taken my complaints or my chest pain, it had been to Dr. G.—who had labeled Len "merely the plumber." Yes, Len was scathing in his criticisms of the other doctors' failings—and there was no question but that he himself was sulky, difficult, and arrogant—but it was also he who had insisted on and referred me to an outside consultant—without whose input I almost surely would have died. Yes, Len had taken advantage of me when I was particularly unable to resist getting involved with him, and his sexual exploitation of me was an unforgivable breach of medical ethics.

But it was also Len who sat holding my hand long hours into long nights in the artificial quiet of the hospital; it was Len who was willing to listen to me and talk with me when I was reduced to babbling like an idiot, who—although he may have known that I was crazed—never treated me like I was crazy. Len was there when I needed him, whatever his motives; Len had been supportive and given me courage when the indicators on my own reserves stuck at Empty.

Len may have fucked me, but he didn't fuck me over.

Michael and I pulled further apart, agreeing to disagree, trying to stay out of each other's way, filling the breach with stone-cold indifference. Even so, it came as a mild surprise to me that my desire for Michael's love had not in fact survived the mutilation of the hospital incident; all that pulpy need for comfort and closeness seemed to have been excised with the other superfluous bulbs of flesh over my heart.

This didn't mean, of course, that I yet thought the marriage itself seriously threatened: as my mother-in-law said, "The only thing worse than divorce is death."

The challenge was to fill the vacuum, but that's what you had a brain for, to know how to substitute, to repress, to sublimate, to keep going . . . and I pumped the vacuum of my life full of activity all that spring. It was now a full year since I had been discharged from Quimby.

I felt I had fully recovered both my health and the capacity to distract myself by keeping moving at all times. I worked half-days at the abortion clinic. I began training as a sex therapist. I studied for my Ph.D. I had friends, the children, the house. If I just kept the pressure on, controlling exits and entrances, I would be all right. I would have purpose. I would know where I was going and what I intended to do when I got there.

And then there was an entrance I couldn't control: I fell in love with a colleague with whom I was working on a special project at school. We tried to stop because it seemed (and indeed it was) irrational and unnecessarily complicated, but the great engines of passion are not easily flagged down by good sense and moral propriety. We were both ready—for our various reasons—and receptive, and we could no more have saved each other than we could have saved ourselves. ("Are you sure you want to do this?" I asked, the first time he kissed me. "No," he said, fumbling at his tie in his haste to get it off, "but I'm going to do it anyway.") I also wasn't sure but I did it anyway. It didn't seem as if there were any longer anything to lose. And there might be something to gain.

September 1973. September, when I always had to start over, the mind freshly sharpened, the pages of the future blank and white. I had to *do* something, because even with all this movement there was somehow no progress. Even my consuming love affair—and this time it *was* love, it felt like love should feel—rather than taking me somewhere helped keep me where I was.

I had fooled myself. I had thought that all I wanted was to get back to what I had had, who I had been. But I was unequal to stoicism and duty, I was unequal to feeling eternally grateful and paying decades of interest on a mortgaged life. Indeed, it looked like I was unequal to *all* my deathbed promises . . . suggesting to me that I may have promised the wrong things because I hadn't had the courage to promise the right ones.

I wanted more than I had, even though what I had promised was to want less. I wanted *more*. I wanted great dollops of life whipped to a froth, rather than the thin watery stuff of my prosaic, temperate existence with its discreet overrun. I wanted to be in love and to be in pain; I wanted pleasure and I wanted the incendiary roar of passion, the fire of emotion so strong you could feel it with the mind closed, the way you can feel the glow of the sun when your eyes are shut. I wanted everything, to do everything, to feel everything. What, after all, had I survived for? What had I regretted all those months, passive and yearning and remorseful in my hospital bed? That I hadn't folded enough wash?

Now, when I looked into the chasm from the safety of my sensible, desiccated marriage, when I teetered on the edge trying to keep my balance and a persuasive voice said "Jump! Jump!" I knew I had to jump. I *had* to. Not to jump was not to move, and not to move meant that you were dead. I had moved with my body but I had not yet moved with my spirit.

I had to stop being afraid of taking a risk. I had to stop being afraid of what I felt. I had to stop being afraid of what I had to do. It was time to start considering the alternatives, thinking the unthinkable.

Michael and I were driving somewhere and the road hummed under us, reeled in by the car. I counted under my breath, thinking that when I got to thirty-nine, my childhood lucky number, I would tell him.

"Thirty-eight, thirty-nine," I whispered, then said loudly, "I want a separation."

It was a prepared speech, a brief for divorce, submitted to Michael's chiseled profile as we sped along. He had known about my affair almost since its inception—because there was no reason *not* to tell him and any number of considerations of convenience in favor of his knowing—but the affair was neither the cause nor the point. (Michael himself was also having an affair, which he had complementarily told *me* about—which was also neither the cause nor the point.) We had regarded ourselves as a modern couple, a product of the freewheeling, freethinking seventies, and had segued into Open Marriage as neatly as we had negotiated the rest of the maze of the visible portion of our lives. "If you're happy, I'm happy for you," is how we thought and how we put it. Michael no longer had the responsibility of my sexual and affectional needs; I no longer bore the resentment of feeling I owed him an occasional servicing. We were both relieved, glad to spread ourselves around in this fashion so that neither of us would put too much weight on a fragile marriage that was likely to splinter and collapse like the baby bear's chair.

I explained that Open Marriage seemed pretty much a farce if there was no marriage—the openness got redundant—so that we were left with only a series of limp, flimsy pretexts for staying in the same house. We regularly manufactured great cheer and optimism—ignoring its built-in obsolescence—but when the illusions ground to a halt, *I* was miserable and he gave every sign of being the same. Furthermore, I had lost all my enthusiasm for shoring up a sham because he contributed so little to the project.

Somehow I thought that he would be relieved that I had taken on the responsibility of suggesting a split. I had thought he would nod in his tight, reflective way and say, "Yes, I've been thinking the same thing." But that wasn't what happened. Instead, when I had finished my petition for a recognition of reality, he said quietly, "Don't leave. I don't want to separate. Things will get better."

I rattled into my rebuttal: it had taken me so long to work myself up to this I couldn't stop. He started shaking his head as if the words were flies he was trying to keep from settling. And then, in the middle of one of my turbid explanations, a tear crested on his lower lid and ran down the cheek I could see. I was astonished. My distant, silent husband—the independent man, the self-contained universe who disdained all my gluey intimacy, my eruptions of emotion, my expressions of need which weighed on him like so much steel scrap—was crying. "You can't leave me," he said.

So we decided to try. Again. Harder. *He* would try this time. I would see. Things would change. I should wait a year.

He was right, as usual. I couldn't leave him. And now I was ashamed of wanting to.

I held on that year the way you cradle your head when you have a headache: it doesn't help the pain but it lulls you into thinking your skull can't explode while braced between your hands. For the first two weeks after our confrontation in the car things really were better. The possibility of significant change condensed out of all the misty half-promises and murky devotion to the idea of family. Then, as swiftly as it had descended on us it evaporated, leaving me feeling cheated, miserable, and trapped.

That year the courage I had been building so carefully—post by beam, clay by wattle—tipped precariously and then began to crumble. Once more I lost faith in my instinct and judgment, in the impluses I had wanted to think were healthy. I had followed those healthy impulses so often in the last two years, having learned to examine them for traces of the anger and frustration that had originally been a prime motivation for their expression: it had always been easier to vent anger than to take the responsibility for saying what you really thought. I had faced up to my problems with Dr. J. and he had inadvertently helped me to solve them when he was able to reply with, "It's not you, but me." (It may have been the only time I could remember a man telling me that what had happened between us was not necessarily my fault, that because I was what I was, I did not necessarily make him what *he* was.) I had finally said to my father—on one of the rare occasions I saw him after that Christmas I was sick (until I was able to come to terms and make my own peace with him)—what I should have said many years before and had always been afraid to: that he had damaged me emotionally if not physically, that he had had no right. (He hadn't said anything, but looked away, lips compressed. He clearly didn't want to talk about it. "Why did you do it?" I had demanded, suddenly inflamed. "You *had* other women. Why me?" He had looked childlike, helpless, but not, strangely, at all chagrined. "I don't know," he said simply. And then, "Maybe because you were mine. And I love you so much." He paused again. "It's so complicated. I hope that one day you will be able to understand. . . ." He closed his eyes for a moment, as if the light hurt them. "Or rather," he continued, opening them, "I hope you don't understand. I hope you never know what the need for love can do to you.")

And now, after all these years—after all these years of knowing in my secret heart that Len had been right so long ago when I sat across from him in his office and he gave my marriage poor odds—after finally being able to admit that I had made a mistake when I joined

my life to that of a man who was in every way a retreat
from all that I feared most rather than an unfolding toward a more complete sense of myself, now, finally, I
had been capable of grappling with that original error
of judgment and flight into a perilous safety by suggesting to Michael that he and I part . . . not because
either of us was truly at fault; not because we *intended* all
the pain we caused each other; but because we were
human and we were fallible and we had allowed ourselves to get married for all the wrong reasons, hoping
that they might turn into the right ones. Now, after all
these years, I had finally faced up to the bleakness of
my marriage and my own responsibility for it; I had
considered the alternatives long and carefully and decided that for both our sakes it must be ended. Now,
after all these years, I had finally taken a positive step
in my own behalf.

I thought those things were *good* to do. That they
meant I had grown up and started to make my own
choices, to make up my own mind, to be more self-
referential and less needy of approval. Why then was I
losing resolve? Why did I start again to question myself
so obsessively, fearing misinterpretation, projection?
Why did I once more inspect every perception, every
decision, for unfairness, ingratitude, and selfishness?

What was the *matter* with me? What was the matter
with *me*? Who was I to go around breaking up a marriage that . . . worked? Who was I to have pretensions to being loved in some complex labyrinthine way
known only to myself when the rest of the world
learned to make do, learned to have strength, learned to
embellish a serviceable character into a monument of
fortitude? Whatever made me think I was special in my
misery? All around me were loveless, sexless marriages
sustained by habit and apprehension: the world was
kept turning by the endless trudge toward the next
meal, the next paycheck, the next birthday . . . the
next forbidden pleasure. Maybe strength was learning
to get used to the sticky caution, the brutalizing civili-

ties, the boredom. Maybe the whole world waited and I simply lacked the courage to accept the commonplace.

Days went by, different in only the smallest ways—like freight cars you counted as you sat at a country crossing unable to see either the beginning of the train or the end. I was set against myself and the two parts were locked in mortal combat. The Good Seedie and the Bad Seedie was what one of my sisters called them, and if the Good Seedie and the Bad Seedie hated each other enough—if they fought and fought and fought—they could destroy the very ground of their battle. The Good Seedie hollered at me, "You selfish, greedy thing! As a wife you promised to honor and love your husband. Forever. You promised to bear his children and stand by him! He stood by *you!* Look what he went through with you, what he did for you! A lot of men wouldn't have done that, they would have left you flat and let you *die.* They wouldn't have put up with your nonsense, all this thrashing and bleating. Look how kind his parents were, look what you owe *them.* How will *they* feel if you separate? What will they tell their *friends*? And the children! Let's not forget your primary responsibility: you gave birth to them. Your life is theirs now, you had your chance. They have suffered enough, don't you think? *Stare decisis,* my dear. *Stare decisis.* Can't you *ever* learn to control yourself?"

And then the Bad Seedie would holler back. "The hell with all of them. It's your life and you almost lost it. You didn't even know what you *had* until you almost lost it. You don't owe Michael anything: you gave him what he wanted. And he gave you what you wanted. Then. You want something else now. That's not a crime. The crime, I'll tell you, is *not* going after what you think you want: it's the worst kind of betrayal. If you give up your life for other people, do you think they're going to get down on their knees and thank you? They're not going to love you for that, they're going to hate you for your sacrifice. It doesn't matter what people think; you haven't learned that yet. It doesn't matter whether your in-laws don't understand

and think you're an ungrateful wretch. Michael will manage. The children will manage: you can't be a good mother when you are so unhappy all the time."

And the Good Seedie would rant, "Do you think you're the only one? What if we all rushed around divesting ourselves of sacred trust and responsibilities? What if nobody knew the meaning of the word duty? How do *you* feel about how you've behaved, what you've done? Proud of your filthy little liaison with Len? Gloating over the irreparable damage you and your lover have done to his marriage in the name of love? Thinking of how many lives *you* have ruined . . . and how many more you could ruin?"

And then the Bad Seedie: "We all have to take responsibility for ourselves, we do the best we can. Sometimes people get hurt, it can't be helped. And when you look back over your life are you going to be able to say you loved life?"

Or was that the Good Seedie saying that? . . . And was it the Bad Seedie . . . that . . . said . . .


Time bent in the strangest way, twisting around on itself. I began to lose weight; occasionally I threw up in the morning. I was so engaged in my internal dialogue—so isolated in it—that life got muffled: the children had to yank my sleeve to get my attention; they said things over and over again before the meaning of the words seeped through. I slept too much and ate too little and couldn't get out of bed in the morning. I was often sick, attracting vagrant flus and fevers the way leftovers invite spoilage.

Michael circled in his silence, his stolid withdrawal. He and I didn't talk because there was nothing else to say, and anyway he was always busy in some other room, reading his books and writing his writings and thinking his complicated thoughts.

I still went to school and went to work and played with the children and made tuna-fish sandwiches, and all the time the Good Seedie and the Bad Seedie hollered back and forth, making a wind tunnel of my head.

I thought I had cancer again. I felt so awful, so wasted.

If only Michael had wanted me. If only he could have showed me—consistently, for more than one effortful week at a time—that I was necessary to *him* rather than just necessary to the management of the household and the family.

If only he had loved me in a way I could understand.

The loneliness was devastating, the loneliness was unbearable. I kept thinking, the children are the key, the children will save me, the children are enough. Children had been enough for generations on generations of women who found themselves less wanted although usually not less needed than they might have wished in a more perfect, more charitable world.

This was the dark part, the dark question that was hard for me to answer. I wanted not to feel alone when I had the children to give my existence meaning and direction, but I did. I wanted to hug my life around me like a heavy cloak with the children inside, to tailor my needs to their small and perfect gifts. "What do we need *them* for?" asked a friend once, jerking her head in the direction of the living room where Michael and her husband sat and talked. She and I were standing in the doorway of her bedroom, having just tucked in all four children—her two and my two—where they fluttered and giggled under the blankets. We stood and watched our miraculous children—our lives and our future—our arms around each other's waists. "It's everything, isn't it?" she said to me. "Everything," I agreed.

But late at night it wasn't everything. Late at night when I had been thinking too much so I couldn't sleep, when I stole out of bed and wandered into the children's room, sitting next to them and touching them and listening to their light breathing, it was harder to convince myself that they were—or indeed should *be*—everything.

And then I would think of my mother, retreating to her room every night in her alcoholic fog (she couldn't get to sleep, she said, without the booze). I thought of how much I had not then understood about the kind of loneliness that cores you like an apple, leaving the hollow white flesh to dry out without its center of seeds and husks and tangled membrane. That was what it felt like to me not to have Michael—my husband, the father of my children—love me, in a way—as Dr. P. said—I could understand, not to have his arms around me at night and even during the day. That was what it felt like to be in a situation in which togetherness was one step closer to abandonment. I understood my mother better now, her thin bitterness, her solitude in her bed with its tight stretched sheets. ("No one wants a woman with four children—except for just sex," she would say in her clenched voice.)

But she had had us! And with the consummate egotism of children the four of us thought we were enough, that we should be enough. We demanded that she be happy because she was a mother and because we wanted and needed nothing more than a mommy. So we never did understand her dragging up to bed early—alone—reeking of alcohol and cigarettes, her lovely face gone slack, her blond hair brittle; we never understood her need to forget and her Lethean dedication to the liquor and the nicotine and the little red pills that one night clotted her breathing so that she had to be resuscitated by the fire department.

And now I knew: the shame of being abandoned and at the same time trapped by circumstance and obligation, the shame of being scorned. I knew what it was like to feel your healthy anger turn into a convulsion of self-loathing and malignant depression, what it was like to be without the kind of comfort we do not speak of and are often ashamed of because it is dark and acrid and not fit subject for polite company. My mother had been trapped in her loneliness and her need—in the end—to be a good girl, immobilized by what was ex-

pected of her in that time and that place (not so different from my time and my place) so that her mourning
was in secret, was self-destructive. We don't want to
know what comforts a woman, what stanches the bleeding of her grief and stoppers her tears. We don't want
to be reduced to that animal state, to be elevated to that
transcendence, feeling as we do that we have no business
in either place—in the mud or the firmament—to which
our coupling can carry us.

If only I could have made them enough, those angel
children: I should have had the strength to dedicate
myself to their future if I couldn't dedicate myself to
mine. But they weren't; I couldn't; I didn't; and so beyond the machinelike activity, in my muffled solitude,
the only thing left throbbing and twitching was my own
dark impulse. Thoreau said, "There are two ways to
victory,—to strive bravely or to yield. How much pain
the last will save we have not yet learned." I thought of
Sylvia Plath, her head in the oven while her two children slept in the icy London flat, turning blue as the
morning, blue as a snail as she curled into the depths of
her own darkness. Or Anne Sexton, gulping the poison
exhaust of her car in her sealed garage, deserting her
daughters to their memories of her torrid affairs with
death. I was no poet, no artist, to make of my death
something I hadn't been able to make of my life, but I
was a woman. Like them. I didn't have their language
and their vision or their long-nurtured intent, but I was
a woman, and I too knew the boot in the face; I was a
woman, and I too could break like a stone.

I lacked courage. I wanted freedom but I couldn't
conceive of it. I was beginning to think that the only
reason I had lived after all was that I hadn't had the
courage to die. Courage must be sought by commission
rather than omission, by subduing the chaos rather than
simply enduring it. I had to have the courage to take a
new life.

Whoever it was that the doctors had saved, Michael

had saved, that my in-laws had saved, that my mother and sister and friends had saved, was not worth saving. Whatever had walked out of the hospital saved was somehow not me; it was what I had meant to be and pretended to be but it wasn't me. I was not worth saving for the bitterness, the isolation, the booze or pills or dope if I was really modern, the drifting in and out of lovers (if I was lucky) to keep myself level. If I was going to survive, I had to save myself.

September again, 1974. September of the new beginnings, September of the mind sharpened like a razor and the future as empty as a porcelain bowl.

We planned a party for Alexandra's sixth birthday. I baked a cake—an elaborate one. I bought the favors and saw that the balloons were blown up. I stood at the door and welcomed the guests—all these little girls rendered strange and unrecognizable, party-blooming flowers dug out from under their grime and overalls. I helped with the presents. I organized the games.

I had the flu again—I caught it regularly, bleeding fever by the phases of the moon—and somehow, as the afternoon wore on and the fever went up and the headache got worse and my stomach kept threatening to climb up into my throat, some linchpin that held the working parts together broke and I spun away from good sense, from moderation, from duty, obligation, and responsibility. I walked quietly, purposefully into my bedroom and closed the door. I changed my clothes and went into the bathroom to stare at myself in the mirror, to see if I could understand what I wanted to do. I looked at my face. I looked into my own eyes. I looked at my neck and my shoulders and the big red apple embroidered on the bodice of the nightgown that might have been the spreading stain of a deep wound to the chest. The Good Seedie and the Bad Seedie were urging death and birth. And I saw myself.

It seemed absurd and terrible to me that I should

have been through so much—have gone so far—and still have gotten nowhere.

So I sweated blood into the sink. I took the indigo blade and pressed it against my flesh to find out whether I could do it. I envied the children and their excitement, their birthday celebrations, their conviction that anything was possible—and what's more, that it was imminent. I envied their abandon. I envied their faith in the future.

Once there were only beginnings.

An affirmation of one's humanness, of one's uniqueness and integrity, of one's right to self-determination, can look very much like despair.

# SEPTEMBER 1974–DECEMBER 1976

BLEEDING. LETTING BLOOD. A POWERFUL AND PRIMI-
tive act of catharsis, atonement, propitiation . . . and
for a woman, much more. For a woman it is also an act
of affirmation and an act of continuity, an act of possibility and an act of finality. From the day we first see
the stains of our own innocent blood in our underpants,
to the time of our life when the bleeding begins to di-
minish, becomes erratic, and then stops for good, that
unbidden flow of life and not-life reminds us who we are
and that we are mysterious—even to ourselves.

We come to recognize the semiotics of the flow: on
schedule or late, heavy or light, a penetratingly vivid
crimson wash or a viscous mahogany deposit. Are we
sick or are we well? Are we pregnant or have we
(whew!) made it through one more month? Are we
pregnant or have we failed—are we barren and bereft—this month also? Carrying a child, we are terrified
of the familiar twinges, the slow wrench of the clasping
and unclasping of the uterus that either means something has gone wrong or means that the body is readying itself for the labor of birthing. At the wrong time
the show of blood is terrifying, horrifying; we dread the
sweet, sticky feel of warmth and wet between our legs.
At the right time the bleeding is the reiteration and
avowal of all that it means to be a woman and the conduit of life. Bleeding is familiar. It is reassuring. And it
is intensely private.

If I had been asked, then, whether I "minded" being
postmenopausal, "minded" no longer having periods, I

would have said no, how could I miss the discomfort, the mess, the odor, the paraphernalia and the inconvenience? It seemed infinitely more important at the time that my missing hormones be replaced so that I wouldn't dry up and blow away, wouldn't have skin like corduroy and a spine like a crumbling obelisk. Dr. J. had finally put me on estrogen—six months after my ovariectomy—when I was in Quimby. But I also knew that my estrogen-supported sense of female well-being was insufficient, and I felt not so much less-a-woman as I felt deprived of some indescribable female resonance, some essential intimacy with myself that was gone forever. I had lost the sense of my own blood and that was one of the things I sought as I stood at my old-fashioned, broad-edged sink, contemplating my face in the mirror.

My "gesture," my experiment, was made both more and less than it actually was—not a cry for help but a howl of defiance: *my* blood, *my* body, *my* life. I knew what I had done and why; everybody else was responding to the act rather than its implications.

Michael called Dr. G., who glad-handed me—plumping up my spirits like a pillow, prescribing antibiotics for complications of the flu, aspirin to keep the fever down, and "careful watching" until I was "myself" again. Friends rallied. My lover—who had since gone on into another excursion from his marriage—came to talk, to scold, perhaps to reassure himself that this had had nothing to do with him.

"Why?" they all asked, over and over again. "Why did you do this," each asked me gently, separately, sadly, "you who have been through so much, you who have so much to live for?"

Why indeed? The answer, like the act, was private although not a secret; it was just that I didn't expect anybody to understand. I did it because I needed to know I could. It was as simple as that. And it was more to the point and less final than stepping in front of that fascinating subway train. Spilling my own blood—after so many others had spilled it for me—became an archetypal act of self-determination.

I did not want to die but I did want to bleed. That is the answer. And it is probably only another woman who will know what I am talking about.

For a month—the month between Alexandra's birthday in September and mine in October—I went nowhere and saw no one except the few people who ventured in to see me. For some whole days I refused to get out of bed; if illness was an excuse for self-indulgent behavior, well, at least it was a familiar ploy. I needed time. I was recovering from a lifetime of indecision, fear, guilt, and paralysis.

I was in no hurry. It had taken this long and this much pain and confusion to bring me to where I was. I could afford to be reflective. I could afford to hang around the house, letting the children climb under the covers with me, burrowing, nesting. I had my whole future and theirs to think about, and a picture of it was forming, particle by particle, like a pile of iron filings orienting themselves to some new source of magnetism. I wasn't yet ready to make a move, but I would be. I would be.

I spent my birthday at home. Originally I had planned a big party for myself, to celebrate the milestone of having survived thirty years. I hadn't had a birthday party since I was little, and since being married to Michael, I had had no party of any kind because he didn't like them. I had wanted so much to celebrate *something*, and was willing to do it for myself and by myself if necessary. But now I didn't have the energy for any social project so ambitious; furthermore, it seemed considerably less important now as a gesture of independence than it had when I had conceived of it.

Michael went out the evening of my birthday. Without me. He had finally engineered his change of career, leaving Wall Street for the arts, and his presence was required at evening functions. He had never been facile at planning occasions, so it was no surprise when rather than arranging some small event—like dinner out—for the night of my birthday, he told me he had to be somewhere. This, in conjunction with the fifty-dollar check from our joint account that he presented me with as a thirtieth birthday gift—urging me to furnish my new desk with office supplies—was just one more slip in a landslide of convincing reasons to end the marriage.

I was home, but not alone. Anya, an old friend from Barnard, had called the afternoon of my birthday to wish me well. When she found I had nothing planned she offered herself as a companion in cake and champagne—which she would also conveniently provide. "We'll celebrate," she said, "and we'll do it just fine without *him*." My gray mood of loneliness and abandonment lifted. Getting drunk with Anya had possibilities that dinner out with Michael lacked.

Anya arrived shortly after I had put the children to bed and we quickly got down to the serious business of getting loaded—which I did with admirable dispatch that was heavily contributed to by my having had nothing to eat all day.

It wasn't long before I was as drunk as I could ever remember being: there's something about bubbles that has more effect on me than alcohol content. "You ought to eat something," said Anya solicitously, her Jewish-mother impulse to feed surfacing. "That cake," I said, leering at her chocolate creation. "That's all. It's just me and the cake." I made creature-from-the-slime grasping motions at it.

"Hey. Hold it." Anya, none too sober herself, pulled the cake away protectively. "We need candles! You gotta make a *wish!*"

"Screw the wish. Where did wishes ever get me? No, thanks. Probably couldn't light the suckers anyway. Scalpel, please."

Anya held out the knife. "Aha!" I said, snatching it. "Is this a dagger which I see before me?" I raised the knife over my head like a mad murderer, then found myself plunging it into the moist center of the cake. The knife went right through its softness, ramming into the plate beneath which made the cake quiver as if it were a live thing I had just slaughtered.

"For God's sake," said Anya. I couldn't tell whether she feared for my sanity or was amused.

I pulled the knife out slowly, voluptuously, and wiped it clean. Stabbing the cake was the most satisfying thing I had done in a very long time; I wanted to do it again and did. Dancing around the kitchen table, muttering incantations, I raised the knife over my head once more—this time with both hands—and slew the cake a second time. Then with the knife buried almost to the hilt in the dark chocolate, I felt a murderous frenzy and stabbed the cake again and again, slashing it, mutilating it, until the table top was a wreckage of hacked chunks and crumbs trailing muddy gobs of frosting. We began to laugh so hard I could no longer stand up and sank to the floor, clinging to the edge of the table, while Anya teetered precariously on two legs of her chair. When we had finally caught our breath and each taken another swig of champagne from the bottle—having long since dispensed with the formality of glasses—I said cheerfully, "I guess we'd better eat it."

Anya seemed less than enthusiastic about consuming anything so savaged and nibbled politely; having no such reticence, I easily disposed of better than half of the carnage. Then we stumbled into the living room and Anya joined me as I flopped onto the thick white flokati rug, scattering bits of cake here and there like an insect strewing pollen. Side by side, floating on the rug as if it were a raft on the open sea, we passed what was left of the champagne back and forth in silence, each lost in our own thoughts.

"I'm getting old," I said finally. "I'm getting old and here I am with my life in the same sorry state it was two years ago, four years ago." I paused reflectively, and then said with conviction, "Eight years ago."

"What are you going to do?" Anya was staring at the ceiling with such concentration one would have thought she was trying to navigate by the stars right through ten sets of floors and ceilings.

"I don't know."

"What do you *want* to do?"

"Get out of here." It sounded so matter-of-fact, so simple, that it took me a moment to adjust to what I had said. "I think I'm finally ready to leave. I think I can handle the guilt. The fear of being alone too."

I didn't believe what I was saying. I had never been alone in my life. It would be like trying to fly without a plane. But I wouldn't think about that now. First things first. Get out first. Then worry about being alone.

There was a long pause as I rummaged through my thoughts, trying to find one or two that weren't too sodden to articulate. "Do you know what?"

"What?" Anya mumbled, still drunkenly engrossed in charting our course by the ceiling.

"I have almost never done anything I really wanted to—but not because nobody let me. Because I was afraid. Because I was afraid of hurting someone's feelings, afraid of doing something wrong. And when I try to be courageous I inevitably wind up feeling guilty, feeling regret because I am denying myself to somebody—denying them the person they have needed me to be. I'm always weighing this aspect with that aspect and I get so tangled in the art of the weighing that I forget to *do* anything." I sat up unsteadily. "I've been functionally immobilized for as long as I can remember. Why, I've been thinking about the inevitability of having to separate from Michael since we first got married. I've *known* all this time and I've needed to pretend that I haven't. I've played 'perfect couple' until I'm not sure at all what real life might be like. I had this idea about how I should be seen—how I should see myself—and I wanted so much to *be* that. It was all surfaces, like being a model: so much effort into getting the picture right so it could be captured forever and treasured as the artifact of what happens between two real, living, breathing people who eat and shit and fuck and fight and humiliate and destroy each other as much as they love each other."

I lay down again. The room was going around the way Central Park does when you're on the merry-go-round. "I don't want halfway anymore. I'm worn out with trying. I'm worn out with pretending so that we don't upset the way other people have to see *themselves*. It's over. I'm through with it."

"Oh, yeah?" said Anya, who tries to be moderate in most if not all things.

"I think," I said.

That year—the school year of '74–'75—is mostly a blank. I must have done the usual things, had the usual desires and frustrations and confusion. I was very busy in school with the Ph.D. program and busy with my job as a co-therapist in a sex therapy (ahem!) practice; I was also beginning to see some clients on my own. I must have thrown myself at a man or two: it would have been inconsistent not to. And the children—the dear children who meant more to me than life—filled what space was left.

It was for their sake I kept trying—we kept trying—cheered on by parents, friends, people who knew we were in trouble. Try! they said. Think of the children! It was one thing to be a bad wife and desert your husband, another entirely to be a bad mother.

Finally, sometime in the spring of 1975, I did think of the children, thought of what Michael's and my deadly silences must be doing to them, thought of the fights that were never had—because of the indecorous behavior they entailed—but festered anyway, ulcerating in small pockets of anger, nagging, and complaints. Half the time I felt like a zombie, ambulating through my well-organized life, staring sightlessly straight ahead, arms out to warn myself of dead ends. The other half of the time I was the florid menopausal erratic, ricocheting from a masochistic lowering passively to malignant depression to fits of rage that had me dancing and hollering like a troll. (Trying to finish a paper one day, interrupted for the umpteenth time by the children who were fighting literally under my feet, I began to screech like a madwoman, quite unable to control myself, "Leave me alone, leave me alone, leave me alone . . ." as the children cowered against each other and backed away carefully, their eyes as big as dinner plates.) Selfish and thoughtless were beginning to look better and healthier than immobilized or out of control.

When I screamed "Leave me alone," it was a huge existential sweep of despondency that whisked through every cell of my life. *Do* something, I chided myself, thinking of the children terrified, the children backing away as if confronted by a huge slavering dog gone rabid. Give this up. Give up the strength of tenacity you pride yourself on. Have the courage—for once—not to hang on but to let go, to give in to what is inevitable.

By the September of 1975 I knew that there was no purpose in continuing even to try. There was nothing at all left except a residual respect for each other which I knew would not survive another year. I had moved into a separate bedroom during the summer, imposing the children on each other, so that I could escape Michael's disapproval, his silence, his hostile taciturnity, his back to me. His presence was a perpetual reproach, a constant reminder to me of my own failure.

We had to discuss logistics, decide who would go where, whether the apartment was to be sold, how to set things up financially. We held off telling the children until I insisted; if they were going to be destroyed, I wanted to know it sooner rather than later. Michael wanted to put it off . . . and put it off . . . and put it off, until it seemed to me that until the children were told, we could not go forward any more than we were ever capable of going backward. Michael wanted to wait until we were *absolutely* sure, until they were older, until our parents were dead—anything. I wanted to have it out and finished, buried and grieved over.

He wanted to be the one to tell them, so one Sunday night after dinner, as we all sat together at the table picking at hamburger fragments and pushing shreds of lettuce in circles, we nodded to each other and Michael began to explain that Mommy and Poppy were going to live in separate houses. But his voice broke, he couldn't get through it, and I had to finish. While Michael cried openly, unexpectedly, unashamedly, I held tight to the rim of the plate to keep my hands from shaking and tried to say the right words, to find some way to help them make sense of this.

The eager faces that had looked forward to this adult discussion seemed then for a moment like perfect wax dolls' features that had got too close to a flame and begun to melt. Zachary's face collapsed inward like crumpled paper, and his mouth opened to emit a wail that never came. He was five years old, and it was his first encounter with harshness and despair. And Alexandra, although she was clearly stricken, had learned something at seven about resignation and restraint. "So we'll have to move," she said matter-of-factly, escaping to the TV to watch the Bionic Woman conquer life and death as Zachary sat and finally wept.

I could, at that moment, have retracted everything, have promised anything, so painful was it to watch. What kind of woman was I? What had I done to these innocent people—this man and these two children? And then I, too, cried and cried.

What had we done wrong? What was our sin except to believe what we were told about how life went, how things were supposed to be? I was a True Believer when it came to Eternal Verities. At least for myself. My parents had not made it, but *I* would make it. I saw so many unhappy people . . . but *I* never intended to be one of them. I planned carefully. I tried to be good. Why hadn't things worked out? And I think Michael felt the same.

I wonder if other people our age—poised, as we were in the mid-sixties, between the conservative, accepting, passive legacy of our parents and our own backgrounds, and the rollicking, free-spirited counterculture that was to come—were so blind, so smug as we were. We had had secret, discreet sex with each other, but we were not free to talk about it and let our parents know about it and live together openly without the benefit of wedlock. We were encouraged to step out of eons of stereotypical proscriptions about and prescriptions for sex-role behavior, and yet so many of us "freely chose" to do (almost) precisely what our parents had done before us—especially the women, who then had to turn into superwomen to handle the complex responsibilities of separate and frequently inimical life-styles. We were free and yet we sought limits; we thought we craved horizons but what we were really looking for was boundaries.

We thought we knew it all; nobody could tell us anything. We thought we had it all, and in a way we did . . . for all the good it did us. We bought into marriage as if it were the bargain of the century, and I think we never really expected to pay for it. We didn't understand ourselves and we couldn't understand each other and we tore our lives down around us because there seemed no way to rebuild but from the mud up.

Stupid. We were stupid. And we were pretentious.

Michael suffered too. His pain was different from mine, but I know he suffered because of me. However, I had no shame about begging, Help me! And that was another thing about us that was so different, perhaps the most important thing: he could never say, Help me! I feel alone. I feel frightened. Help me!

Michael, of course, had his own view of the marriage. He wrote to me:

I was an English Lit major when I met you in the spring of my senior year. Intending to study, write and travel abroad for a year after graduation, I decided over the summer to stay home with you. We would be married the following June. A Master's in English gained over the ensuing academic year dissuaded me from a teaching career. What to do? My upbringing and you conspired to suggest business school. I pointed myself in the direction of Wall Street.

The sensitive and sheltered number one Jewish son with a full cargo of dreams and illusions hit the stone wall of business school and business. From day one there was ambivalence tending to outright, downright unhappiness. The abandonment of words for numbers, the narrowness of the subject matter, the outrageous price paid by the psyche in the name of profit, these were the nemeses from which there was no escape short of resignation. And even that didn't work.

The pressure had been building for three years when I walked into my boss's office and resigned. Just like that. (This was after Zachary's birth but before your first hospitalization.) Investment banking couldn't be the way I was intended to spend my professional life. What was the firm's reaction to this most surprising development? I was told I "couldn't" leave, that I had a "brilliant" future. So said the head of corporate finance in one of the world's finest investment banking firms.

I was not unaware that the Wall Street experience was extremely worthwhile. The travel, the training, the responsibility, the opportunity to measure myself against the best: one could not help but know one was working in a privileged environment. Yet the costs outweighed the benefits. I have said for years I finally left Wall Street because I was dying. Sound familiar?

I withdrew my resignation and three months later you were in the hospital. The firm could not have been more understanding. The bottom line of your illness for me was that one is all too clearly allotted a single life. After your recovery I waited for what seemed a decent interval and then resigned permanently to become, as you know, the financial administrator of [a large performing arts organization]. This proved to be an enjoyable and extremely gratifying experience but three years later the idea erupted in my mind to write a book, a philosophical meditation and a very long way from Wall Street.

What would I say were the dynamics of our

relationship? I would trace our early problems after a lovely courtship to the fact that we were married one week after I started business school. There was no honeymoon because accounting and statistics beckoned. Then I was trapped on Wall Street and I never fully understood how miserable I was until after I left. My relationship to my job paralleled your relationship to me: pervasive and problematical.

You invested me with an almost totemic power to control you, a power I did not seek nor enjoy. Endowed with considerable self-confidence myself, I never fully understood the extent to which you, someone so gifted, had such a wretched self-image. Admittedly, I was judgmental, which served to exacerbate the situation. I felt suffocated by what I felt was an excess of need on your part: the more you pushed, the more I withdrew. What you didn't understand was that I, too, was fighting for my life. I was caught in a vise between you and my work.

Neither of us adequately communicated our problems to the other. And if I was not fully responsive to your needs, I myself felt equally badly served. We were both self-absorbed. You were never really interested in what I actually did on Wall Street and you never helped me to sort out my work problem. If I broached the possibility of a change, your reaction was "Don't talk about it, do it." You became intensely jealous of a screenplay I was writing to keep alive the creative side of me. In your focus on the tangible and practical, you were never sympathetic to or even tolerant of my mystical aspect. You never asked yourself why I changed from a sensitive dreamer to a somewhat callous businessman. It is the law of relationships that the failure is always mutual. There are two sides to every story.

Why didn't *I* leave *you*? Two reasons. First, work was the major problem I had to resolve. Second, the children. The children were the receptacle into which I poured all the emotion frustrated by you and my job. Too, I had been their mother and father when you were in the hospital. I could not imagine being separated from them.

You never understood me and you never loved me any more meaningfully than I loved you. Whoever you thought you loved, it wasn't the real me.

So. I guess it is your illusions that kill you, not the lack of them.

What I remember most about the end of 1975 and the first half of 1976 is how frightened I was, with a fear that trickled around the edges of my tight, tight schedule, that ran in rivulets around me as I lay in bed at night. How could I be sure I was doing the right thing? I was so brave, here, with my fancy co-op and my husband—if not in the same bed, at least in the next room—and my splendid, cherished children. What if the children broke down or I broke down? How would I feel, *living* alone, without much money? How would I feel *being* alone, as my mother had been? Would I end up one of those strident, glacial women who can never again melt to love, who devours her children in her own need to be fed, who belongs to no one and therefore belongs nowhere?

Ironically it was my mother who was most supportive to me during this woeful period. She called regularly—in spite of the long-distance rates—and wrote funny and encouraging letters about learning to rely on oneself and not allowing any man to relieve you of your self-respect. We began to be able to say "I love you" to each other and it no longer felt awkward and forced. She herself was calmer and less bitter; her remarriage a couple of years before to a man who was able to show her he loved her had taken her edges off, had warmed her and made her more forgiving, less rigid.

I suppose all this was a process of mutual forgiveness, pardon—each to the other—for all the imperceptible wounds inflicted all these years. I forgave her for closing me out; I think she forgave me for achieving so apparently easily what she had herself had to forfeit—

that life of glamour and spoon-fed admiration, the modeling, the traveling, the successes. She forgave me for getting beautiful—like her—when I had seemed to have so little promise in that department when I was growing up. She forgave me for stealing her fire.

And I forgave her for her abandonment of me to my father—and her punishment of me for loving him—although at that time I felt sure she knew nothing of the real nature of our relationship (now I am not quite so sure).

I forgave her for not protecting me from what she chose not to see, hoping at the same time that she would forgive me for what she knew nothing of.

Michael and I were finally separated in May of 1976, renting apartments two floors apart in the same building so that we could better share the children. They circulated easily between our separate quarters, and seemed much more sanguine than they had before the move. Zachary was once more cheerful and bouncy, and Alexandra no longer brought home drawings like the one she had produced after our announcement of intent, in which a little girl stood, arms akimbo, her tiny family and house dashed around her ankles like broken toys, while across the top was written, "The sun is gone today." We seemed to have survived the modern-day catastrophe of the broken home with minimal dismemberment.

I was still painfully lonely. Worse, immediately after the split, I found myself hopelessly involved with a man I adored, a man who was never to be either right for me or completely available to me. (I still don't know why I didn't see it; everybody else did.) Although I loved him more than I had ever conceived of being able to love a man, it wasn't that I wanted to marry him; it wasn't that I needed him to be around all the time. It was just that I wanted . . . *him*. To be *with* him.

It was going badly . . . the life semi-alone, the love affair (as had all the love affairs), all the schoolwork I couldn't concentrate on because when I wasn't working or taking care of the kids or the house, I was trying to understand why something so wonderful as love should hurt so much, because I was trying to understand *him*. When it came right down to it, all I really wanted to do was go home, to my *old* home . . . to have someone take care of *me,* to be the baby—the one who is understood, the one who is tolerated and interpreted.

My mother and I had spent very little time together since I had married Michael; my commitment to him was a wedge between her and me because she knew he didn't like her. So I was pleased and surprised when she called me in November and suggested that I come home for Christmas. "It will be crowded but we shall manage," she said. "I can't think of anything nicer. It will be just like old times and the children will have a real, traditional Christmas with all the trappings." She sounded genuinely excited, genuinely welcoming. "Come for a long stay if you can. I'm sure it will help to get away." She knew that I felt nothing was going right, that I was again miserable in love without much chance of being happily in love, that I was in despair. I just couldn't seem to get a good fix on anything.

"Yes," I said. "Yes, of course. It will be wonderful. I need to be home and to be with you."

"When can you come?" She had a thing about making plane reservations way ahead of time.

"I don't know, I'm not sure. I have so much school-work to do. I have to leave time for that."

"Look, why don't you come as soon as the children are out for vacation? I can watch them and you can go to the library and catch up." She had never been so solicitous. My dear, dear mother.

"You've convinced me. I'll be there on the . . . uh, let's see . . . the sixteenth. How is that for you?"

"That's great. That's perfect. The sixteenth it is."

I felt a wave of gratitude for the mothering instinct, for all mothers who, through everything, love their children. Mother is always to go back to. There is always Mother when you are alone and nobody loves you anymore—at least when nobody loves you in a way you can understand. I had been rescued.

"You have no idea how much I'm looking forward to this," I said. "It will feel so good to be home." I paused. "Mother. I love you."

The few weeks before Christmas were filled with the usual frantic rush even though I had decided to leave all the Christmas shopping until I got home. I had meetings, school; I had the children.

And then on the eighth of December, I rushed in from one meeting, about to be late for another. My baby-sitter, who watched the children afternoons, looked up from the sink where she was washing dishes. Her face was gray. "Are you all right?" I asked, concerned, as I tossed my books on the sofa. "You look awful."

"Call home," she said. "Your brother has called twice."

"Did he say what he wanted?" I grabbed a carrot stick and began to dial the phone.

"You mother isn't . . . feeling well, I think. . . ." She looked more closely at the dish she was washing and seemed to be trying to get some resistant speck of something off.

"Hi," I said as my sister-in-law answered the phone. "What's up?"

"Your mother—your mom. She's had it." Had it? At the same time my heart stopped I remember thinking, what an *odd* thing to say, what a quaint way of announcing disaster.

"What do you mean, she's 'had it'?" I tossed the carrot in the wastebasket. The baby-sitter was watching me. She *knew*, I thought, that's why she looked so terrible.

"She's dying, and if she lives she'll be a vegetable. She had a massive stroke this afternoon, blew an aneurysm. Christmas shopping. She's been in a coma almost since it happened. They said she'll never come out of it."

"Are you sure? How do they know? Does she have a flat EEG?" I was trying to respond practically, level-headedly.

"EEG? I don't know about that. But everyone has been at the hospital all afternoon. Nobody has much hope. There's nothing to do but wait."

"I'll be on the next plane."

"There's no hurry." How *could* she be so matter-of-fact, I thought, but then, it's not her mother. "She won't regain consciousness, they're sure of that, and they don't expect her to live through the night. You might as well wait to see what happens."

*Wait?* Wait here in New York while my mother dies? "I'll be on the next plane," I repeated.

"Well, that's up to you, but there's no need to come right now."

"Don't let them put her on a respirator. Let her go in peace," I said, and hanging up, I caught my breath in a single, grotesquely noisy sob.

I just shook on the way to the airport, ashamed of myself for the selfish reaction I was having. How could she die now, now when we were going to be together after all these years, now when I needed her so much? My poor mother, who would never know now how much I loved her—what a compelling, tragic figure she was for me, with her harsh pride and her loneliness—how I had admired her even through the resentment and critical feelings I had often borne her! Poor me, who would never have the comfort of knowing that *she* knew what she meant to me; poor me, who would bear the burden of not having told her often enough or well enough that I loved her, that all was forgiven. Losing a mother feels like total abandonment, because a mother can abandon you in a way no one else can; she has always been there, and until she dies, she *is* always there—at least in one's regressive fantasies—to go back to. She is *there;* she is a presence. The only thing that I can imagine is worse is losing a child, for then the potential abandoner is herself abandoned.

I had always feared abandonment. More, even, than death.

I had two very stiff drinks on the plane, which was a mistake, because the shaking and the fear were transmuted into weeping. I used to tell myself that I couldn't imagine what kind of grief I might feel when my mother died—this event was supposed to take place in the far distant future—but I thought (what callousness!) it likely that I would feel little or nothing, so incompletely had we understood each other and so little had we appreciated each other. How wrong and how stupid. How blind not to see—not to be willing to see because of blinding hurt or anger!—what another person means to you, how much he or she is the warp of the weave of your life!

Somewhere over Ohio I suddenly knew she had died; I had the sense of the plane's having flown into a cloud of her spirit released. She's dead, I said to myself. I know she's dead. Now everything was finished. I would have to live forever with the sin of my ambivalence toward her. I sent my thoughts and my skeletal, functional prayers beaming at her like a laser cutting through thousands of miles of star-pocketed night sky, wanting to catch her soul in transit. God gather her in. God keep her.

God help me.

As soon as the plane had landed I ran to a telephone and called my brother.

"Don't hurry," he said, sounding as if his head were in a barrel. "She died an hour ago. There's nothing you can do."

* * *

"There's nothing you can do." How many times was that true? How many times did I *think* it was true even if it wasn't? There's nothing you can do. Sure. It was the story of my life: I specialized in a peculiarly female impotence.

\* \* \*

Once I was a good little girl. And because I was both good and little, I did what I was told. Daddy said, "Climb up here on my lap, sweetheart, and let Daddy give you a hug." And I did. And Mommy said, when I was a mite older, "Be careful. Never do anything . . . dirty. You will be punished." And I was afraid of that punishment.

I should have grown out of the habit of compliance and fear, but I didn't. Michael said something like, "We belong together" (which meant, "A girl like you ought to be married to a guy like me"), and for reasons I didn't fully understand I thought he was right. My mother-in-law said, "You have certain responsibilities now," and she was right too. There was always someone else to please and to pacify, someone who could be disappointed, someone who could be angry and judgmental.

Please don't misunderstand: I *chose* this role. The victim chooses the oppressor; the prey offers herself to the predator.

The world was my observer and I was the observed. I felt myself looked at and took that for evidence of my worth.

My idea of being a woman was filled in with the same comic-book primary colors as my picture of marriage. A woman was beautiful and she worked to get herself that way and then keep herself that way. It was like a job. It was something she owed the observers, the men. She was as sexy as she dared to be without sliding over into the category of tramp, because sex—like illness—is a guaranteed attention getter; sex—like illness—is a disposition of the body. It was the supply and demand of the economy of human relations: you notice me and I will notice you and we will reassure each other of our value.

The rest of the observant world required more. A real woman understood instinctively that things were as they always had been for a reason indistinguishable from a divine imperative. A real woman devoted herself unthinkingly to the welfare of husband and children and *loved* doing it. (Loving it was the salient feature.) She never gave in to failure; why, she just tried and tried and *tried* and *never* gave up on what she was meant to be and do and complete.

It was all surfaces—a trick done with mirrors—like the hundreds of pictures that were taken of me as a model. (Alexandra would sit for hours with my old modeling book, turning the pages thoughtfully, folding one magazine cover against another so that the slick print faces seemed to be kissing their own reflections. I would think, Is that me? Does she think it is me?) You look a certain way, you sell the product and convince the observer that you're happy to be doing it, you put the thing across for the audience. For the men especially; the men were suckers for surfaces: more, they created and then supported those surfaces—perhaps because anything more profound was engaging and therefore threatening. They wanted the exterior, they wanted the ownership and the title, they wanted me in the dead eye of their memory as if they were the camera and I were film to be developed. They projected their fantasies and needs onto and into me. But that was what I wanted to happen. The surfaces evolved as a function of the way I was seen, which then became the way I saw myself. I was my own observer.

That was how my new vision—my magical third eye, the third eye that grew from experience and pain, from months of staring at hospital room ceilings and into my own soul, the third eye that was trained on hypocrisy and doublethink and the faces behind the masks—that was how my new-seeing caused me trouble. It caused me to look at myself and see what I had hidden; it caused me to be addicted to the truth and plain saying; it caused a curious kind of distortion that allowed me always to see the end of my life close up, to remember how near to dying we are. I could never again look at a surface without wanting to see beneath it; I could never look at life without seeing it wreathed with death.

I had always known, somewhere beneath that glossy surface I sustained, that I was not what I was seen to be. The new discovery was that I was no longer to be looked at.

I am not to be looked at. I am someone who sees.

# EPILOGUE

# SEPTEMBER 1978

LABOR DAY. IT'S JUST ME AND THE KIDS AND WE'RE stuck here in the city for one of those long, breathless holiday weekends that make it easy for you to notice that you are alone. I have the kids, of course, and they root me, need me, feed me; I have my work. But this is the kind of beautiful, brilliant day that can get to you; the trick is not to hold still long enough to let it gain on your sense of isolation. I've got to get moving. I call the kids.

"Let's go to the park." (I will *not* sit and brood.) "It's too nice to stay inside."

Zachary appears in the doorway. "I'm taking my kite. I want to fly it in that big field."

"But there's no wind, baby." I check out the window just to make sure. "There's no point in taking a kite." Alexandra, always more practical, is already tucking her skateboard under her arm.

"No, I'm going to take my *kite*," says Zachary. He joins me at the window, gives himself a moment of pause for impact, and then says confidently, "I think the wind's about to start up. I'm going to take that kite and fly it very very high."

I try to keep the edge of parental exasperation out of my voice. "Look, sweetheart, the weather is hot and still and likely to stay that way. . . ." He is less sure of himself, but he assumes a stolid, eight-year-old posture of determination, hands on hips, feet apart. "All right," I say. (What the hell? What's the difference?) "Take the kite. Who knows? Maybe the wind will come up after all. We only need a little breeze."

We romp off to the park, splashing through pools of sunshine, into the big field that's jammed with kite-flyers in the fall and spring when Central Park rarely lacks for a serious, kiteflying wind. The softball players near us look amused.

Zachary plants himself in the middle of the great ellipse of trampled grass, keeping clear of four different outfields. "I can feel the breeze, Mommy," he shouts excitedly. He is arranging the line, the tail, on the brown stubble. Alexandra, on her skateboard, is tearing around the path that bounds the playing fields, describing graceful arcs through the groups of strollers, her long hair rippling out behind her. I lick a finger and hold it up. "I don't know, baby, I wouldn't count on it. . . ." I hate for him to be disappointed.

"You just can't feel it yet, Mommy. I know it's coming. Just wait. You'll see." He tends to the kite, stroking, straightening, flicking off grass shreds and tiny chunks of dried mud. And then he is running, the kite bouncing after him over the scruffy vegetation and summer dust. His small-boy speed creates the wind resistance the red kite needs to lift, and it follows him in lurching swoops as he runs through the games, past the pitchers warming up, among the kids on bikes.

"See, Mommy," he hollers triumphantly as he dashes past, his blond hair dark and wet where it is plastered to his temples, "you were wrong! There *is* wind! I *knew* the wind would come up. I could *feel* it."

There are many things I am wrong about, but this is not one of them. I don't intend to tell him that his nodding construction of paper and wood will be up there only as long as he keeps moving. He will find out soon enough.

Anyway, it doesn't matter. Perhaps there will be wind before he tires and has to stop.

# CODA

---

"WHAT ABOUT YOUR DREAMS?" ASKED MICHAEL THE other day. (He didn't mean the ones I have at night, which are many and vivid.) "You seem so cynical."

"I don't have any, not any more, not really."

"Did I do that to you?" I could see by the look on his face that he sincerely wanted to know.

"Nobody did that to me," I said. "I did it to myself. Chose it, actually."

He shook his head. "How can you live like that, without hope?"

"Without illusions," I corrected him, although perhaps it is the same thing. "I live quite well like that: you can't imagine how much better off I am. I don't miss those dreams, I really don't."

Which is the truth.

# COPING, LOVING and SUCCEEDING

## Ballantine has everything to help the modern woman in today's world.

16                                               TA-15

# HELP FOR THE WORKING WOMAN